Cases in Financial Management

Sidney R. Finkel

Vice-President, Strategic Planning
Goldome Federal Savings Bank

D0104716

Macmillan Publishing Company
New York

Collier Macmillan Publishers
London

Macmillan Publishing Company
866 Third Avenue, New York, New York 10022

Collier Macmillan Canada, Inc.

Library of Congress Cataloging-in-Publication Data

Finkel, Sidney R.   (date)
    Cases in financial management.

    1. Corporations—Finance—Decision-making—Case
studies.   2. Corporations—Finance—Data processing.
I. Title.
HG4026.F523   1986   658.1'5   85-18728
ISBN   0-02-337710-0

Printing: 1   2   3   4   5   6   7   8   Year: 6   7   8   9   0   1   2   3   4   5

ACKNOWLEDGMENTS

Original Business Logos by Anna Whitaker
1-2-3 is a trademark of Lotus Development Corporation
SuperCalc^3 is a trademark of Sorcim Corporation
Multiplan is a trademark of Microsoft Corporation
IBM is a trademark of International Business Machines Corporation
Apple II and Macintosh are trademarks of Apple Computer Inc.
DEC Rainbow is a trademark of Digital Equipment Corporation

ISBN   0-02-337710-0

Preface

This book contains forty cases that involve financial management decisions, and a supplemental section on using personal computers and spreadsheet programs. The cases can be analyzed either by using traditional methods or on a spreadsheet program. Each case has been designed so that spreadsheet techniques can be applied easily.

Each case is designed around three objectives. The first is to illustrate a problem in financial management. Financial techniques are designed and developed to solve management problems—that is, to make a decision that increases the value of the firm. Each case makes use of at least one quantitative technique in finance, and all major topics are covered. The key on pp. vii–viii links each case to the appropriate chapter of various texts in Basic or Intermediate Financial Management.

The quantitative techniques are not, however, an end unto themselves. Quantitative analysis is only a tool and represents only part of the solution to a management decision. In many of the cases, the decision is still unclear after the analysis; that is, there are factors present in each case that might argue against the decision indicated by the financial analysis. Thus the second objective of the cases is to illustrate how nonfinancial criteria interact with quantitative financial analysis in the decision-making process.

Finally, the third objective of the cases is to present real-world situations without real-world complications. The companies and the situations in the cases are fictional. However, this is not to say that the material in the cases is not real or that the description of the industries and the problems do not mirror real-world situations. The cases and problems have been drawn from real-world examples, either through the author's own consulting and management experience, or from write-ups and descriptions of companies in business magazines and newspapers. The problem with using real case studies in many courses is that the noncritical variables often obscure the important elements of the problem. By using fictional companies and financial data, these complications can be avoided, yet the reader should obtain a flavor of how the company and industry works, and what their problems are.

The chapters on computers are designed to provide sufficient information for a student who has access to a personal computer to use a spreadsheet program to help analyze the cases. Personal computers and spreadsheet analysis are ideal for financial analysis. Indeed, if microcomputers had no other application than spreadsheet programs, their development and cost could probably be justified. The computer section demonstrates that the ease of use of computers and spreadsheet programs is so great that they can be integrated into financial analysis with very little outside personal instruction.

In working with computers, a user is advised to set up the problem in a format that is easy to work with, print out that format, and then try to develop the computer logic that will solve the problem and produce the answers. Users will find this method much faster and a better learning experience than trying to solve the cases "on line"— that is, while sitting at the computer. You will find it much easier to think about the solution when you do not have the computer blinking at you, impatiently waiting for a response.

Finally, problem solving and decision making is a fun exercise. Each case has a unique quantitative decision, and the quantitative decision can be weighed against the qualitative factors in determining the final solution. If you look upon the cases as puzzle-solving exercises, they become much more interesting and even fun.

I would like to take this opportunity to thank the following individuals who provided reviews of the manuscript:

Keith Howe—Iowa State University
Anthony Jackson—Miami University
James Scott—Columbia University
Joseph D. Vinso—University of Southern California
Kent Zumwalt—University of Illinois, Urbana-Champaign

The comments of these people were of considerable help and were responsible for significant improvements in the manuscript.

S. R. F.

KEY TO TEXTS IN MANAGERIAL FINANCE

The following section keys each case to a specific chapter in the most current edition of texts used in basic, intermediate, and MBA courses in financial management. For some texts, more than one chapter may relate to the specific case, in which event the most relevant chapter is listed. This section should be used as a reference in working the cases, as most texts will provide illustrations of the methodology, if not the specific problem, contained in each case.

Text	1	2	3	4	5	6	7	8	9	10	11	12	13	14	15
Bierman and Smidt FINANCIAL MGT. FOR DECISION MAKING	2	2	2	3	3	3	7	7	10	11	11	8	7	16	16
Moyer et al. CONTEMPORARY FIN. MGT.2E	3	3	3	4	4	3	10	10	11	11	—	—	—	12	12
Keown et al. BASIC FIN. MGT. 3E	9	9	9	12	12	9	10	10	11	11	11	—	—	13	12
Gitman PRINCIPLES MANG. FIN. 4E	6	6	6	8	8	8	10	10	11	11	—	—	—	12	12
Weston and Brigham ESSENTIALS MANG. FIN. 7E	11	11	19	14	14	11	12	12	13	13	13	—	—	15	15
Weston and Copeland MANAGERIAL FINANCE 8E	5	5	5	23	23	5	6	6	17	17	17	—	6	21	21
Brealey and Myers PRINCIPLE CORP. FIN. 2E	2	2	2	4	4	3	6	6	7	7	7	6	6	—	9
Van Horne FUNDAMENTAL FIN. MGT. 5E	4	4	4	5	5	4	13	13	14	14	14	—	13	15	15
Van Horne FIN MGT & POLICY 7E	2	2	2	—	—	5	5	5	6	6	6	—	5	8	7
Henderson et al. AN INTRO. TO FIN. MGT.	3	3	10	4	4	5	5	5	6	6	6	5	5	4	4
Gitman,Joehnk,Pinches MANAGERIAL FINANCE	5	5	17	7	7	5	13	13	14	14	14	13	13	17	17
Brigham FINANCIAL MANAGEMENT 4E	4	4	4	5	5	4	8	8	10	10	10	9	9	7	7
Brigham and Gapenski INT. FINANCIAL MGT.	2	2	2	3	3	2	7	7	9	9	9	8	8	4	4
Schall and Haley INTRO TO FIN. MGT. 3E	4	4	4	—	—	4	8	8	9	9	9	8	8	7	7
Neveu FUND. OF MANAG. FIN. 2E	10	10	21	13	13	10	10	10	11	11	11	11	10	14	14
Halloran and Lanser INTRO TO FIN. MGT.	5	5	14	7	7	5	9	9	10	10	10	10	9	11	11

Text	16	17	18	19	20	21	22	23	24	25	26	27	28	29	30
Bierman and Smidt FINANCIAL MGT. FOR DECISION MAKING	16	13	14	13	12	18	—	—	18	—	19	19	19	20	20
Moyer et al. CONTEMPORARY FIN. MGT.2E	12	16	17	16	13	6	7	7	8	7	8	19	19	20	20
Keown et al. BASIC FIN. MGT. 3E	13	19	20	19	15	3	4	4	3	14	6	6	6	7	7
Gitman PRINCIPLES MANG. FIN. 4E	12	19	20	—	13	4	5	5	4	—	5	16	16	17	17
Weston and Brigham															

Text	Cases 16	17	18	19	20	21	22	23	24	25	26	27	28	29	30
ESSENTIALS MANG. FIN. 7E Weston and Copeland	15	19	18	19	16	3	4	4	4	16	5	9	9	8	8
MANAGERIAL FINANCE 8E Brealey and Myers	21	26	25	26	20	8	10	10	9	9	9	12	12	14	14
PRINCIPLE CORP. FIN. 2E Van Horne	—	22	23	22	17	25	26	26	25	—	27	19	29	28	28
FUNDAMENTAL FIN. MGT. 5E Van Horne	15	21	23	21	16	6	7	7	7	16	7	9	9	10	10
FIN MGT & POLICY 7E Henderson et al.	8	22	—	22	10	27	28	28	28	6	28	14	14	15	15
AN INTRO. TO FIN. MGT. Gitman,Joehnk,Pinches	4	12	13	12	—	2	2	7	7	12	7	9	9	9	9
MANAGERIAL FINANCE Brigham	17	21	20	21	18	3	4	4	3	3	4	9	9	10	10
FINANCIAL MANAGEMENT 4E Brigham and Gapenski	7	15	14	15	12	22	23	23	23	12	23	20	20	21	21
INT. FINANCIAL MGT. Schall and Haley	4	12	12	12	5	20	21	21	21	6	21	18	18	19	19
INTRO TO FIN. MGT. 3E Neveu	7	21	20	21	10	12	14	14	12	13	14	15	15	15	15
FUND. OF MANAG. FIN. 2E Halloran and Lanser	14	19	20	19	15	3	4	4	3	5	4	7	7	7	7
INTRO TO FIN. MGT.	11	14	15	14	16	3	4	4	3	4	4	21	21	22	22

Text	Cases 31	32	33	34	35	36	37	38	39	40
Bierman and Smidt **FINANCIAL MGT. FOR DECISION MAKING**	20	—	21	22	—	—	24	24	25	40
Moyer et al. CONTEMPORARY FIN. MGT.2E	21	22	15	25	2	9	23	23	17	6
Keown et al. BASIC FIN. MGT. 3E	7	8	18	23	2	10	21	21	20	3
Gitman PRINCIPLES MANG. FIN. 4E	17	18	21	19	2	2	23	23	22	4
Weston and Brigham ESSENTIALS MANG. FIN. 7E	7	10	21	24	2	2	22	22	20	3
Weston and Copeland MANAGERIAL FINANCE 8E	13	15	27	32	4	6	30	30	28	8
Brealey and Myers PRINCIPLE CORP. FIN. 2E	—	30	24	32	—	—	31	31	23	34
Van Horne FUNDAMENTAL FIN. MGT. 5E	10	12	20	25	2	13	24	24	23	6
Van Horne FIN MGT & POLICY 7E	16	17	19	25	—	—	24	24	23	27
Henderson et al. AN INTRO. TO FIN. MGT.	9	10	11	16	5	5	17	17	14	3
Gitman,Joehnk,Pinches MANAGERIAL FINANCE	10	11	22	—	2	12	—	—	23	3
Brigham FINANCIAL MANAGEMENT 4E	19	18	17	26	2	8	24	24	16	22
Brigham and Gapenski INT. FINANCIAL MGT.	17	16	14	24	7	7	22	22	13	20
Schall and Haley INTRO TO FIN. MGT. 3E	15	16	19	24	3	8	23	23	22	12
Neveu FUND. OF MANAG. FIN. 2E	7	8	21	23	2	2	24	24	19	3
Halloran and Lanser INTRO TO FIN. MGT.	22	20	23	25	2	2	24	24	23	3

Contents

PART II. CAPITAL BUDGETING

PART III. LONG-TERM FINANCING

PART V. SPECIAL TOPICS IN FINANCIAL MANAGEMENT

PART VI. MICROCOMPUTERS AND SPREADSHEET PROGRAMS

PART VII. APPENDICES

PART I

Introduction to Financial Management Concepts

Gold Coast
Financial Services

*Constructing Future-Value
and Present-Value Tables*

Gold Coast Financial Services had been organized in Palm Beach, Florida, for the specific purpose of providing personal financial investment services to wealthy residents of that community. The company's founder, J. P. Sloan had left a Wall Street brokerage firm to retire to the community in the early 1950s, and soon after moving to Palm Beach he discovered that none of the brokerage firms were set up to do business in the unique community known as the Gold Coast of Florida. The major stock and bond brokerage houses maintained offices in the larger cities of Florida and serviced communities such as Palm Beach through the use of "travelers." These were usually young, inexperienced brokers who literally operated out of the trunks of their cars.

Thus, in 1953 when Sloan moved to Florida the sole source of individual investment services in the area was the retail brokerage representatives of some of the larger national brokerage houses. These operations were similar to operations all across the country, staffed by account executives who were paid on commission and, hence, motivated to build the largest number of accounts and give very little personal service to any one client. While Sloan as a veteran of the world of Wall Street did not need any specialized investment counseling, he found, from the frequent requests for advice from fellow retirees, that there appeared to be a lack of investment advisory services available to the general public. Despite the fact that he was retired, Sloan could not resist the opportunity and founded Gold Coast Financial Services to meet this need.

GCFS was founded on the belief that there were wealthy individuals who knew they needed financial advice and would be willing to pay for an honest, unbiased appraisal of their financial situations. Sloan also felt that these same individuals would like the opportunity to invest under the guidance of an investment counselor, but would not like to feel that they were obligated to do so. Therefore, Gold Coast's program consisted of a four one-hour investment-counseling sessions, costing $100.00, in which a trained investment counselor would review the financial status of a client and produce a detailed analysis and proposal of an investment strategy for the client. The client was then free to take the report to any financial services company he chose to make the appropriate investments.

It was the goal of Sloan to use the client's report ultimately to sell the client investments that were marketed by Gold Coast. To do this and still maintain that the analysis was an independent evaluation and not influenced by products Gold Coast had available, Sloan created an alternative section of the report. In this section, the report listed a series of investments that were available through Gold Coast, which would meet the investor's needs, along with at least two alternatives for each investment from competing sources. In this way Sloan sought to convince a client that the analysis and evaluation were truly objective and not a ruse to sell investments from Gold Coast.

It was Sloan's objective to make most of the money for the firm on the sale of investments as opposed to fees from financial counseling. He believed, correctly as it turned out, that once clients developed faith and trust in the investment counselor and his recommendations, the client would naturally select the investments from Gold Coast as being the easiest and most practical way to implement the recommended strategy. Consequently, the financial counselors were to receive a large portion of the advisory fee, in order to provide them with an incentive to obtain a client and produce the investment recommendation. Once the client was sold on the investment analysis, the client would sell himself on the Gold Coast investments. Thus, a counselor could expect his income to be made up of 75 per cent of the advisory fees and 25 per cent of the total commission generated from the sale of investments.

The strategy worked very well, and although Sloan had originally set up the firm almost as a hobby, it became sufficiently successful that by 1984 it was supporting a field staff of seventeen investment counselors. At that time the company was operated by Stephen Sloan, a grandnephew of the founder who had purchased the company from the heirs of J. P. Sloan when the latter died in 1967. Stephen Sloan has resisted all offers to expand outside the Florida East Coast region, feeling that to do so would compromise the quality of the service and raise operating costs. Other than the field investment counselors, costs consisted of a small computer-analysis group and a management team consisting of Sloan and a secretary. As counselors were paid totally on commission, and since most clients who received an investment report ultimately purchased at least some investments from Gold Coast, the firm was very profitable and provided Sloan with a very comfortable living.

In mid-1984 the original cost of $100.00 for the investment session had risen to $800.00. Gold Coast found little resistance at that price among serious clients, who felt that if the service was in any way valuable, it should cost a fair amount. A counselor was expected to sell about sixty investment studies a year and make about $36,000 in commission from those reports. A good counselor could add an additional $10,000 to $15,000 from his share of commissions on investment purchases. This additional income would come only if Gold Coast investments were equal to or better than the competing investments listed in the analysis. Thus, Gold Coast was under constant pressure to develop new and better products for their clients.

In late August, 1984, the company's best-selling product was a line called 30-50-100. The numbers referred to the amount of money invested or an amount of annuity purchased. Higher interest rates were paid on larger amounts, the then current rates being 11 per cent on $30,000, 12 per cent on $50,000, and 13 per cent on $100,000. For several months, however, the company had noticed that its investment counselors had not been able to sell as much of the company product at they had in the past. More and more clients were taking the report and seeking other companies with whom to do the actual investing.

A marketing survey of the customers showed that there was no change in customer attitudes about Gold Coast or about its investment counselors. However, interest rates had been rising all during the year, and many investors were putting their money into certificates of deposit with out-of-state banks, which were offering slightly higher interest rates than Gold Coast. It was clear that if Gold Coast was going to obtain the bulk of the investments made by its clients it would have to raise its interest rates.

The investments were packaged as a lump-sum product or as an annuity. For the lump-sum products, investors were guaranteed an amount at the end of each year for up to five years, and had the option of withdrawing their funds on the anniversary date of their investment in any of the five years following the investment. Investments of $30,000 to $50,000 earned 11 per cent, $50,000 to $100,000 earned 12 per cent, and investments over $100,000 earned 13 per cent. For annuities, investors could purchase an annual, single-payment annuity for one to five years. The same breaks held for annu-

Part I: Introduction to Financial Management Concepts

Exhibit 1-1   Selected Present-Value Factors
Interest Rates

Years	8%	10%	12%	14%
1	.926	.909	.893	.877
2	.857	.826	.797	.769
3	.794	.751	.712	.675
4	.735	.683	.636	.592
5	.681	.621	.567	.519

ities; an investment which returned an annuity of $30,000 to $50,000 earned 11 per cent, $50,000 to $100,000 earned 12 per cent, and an annuity that paid in excess of $100,000 each year earned 13 per cent.

The major selling tool for each of the investment counselors was a table of future-value and present-value factors. A sample table is shown in Exhibit 1-1; more tables appear in Appendix A. These tables show the future value of single investments or the present value of a single future payment or of an annuity for given levels of interest rates.

The table of future values shows how much a single investment grows to when invested for a given number of years at a fixed interest rate. The factors, when multiplied by the amount invested showed the value of the investment at the end of the year chosen. The present-value tables have two uses. The present value of a single investment is used for financial planning. Typically, investors had a future goal and were concerned about how much money had to be invested today to reach that goal. The table of present values provides factors to compute the initial sum of money that must be invested. The table of present-value factors for an annuity is used to price the annuity. For a given annuity, the data in the table would be used to compute the amount of money that must be paid into the investment account today.

In deciding to become more competitive, Sloan felt he must raise his interest rate by at least one-half of one per cent. Thus he proposed to increase the investment returns to 11.5 per cent, 12.5 per cent, and 13.5 per cent. In doing so he knew he would have to compute a table of future values and present values for these rates to support the investment counselors in their determination of how much a client would have to invest to have a certain sum.

SUGGESTED QUESTIONS

1. Compute a table of future-value interest factors for 11.5 per cent, 12.5 per cent, and 13.5 per cent for years 1–5.

2. Compute a table of present-value interest factors for 11.5 per cent, 12.5 per cent, and 13.5 per cent for years 1–5.

3. Compute a table of present value of annuity factors for 11.5 per cent, 12.5 per cent, and 13.5 per cent for years 1–5.

4. Use the tables to answer the following questions.

    a. What is the future value of an investment of $75,000 at 12.5 per cent for four years?

    b. What is the present value of an investment of $60,000 at 11.5 per cent for five years?

    c. What is the present value of an annuity of $80,000 at 13.5 per cent for three years?

New Jersey Social Advisory Services

Computing Present Value, Future Value, and Annuities

The New Jersey Social Advisory Services was a unique state agency set up on the principle that state social services would be far more effective if they could prevent problems and not just try to solve them after they occurred. The thrust of the agency was to provide a counseling service on a wide range of issues and areas where individuals and families could seek advice and assistance. One of the unique aspects of the organization was that it regarded personal financial problems as a major cause of social and family problems and so set out to provide families with financial advice and assistance.

Traditionally, government eschewed financial advisory services in the belief that (1) the individual is the best judge of what is right for him and (2) government advice on family financial planning leaves the state open to charges of bias toward certain financial practices. Long experience in social work had shown Barrie Larson that the first principle was not the rule for a large number of people. Since becoming head of the Family Financial Services Division of the agency, she had been surprised and amazed at the lack of understanding of various aspects of personal finance shown by many of the clients. This lack of expertise was not the result of a lack of education: many users of the service were college-educated.

On the second objection, involvement of the state in rendering opinions on financial matters, Larson, who had lobbied for, and been the impetus behind, the formation of the organization, argued that unbiased financial advice could be given which would still leave the actual decision in the hands of the individual involved. She had personally been responsible for the limitations on the services that had been placed on the Family Financial Services Division. These limitations included a ban on recommending any specific financial investment, a ban on any opinion regarding a financial institution or financial-services company, and a general restriction of the service to answering questions and providing broad-based financial advice. Larson was not necessarily in agreement with these restrictions but felt they must apply in order for the controversial agency to survive in a treacherous political environment.

The first office of the agency was set up in Atlantic City, staffed by Larson and several assistants. That location was chosen because the introduction of legalized gambling and the resultant real-estate boom had brought windfall real-estate profits to many people who were unused to having large sums of money. Larson felt that the agency could in many cases prevent these people from being "conned" out of their money, and that with proper investment strategies the money could serve as a stabilizing rather than disruptive influence in the lives of these individuals.

Initially, the acceptance of the state as a provider of personal financial-investment advice had been slow, but by mid-1982 the case load of the office was such that the agency was being utilized to full capacity. Larson felt that the agency had served its purpose in preventing many people from losing their money in speculative and unsound investments, while at the same time remaining neutral in terms of passing on the quality of any specific institution or investment.

Although the agency was free to work with clients in any way, typically a client would have two sessions with a counselor. In the first session, the client would provide all necessary financial information and discuss the particular problem he or she was experiencing. The counselor would write up the case and, either alone or through consultations with other staff members, would make recommendations within the framework of the restrictions on the agency. A second meeting was then held with the client in which the recommendations were presented in a written report. Occasionally a follow-up session was required, but in most cases the client was able to take the report and use it as a basis for "shopping around" for the proper investment.

Larson had an M.B.A. in finance from Princeton University, and her background was in the mathematics of investments. Consequently, she often received the cases that required a quantitative answer or analysis. She was currently working with four such cases.

CLIENT 1

Mrs. Adele E. had four grandchildren, the oldest of which would be entering college in ten years. She wanted to provide assistance for their education by giving each child $10,000 a year for the four years that each would be in college. She currently had about $40,000 in the bank from the sale of a small house near the Boardwalk and was wondering whether or not this could be invested to earn enough to provide for the $160,000 that would be needed for the four grandchildren.

In reading the file, Larson learned that the first child would start college in exactly ten years, the second two years later, the third one year after that and the fourth two years after the third. The funds would be left in the investment and withdrawn only as needed. The expectation was that at the end of the last year of the last child's college experience, the account would be exhausted and have a zero balance. Larson felt that 12 per cent per year, compounded annually would be a reasonable estimate for a return on the $40,000 investment over its life.

CLIENT 2

John and Mary C. were a middle-aged couple in the midst of planning for their retirement. John was fifty-five and had decided to put the maximum amount, $2,000, into an IRA account for the next ten years. He was planning to retire at sixty-five. The couple felt they should make arrangements for the following twenty years and were not concerned about planning beyond the age of eighty-five. They wanted the funds that accumulated in the IRA to purchase a twenty-year annuity. They had one child, whom they wished to leave or give $50,000 when they reached eighty-five.

Based on the investment opportunities available, Larson felt that a 13 per cent interest rate should be used in evaluating their situation. The couple was concerned about how much of an annuity to purchase at retirement that would still leave enough in their investment to grow to $50,000 in twenty years.

CLIENT 3

Ansel and Harriet W. were a young, highly educated professional couple both employed by one of the leading resort hotels in the area. They were planning on saving for a new house, which they expected to purchase in seven years. In addition to that financial requirement, they felt that Harriet would quit working at that time to care for their expected family, and that the loss of her income would make them unable to keep up payments on the house without an annuity to supplement his income.

The couple felt that they needed $1,500 a year in supplemental income beginning at the end of the eigth year to assist with the house payments, and that they needed this for each of the next thirty years. They also wanted to have $50,000 with which to make the down payment in seven years when they planned to buy the house. As both were working, they had plenty of funds for savings and were wondering how much they should put away at the end of each of the next seven years to be able to make the down payment and buy the annuity. Larson felt that an 11 per cent interest rate applied to their situation.

CLIENT 4

Arthur F.'s situation also involved the amount of $40,000. He had received an inheritance of $40,000 from a great-aunt and had been offered an annuity of $5,000 a year for twenty-five years, or a total of $125,000 at a cost of $40,000. He also had a number of alternatives available, the lowest of which offered a 12 per cent annual compounded return. Arthur F. liked the annuity, but was willing to invest in it only if it offered a 12 per cent return or better.

SUGGESTED QUESTIONS

In the following questions, assume that no individual income tax considerations are present and that investments can be made at the interest rate stated in the case.

1. For Case 1, is the $40,000 sufficient to provide for the four scholarships, paying the money as needed?

2. For Case 2, how much of an annuity will the couple be able to purchase at retirement, leaving enough in the account to grow to $50,000 in twenty years?

3. For Case 3, how much must the couple save each year and deposit at the end of the year at 11 per cent interest to meet their goals?

4. For Case 4, should the individual accept the annuity?

Northwestern Yachts, Inc.

Loan Payments and Amortization Schedules

Jack Zalig, president and founder of Northwestern Yachts, Inc., liked to brag that his company was set up, organized, and run on more marketing research than any other boating company along the Pacific coast. Regardless of the accuracy of that statement, it was true that the company was one of the most successful small-boat sales companies in its sales area. In 1981, seventeen years after its beginnings, the company had sales in excess of $20 million and profits close to a 10 per cent after-tax margin. With the exception of its first year and two years in the early 1970s when Boeing Aircraft severely cut back production, Northwestern had never had a losing year.

Northwestern was located just north of Seattle, Washington, and had a customer base that extended as far south as Portland, Oregon. The compnay was started by Zalig and two other partners in 1964, but a clash over ideas for running the company had led Zalig to buy out his partners less than one year after the company opened for business. Zalig's interest in sail-powered yachting as a business was a natural one, as he had grown up along the Pacific coast and had been sailing since he was seven. In 1964, after a hitch in the armed service, and six years as an industrial engineer at Boeing, he took a small inheritance, quit his job, and set up Northwestern Yachts.

The core businesses of Northwestern Yachts were the sales and service of small- to medium-sized sailing craft. Northwestern acquired the exclusive rights to two small but popular lines just making their entrance into the Northwest market, and it developed a small service staff that would repair almost any make of sailing vessel. The strong Northwest economy, an increasing use of outdoor recreation by the public, a quality line and good service, along with creative management by Zalig, made the company a financial success in all years except those already noted. Zalig had inspired several competitors, but since none copied his operations directly, he was able to successfully compete in the market, and ultimately absorbed two of the smaller competitors who never recovered from the 1975–1976 recession.

Before beginning the business, Zalig had hired a local consulting firm to survey the market. The consulting firm reported the following results.

1. Customers were likely to be male, aged twenty-five to fifty with annual incomes greater than $20,000.

2. While price would be an important element in choosing a dealer, quality of product and of service would be equally important. Most customers would be willing to pay a higher initial price and a higher service cost if the product were of high quality, the service good, and the customer were treated in a deferential manner.

3. Customers would have a very low tolerance of inconvenience. They wanted a full-service dealer who would take care of all aspects of yacht ownership at one place. This meant sales, service, storage, and insurance should be handled by one individual and one source. Customers would not respond well to "I don't know about insurance, why don't you see someone else about it."

4. There was a strong identification among customers for the type of craft they were purchasing. Boaters were either "sail" or "power," and each side had a very strong identification with one type or the other. In addition, each type of boater tended to feel his method was superior to the other and regarded the other as belonging to a lower class of outdoorsman. The consultants recommended that Zalig set up either a power-boat operation or a sail-boat operation but not mix the two together.

Zalig followed this advice faithfully and believed that the success of his operation would depend almost entirely upon his ability to operate as the consultants described. His advertising stressed sailing and sail power; his sales personnel took care of every detail except financing for the customer. He assisted in getting insurance, obtaining a license, setting up training, completely outfitting the boat and everything else needed for a turnkey operation. A customer needed only to talk with one person from Northwestern Yachts to be completely supplied with a boat, mooring slip, and everything else needed to set sail.

Zalig had wanted to offer financing, not as a money-making part of his business but in order to be able to take care of every detail for his potential customer and truly make his business a one-stop boating center. However, as a start-up business this had been impossible. Finally, in 1977 he negotiated an arrangement with a local bank whereby the bank would purchase an installment note from Zalig at one-half to one percentage point discount from face value, so long as the customer had a good credit rating and the interest rate on the note was at the current market rate. This arrangement allowed Zalig to close the loop and now provide complete sales and service facilities to a customer. From the customer's point of view, he dealt only with Northwestern and rarely knew that the note for the purchase of the boat was actually held by a bank.

Continuing to innovate, Zalig soon introduced an annual payment program, or APP, for the financing of boat sales. His marketing studies had told him that many customers on the upper end of the income scale had wanted to finance purchases, even though they could afford to pay cash, in order to preserve liquidity and take advantage of the tax deductibility of interest costs. However, these same customers disliked the bother of monthly installment payments. They preferred to make one payment a year. Because bookkeeping for a single yearly payment was much easier than twelve monthly payments, and because the credit rating of the customers was triple A, Zalig had no difficulty in introducing the concept of a note with annual payments to either his customers or the bank. The program proved an immediate success and stimulated business; 72 per cent of the loans on sales of $40,000 and up were financed this way.

Under the APP arrangement, a customer could negotiate a payment program for three to eight years. Current interest rates for those maturities are shown in Exhibit 3-1. The higher rates for the longer-term loans were to satisfy credit considerations at the bank, and other than rates the program was identical for all loans. A customer wishing to use the APP finance method would put down a minimum of 20 per cent of the price and pay off the remainder in equal annual installments on the anniversary of the date of pur-

Exhibit 3-1   Loan Payment Terms

Years	Rate
3	12.00%
4	13.00%
5	14.00%
6	15.00%
7	15.00%
8	15.00%

chase. A customer buying a $100,000 yacht, for example, would pay $20,000 down, and if he elected the five-year plan, would make five annual installment payments at the end of each of the next five years, paying interest at a rate of 14 per cent.

Zalig's immediate problem involved a customer who wished to purchase a $50,000 Sky Star, a thirty-foot boat that slept four. The customer wanted to finance the purchase using the APP arrangement, but was uncertain which maturity he would take. He also indicated he was most likely to take a five-year note at 14 per cent and in doing so wanted to know what his payments would be, and what portion of the payment would be tax-deductible interest. Finally, the customer wanted to know the impact of prepayment of the loan.

The program allowed for prepayment of the loan by up to $1,000 on each payment. That is, a customer could pay $1,000 more on his annual payment each year, with all of the $1,000 going toward reduction of the principal outstanding. However, any prepayment did not affect the amount of the subsequent payments until the final payment. The prepayment was subtracted from the principal outstanding in computing the interest component of the payment. The adjustment was made on the last payment; that is, the final payment would be recomputed so that it made the final interest payment and reduced the principal to zero.

SUGGESTED QUESTIONS

1. Compute the annual payments for each rate and maturity in Exhibit 3-1 for a $40,000 note.

2. Assume the purchase of a $50,000 sail boat with 20 per cent down. Construct an amortization table for the five annual payments at 14 per cent.

3. For the situation in Question 2, assume that prepayments of $1,000 are made in years 2, 3, and 4; that is, the payment made at the end of the years is $1,000 more than required and that the payment is used to reduce the principal with the payment amounts unchanged.

    a. Construct the new amortization table.

    b. How much is the final payment reduced?

    c. How much in interest costs are saved by making the prepayment?

4. Under what circumstances would you recommend prepayment?

Pilgrims Bank and Trust (A)

Bond Prices and Bond Price Elasticity

The Fixed Rate Securities Committee of the Pilgrims Bank and Trust of Providence, Rhode Island, was a group that, until recently, was rarely noticed and went about its work with almost no controversy. Its members had almost always been able to produce a uniform recommendation for additions to the Bank's portfolio of fixed-income investments. However, in early 1982, the bank had just been through record-high interest rates and fluctuating bond prices; at times, these had caused the bond markets to resemble the gyrations of the stock market more than their own usual quiet and stability. Suddenly, the committee found itself sharply divided on investment policy.

Pilgrims Bank and Trust was a moderate size commercial bank serving Rhode Island in general and the city of Providence in particular. Its assets and liabilities were typical of most commercial banks, with about 35 per cent of its investments in the securities markets and the remainder in loans, primarily commercial loans tied to the prime rate. Its deposits were primarily checking accounts (demand deposits) and short-term CDs. The balance sheet for Pilgrims was relatively strong for a commercial bank at the end of 1981. Pilgrims had earned 1.25 per cent on its assets in 1981 and a 14.7 per cent return on equity. It had a reputation as a well-managed operation, and its financial performance was usually among the top in its size and geographic area.

Overall bank policy was determined by the Asset/Liability Executive Committee, made up of the chairman and chief executive officer, Roland Briggs, the president and chief operating officer, Harold Downs and the chief financial officer, Donald Riser. These three men met each Monday afternoon to hear reports on the bank's condition, economic forecasts, and special analyses and to make decisions with respect to the bank's investment and funding strategies. Depending upon how it saw future economic conditions and the type of funding available, the Committee might recommend shifting into or out of commercial loans and out of or into fixed-rate securities. The goals of the committee were to keep the maturities of assets matched with the maturities of the liabilities and to take advantage of economic trends by moving to longer-term or shorter-term investments as interest rates and economic conditions dictated.

The Fixed Rate Securities Committee (FRSC) was the group responsible for making recommendations to the Asset/Liability Executive Committee with respect to specific investments in fixed-rate securities. The banks nonloan portfolio was primarily composed of medium- to long-term government and high-grade corporate bonds, with a lesser amount in short-term government securities such as T bills for purposes of liquidity. The FRSC was the vehicle through which recommendations for purchase of fixed-rate securities received approval from the bank's senior managers. The committee was made up of the vice-president for fixed-rate investments, who was responsible for actual trading of the bank's fixed-rate portfolio, the vice-president, treasurer, who was responsible for overall asset/liability management, and the chief financial officer who headed the committee.

The individual portfolio managers, who actually bought and sold the securities, made recommendations for approved purchases to the vice-president for fixed-rate investments. If he approved, he took the recommendations to the FRSC who made their own evaluation. If they approved the recommendation, it was taken to the Asset/ Liability Executive Committee whose ultimate approval was needed before purchases could be made. While this appeared to be a cumbersome procedure, the Asset/Liability Committee met every week so that actions could be taken very quickly, and the approval process made certain that any investment strategy had been thoroughly reviewed and met with approval from all key members of the executive team.

In the past, the work on the Fixed Rate Securities Committee had been somewhat dull and unexciting. As long as the credit quality of the securities that were recommended was at an investment-grade level, recommendations of the individual portfolio managers were rarely challenged. However, the rapid rise in interest rates in the 1980–1981 period had changed all this. (See Exhibit 4-1) The bank had been caught with a large portion of its fixed-rate portfolio in

Part I: Introduction to Financial Management Concepts

Exhibit 4-1 Interest Rates (in Per Cent)
1976–1981

	3 Month T Bill	3 Year Notes	10 Year Notes	Corp AAA Bonds
1976	5.00	6.77	7.61	8.43
1977	5.30	6.69	7.42	8.02
1978	7.20	8.29	8.41	8.73
1979	10.40	9.72	9.44	9.63
1980	11.50	11.55	11.46	11.94
1981	14.10	14.44	13.91	14.17

long-term, relatively low-yielding assets. When rates rose, these securities went "underwater"; that is, their value dropped substantially below their initial cost. While the portfolio was carried at original cost on the balance sheet, so that the decline in value was not reflected on the financial statements, the sale of any portion at a loss would result in a loss on the income statement and a consequent reduction in capital. Thus, securities with a substantial loss were permanently frozen in the portfolio, unable to be liquidated until interest rates fell or until they matured. With rates at near-record highs in early 1982, the large majority of the portfolio was, as one member of the committee put it, "just laying there, moaning and groaning."

In order to avoid this type of problem in the future, the recommendations of the committee had now come under severe scrutiny. The result was that in addition to looking at the credit risk of corporate issuers of bonds, the committee focused an equal amount of time on interest-rate risk and the possibility of taking capital-gains profits from trading in corporate bonds. If interest rates were to decline, the value of high-yielding bonds would rise above their purchase price and could be sold at a profit. Success in this area would significantly offset the losses suffered on existing low-yielding investments.

In early 1982 the committee met to consider the recommendation of adding corporate bonds issued by International Motors. International Motors was a manufacturer of small cars and light trucks. It had suffered severe financial losses in the late 1970s, but a new management team, cost control, and a new line of vehicles had turned the company around. The debt of the company was now rated as investment quality by the major rating services, but because of the past history and problems of the company, the yields were slightly above yields of similar maturity and credit quality. Several of the portfolio managers felt that the bonds should be acquired because

Exhibit 4-2 Bond Listings

	Close Jan. 15, 1982	Code
Int. Motors 14s87	100	A
Int. Motors 14s02	100	B
Int. Motors 6s87	72½	C
Int. Motors 8s02	60¼	D

they would improve overall yields on the portfolio without adding substantial risk.

The critical question in approving the addition of International Motors to the portfolio was which bonds to add. Four issues were available, as shown in Exhibit 4-2. The issue code-named A had a 14 per cent coupon and was due in five years. It was selling at par. The issue code-named B also had a 14 per cent coupon, was also selling at par, but it was due in twenty years. Two issues were available at a substantial discount from par, a 6 per cent coupon issue that was due in five years and sold at 72 1/2, code-named C and an 8 per cent coupon issue that was due in twenty years and has a price of 60 1/4, code-named D.

While all of these bonds had an approximate yield of 14 per cent, they were not all necessarily desirable. Because each bond was different in either its length of maturity or its coupon rate, each bond would react differently from the others as interest rates changed. Some of the bonds would be more profitable than others in the event of a drop in interest rates, while some would offer more protection than others in the situation where interest rates rose. The recommendation of the committee would depend upon the committee's forecast of the future movement of rates. Strategies would differ depending upon whether or not the committee felt rates would rise or fall during the next twelve to eighteen months.

The committee generally relied upon two economic advisory services for its economic forecast. These were Econometrics, Inc., whose large econometric model gave quarterly forecasts for a period of up to four years, and Futures, Inc., a forecasting service primarily using the qualitative estimates of its staff. Unfortunately, the two services were diametrically oppposed in their outlook on the future. An excerpt from Econometrics went as follows:

Interest rates are likely to rise throughout 1982 and well into 1983, possibly reaching record levels by year end 1983. The recent tax cuts will lift the government deficit to record levels, increasing pressure on credit markets and producing somewhat of a crowding-out effect as government competes with business and consumers for loanable funds.

Part I: Introduction to Financial Management Concepts

Later in the year, the fiscal stimulus of high rates of government spending, particularly in the defense area, and consumer demand, stimulated by tax cuts, will push interest rates 100 to 200 basis points above current levels. Inflation, while declining, is not expected to fall much below current levels, and lenders, having been burned by negative real-interest rates in the past two years will demand an inflation premium for their funds.

The other advisory service took a much more favorable view of the future of interest rates, at the expense of the health of the economy.

Interest rates have probably peaked or will do so very soon and then head dramatically downward. The government's level of borrowing will be high, but the economic recession that began last year will continue, reducing both consumer and business demands for funds. The level of inflation should continue to drop as the recession cuts into demand for goods and services and as a rising unemployment rate moderates wage increases.

We see action on the part of the Federal Reserve System to expand the supply of credit and increase the money supply in the second half of 1982 and all through 1983. On the fiscal side, the impact of the three-year tax-cut plan will probably not take place until 1983 and 1984 and, historically, during a recovery period, now expected for late 1983 and 1984, interest rates, prices, and wage rates have had only moderate increases. We do not forecast sharp increases in rates until late in the recovery, which may be as much as four or five years away.

Opinion in the committee was divided along similar lines. One faction felt that interest rates would continue to rise, and that while the high yields associated with the International Motors should be accepted, investment policy should be defensive and choose those issues which would react the least to an increase in rates. A second faction felt that just the opposite was the case. They argued that rates would be falling and that some of the issues of International Motors offered a great opportunity for capital gains. They felt the committee should recommend only those issues which showed maximum appreciation in the event that interest rates fell.

SUGGESTED QUESTIONS

1. Compute the price of each bond for the following interest rates:
   a. 10 per cent
   b. 12 per cent
   c. 14 per cent
   d. 16 per cent
   e. 18 per cent

2. Compute the percentage change in price for each bond from the current 14 per cent yield for each of the above interest rates.

    a. Which bond is best if interest rates rise?

    b. Which bond is best if interest rates fall?

    3. Compute bond price elasticities for interest rate changes from the current 14 per cent for interest rates 10 per cent, 12 per cent, 16 per cent, and 18 per cent for each bond. Explain why the results differ between bonds and within each bond.

    4. Look up movement of interest rates in 1982–1985. Which bonds should have been chosen and why?

CASE 5

Pilgrims Bank and Trust (B)

Bond Yields with Taxes

At its regular meeting in late January, the Asset/Liability Executive Committee of the Pilgrims Bank and Trust of Providence was considering a recommendation to authorize investment in International Motors 14s, 2002 corporate bonds. Executive Committee authorization was the final step in giving portfolio managers the right to add the bonds to the bank's portfolio of fixed-rate investments. The recommendation came from the Fixed Rate Securities Committee, a group charged with evaluating and recommending fixed-rate investment for the bank.

In part, the Fixed Rate Securities Committee's recommendation read as follows:

We have examined four possible issues for International Motors, the 14 per cent, 1987 maturity, 14 per cent, 2002 maturity, 6 per cent, 1987 maturity, and the 8 per cent, 2002 maturity. All four issues are currently priced to yield 14 per cent, an attractive rate in view of other opportunities. We recommend the purchase of the 14 per cent, 2002 maturity for two reasons. The first is that we feel interest rates will decline in the next several years below current levels, and this issue gives us a greater opportunity for capital gains than the same coupon maturing in 1987. If we wish to sell we should be able to do so at a gain, and if we wish to hold we will have locked in a 14 per cent return for twenty years.

The second reason for recommending this issue as opposed to the other long-term issue, the 8 per cent maturing in 2002, is that we are not quite as vulnerable if the interest rates rise. We feel this issue gives us the best opportunity for profit with a reasonable risk.

After reviewing this report, Harold Downs, president and chief operating officer of the bank, asked if the 8 per cent issue, now selling for 60 ¼ had been originally issued at par. If it had, he pointed out, the bond's gain in price as it gradually reached par value would be a capital gain, and taxed at a favorable rate of 28 per cent, as opposed to the bank's tax rate on ordinary income and interest income of 46 per cent. He wondered if this aspect of the investments had been taken into account when the recommendation for the 14 per cent issue had been made.

Donald Riser, chief financial officer of the bank and a member of both the Asset/Liability Executive Committee and the Fixed Rate Securities Committee, indicated that the discount on the 8 per cent bond was indeed the result of interest-rate movements since the bond had been issued at par, and that any gain on the sale of the bond would be taxed at the capital-gains rate. He suggested the recommendations be returned to the FRSC for further review.

The instructions to the FRSC were to evaluate all four potential bonds available from International Motors with respect to their after tax yields. He knew that the before-tax yields were approximately 14 per cent on all four bonds, but under the assumption that all four bonds were held to maturity, the after-tax yields would be different. The coupon payments would be taxed as ordinary income, but any gain in the price of the bonds that were selling at a discount would be taxed as a capital gain.

SUGGESTED QUESTIONS

1. Compute the after-tax cash flows from holding each of the four bonds described in Case 4 to maturity. Assume a corporate-tax rate of 46 per cent and a capital-gains rate of 28 per cent. Assume annual interest payments, beginning in exactly one year.

2. Based on current market prices given in Case 4, what is the after-tax yield to maturity on each issue?

3. Other than taxes, list and explain any other reasons why the 8 per cent bond might be preferred to the 14 per cent bond.

Thackery Capital Company

Internal Rate of Return

Bill Thackery, chairman of the Thackery Capital Company, was the fourth generation Thackery to head the diversified investment company. The company had been founded as a holding company by William M. Thackery of Wilmington, Delaware, in 1885 as a corporate "shell" to hold stock in the various steel companies, railroads, and manufacturing concerns controlled by William Thackery. Thackery had been what today is commonly referred to as a "robber baron," and in the early 1900s came under severe attack by the government for anticompetitive practices. Ultimately the holdings were sold off, and all that remained of a financial empire that rivaled Carnegie and J. P. Morgan was the holding company, Thackery Capital.

Thackery Capital was a closely held corporation, with almost all of the shareholders the descendants and heirs of William Thackery. Following the forced sale or liquidation of most of the Thackery assets in the trust-busting era of the early 1900s, William Thackery retired and turned the operations over to his son, William Thackery, Jr. The second Thackery's objectives were to make money solely on investments, rather than operations, and he used Thackery Capital as the vehicle to make equity investments in various companies, with his source of funds being the proceeds from the sale of companies and long-term borrowings. William Thackery, Jr., died with no direct family, and the shares of the company were dispersed into the hands of the nieces and nephews of the founder.

The current chairman, William H. (Bill) Thackery, joined the company fresh out of business school in 1963, and in 1976 became its head. Since World War II, the company's sole line of business has been investing in small to medium-sized growth-oriented companies. Thackery Capital takes a minority interest, a majority interest, or entire ownership of the companies it invests in; but in all cases it remains a shareholder and not a manager. Bill Thackery's predecessor's philosophy had been to "hire good people and listen to them." Thackery Capital's income came from dividends from the companies in which it held shares and from capital gains when the companies were sold. On the average, Thackery Capital held an investment about 7.2 years.

When Bill Thackery took over the company there were about 235 shareholders, some of them charitable institutions who had acquired stock as bequests or gifts from members of the family. For the institutions and for many of the other shareholders, income from Thackery Capital represented a significant portion of their total income. As a result, the investment policy of Thackery had been to invest in companies whose cash flow allowed them to pass a large percentage of their net income through in the form of dividends, which in turn were paid out by Thackery to its shareholders. This policy was very popular, and Bill Thackery had taken over Thackery Capital with the stipulation that, while he was free to implement whatever policy he felt best for the long-term growth and survival of the company, he would not radically alter the flow of income to the shareholders.

In the early 1980s Thackery became concerned that a policy focusing on investments with high-dividend yields was becoming detrimental to the company. The reason for this was that the high-dividend payments by the companies that were owned by Thackery left them little retained earnings for expansion and growth. Thus, the high-dividend companies tended to have little or no growth, and some were vulnerable to aggressive competitors who paid little or no dividends. Thackery was convinced that unless the policy was altered he would be presiding over a declining company.

The situation was becoming critical in Thackery's view because his father's generation was passing on and distributing its shares to more individuals and institutions. As the number of shareholders grew the income per shareholder dropped; ultimately, it would drop to an unsatisfactory level. Thus, in Thackery's opinion, unless the investment philosophy was changed, income per shareholder would gradually diminish and result in exactly what the shareholders had sought to prevent, a decline in their earnings from the company.

Thackery proposed to solve this problem by shifting the investment philosophy of the company away from high-dividend companies toward high-growth companies. He would meet the objective of current income needs by shortening the holding period of the investments; thus, substituting capital gains for dividend income. He hoped that by pursuing this new strategy he could maintain the distributions that Thackery Capital made to its shareholders at 80 per cent of its 1982 level until the new strategy began to generate its own cash flows. At the same time, the new strategy would significantly increase the total value of the company. It was his intention to have the company large enough so that the 1982 income level could be restored by 1987 and to change the company's current income composition, 90 per cent dividend income and 10 per cent capital gains, to 40 per cent dividend income and 60 per cent capital gains.

In order to implement this strategy, Thackery had to convince the Board of Directors. There was severe resistance by a minority of the board, comprised mainly of those members whose current income would be cut by the change in policy. However, at the end of 1984 Thackery had succeeded in convincing a majority of the board to approve investments where the dividend payout ratio of the companies was between 15 per cent and 40 per cent. However, in the board's January 1985 meeting Thackery was going to propose purchase of Aqua Chemicals, a company whose dividends would be zero at least for the next five years and probably for the foreseeable future.

Aqua Chemicals was a specialty chemical company, founded in the late 1960s by a trio of chemical engineers who had bought out the operations from a large, diversified chemical producer. It had taken over a decade for the company to achieve the type of growth that had been expected of it, but in 1984 its sales were up over 50 per cent from the two previous years, and net income, while not increasing as fast, was up substantially. Bill Thackery believed the company had a strong five years ahead of it, and the owners were intrigued by the thought of selling the company but staying on to manage it. As a part of the deal they would participate in a profit-sharing plan; so, from their point of view, operations and remuneration would be the same as if they continued to own it. The 1982–1984 income statement for Aqua is shown in Exhibit 6-1, and Thackery's own forecast of growth and earnings, which he considered conservative, is shown in Exhibit 6-2.

In preliminary discussions with the owners and their agents, Thackery felt, based on the current price of similar companies, that the company could be acquired for fourteen times 1984 earnings. He planned to hold the company for five years then take it public or sell it to another company. While it would be impossible to forecast a price in five years, Thackery felt certain that the company would at least bring the same multiple at the end of 1989 as he had paid for it. Given the earnings projections of Exhibit 6-2, Thackery argued that the investment presented an excellent opportunity to implement his high-growth strategy.

Exhibit 6-1 Aqua Chemicals, Inc.: Income Statement (in $000)

Year Ending Dec. 31

	1982	1983	1984
Net Sales	22,054	29,047	35,763
Cost of Sales	11,345	13,985	16,542
Gross Profit	10,709	15,062	19,221
Operating Expenses			
Sales Expense	3,256	5.678	6,730
Administration Expense	4,321	5,549	7,643
Total	7,577	11,227	14,373
Operating Income	3,132	3,835	4,848
Other Income (Expenses)	(1,234)	(1,432)	(1,543)
Income Before Taxes	1,898	2,403	3,305
Taxes	423	1,043	1,356
Net Income	1,475	1,360	1,949

Controversy had erupted over the proposed purchase within the board, and even Thackery's supporters were concerned. Purchase of Aqua would be the first company ever bought that did not pay any dividend and for which no future dividend was expected. At its proposed cost, Aqua would represent over 15 per cent of Thackery Capital's assets, and the sole prospect for income would be a capital gain to be realized in the future. While Bill Thackery was confident of the future prospects of Aqua, several board members pointed out that there was no guarantee that the forecasted growth would take place. Even if it did, they argued, there was no assurance that Aqua could be sold for fourteen times earnings at the end of 1989. If P/E ratios of similar companies was ten times earnings; the sale of Aqua would make very little contribution to Thackery.

As an alternative, several members of the board proposed the acquisition of Ellis Parts, Inc. Ellis Parts was a Cleveland based

Exhibit 6-2 Aqua Chemicals, Inc.

Sales, Earnings, Dividends Forecast

Year	Sales	Net Income	Dividends
1985	43,254	2,214	0
1986	48,976	2,567	0
1987	51,234	2,896	0
1988	59,876	3,198	0
1989	67,543	3,589	0

Exhibit 6-3   Ellis Parts, Inc.: Income Statement (in $000)

Year Ending Dec. 31

	1982	1983	1984
Net Sales	32,567	34,523	35,643
Cost of Goods Sold	14,387	15,432	16,854
Gross Profit	18,180	19,091	18,789
Operating Expenses			
Sales Expense	3,134	3,218	3,365
Administration Expense	5,476	6,754	6,233
Total	8,610	9,972	9,598
Operating Income	9,570	9,119	9,191
Other Income (Expenses)	(2,214)	(2,453)	(2,563)
Income Before Taxes	7,356	6,666	6,628
Taxes	3,045	2,765	2,616
Net Income	4,311	3,901	4,012

manufacturer of automobile parts for both the original-equipment market and the replacement market. While the past growth of Ellis was not as spectacular as that of Aqua, as shown in Exhibit 6-3, Ellis had a very healthy return on sales and a dividend payout ratio of approximately 75 per cent. The company had a long history of stability, and its future sales and incomes could be forecasted with a relatively high degree of accuracy. The forecast for sales, income, and dividends for Ellis is shown in Exhibit 6-4. As a mature company, Ellis could be purchased for seven times 1984 earnings, and the dissident group of the board pointed out that the company could also be sold in five years, probably at the same multiple, which would contribute some capital gains to Thackery.

As the January 1985 board meeting approached, Bill Thackery realized he would have to analyze both investments and give the board the opportunity to select the one it felt would be best.

Exhibit 6-4   Ellis Parts, Inc.

Sales, Earnings, Dividends Forecast

Year	Sales	Net Income	Dividends
1985	38,976	4,123	3,250
1986	41,236	4,232	3,250
1987	43,987	4,297	3,350
1988	47,864	4,312	3,350
1989	49,873	4,321	3,450

SUGGESTED QUESTIONS

Assume away all tax computations and effects.

1. **a.** Based on a multiple of fourteen, what is the current price for Aqua Chemical?
   b. Based on the same multiple, what is the value of Aqua at the end of 1989?
   c. What is the rate of return on the purchase and subsequent sale in five years of Aqua assuming it was purchased for the price in **a** and sold for the price in **b**?
2. **a.** Based on Exhibit 6-3, and a multiple of seven, what is the current cost of buying Ellis Parts?
   b. Assuming the dividends on Ellis as shown in Exhibit 6-4, and that the company could be sold at the end of five years at seven times earnings, what is the rate of return on the purchase of Ellis at the price computed in **a?**
3. **a.** What is the total cash flow regardless of source or timing from buying Aqua and selling in five years? From buying Ellis and selling in five years?
   b. Since both investments return about the same rate, how do you explain the fact that the total dollar profit from Aqua is higher than that of Ellis?
4. What assumptions are implicit in the acceptance of the rates of return that are computed in Questions 1 and 2?
5. Make a recommendation for Thackery as to the purchase of Aqua or Ellis and support it with facts from the case and from your analysis in the previous questions.

PART II

Capital Budgeting

Bonar Graphics Corporation

NPV-IRR for a New Project

Daniel Ellis, vice-president of administration and finance of the Bonar Graphics Corporation had rapidly come to the conclusion that building an extra 37,000 square feet in the company's new plant to accommodate growth had been an economic success but an administrative failure. The plant had been finished eleven years before. It was a modern building, on a small parcel of land in an industrial park outside Rochester, New York. The plant had been designed to hold all of Bonar's manufacturing, distribution, and service operations under a single roof.

Bonar Graphics had been founded in the mid 1960s by several engineers who had left the Jennings Camera Company, one of the country's largest manufacturers of graphics equipment and supplies. Bonar had originally been set up to manufacture a line of specialized graphics equipment that its founders had helped design, but which had generated little interest at Jennings Camera. However, the founders soon learned what Jennings' marketing people already knew, namely, that this line did not have sufficient potential to carry the company. Rather than abandon the project they expanded the business to include a distributorship of other manufacturers' products and a service department to repair and install not only their own equipment but other major manufacturers' as well.

Based on a combination of technical expertise and high service quality, the company had grown and prospered as high-tech firms expanded in the Rochester area. In early 1970, the company secured government-assisted financing to build its own facilities in a newly formed industrial park. Anticipating growth, the company built an additional 37,000 square feet of plant space onto the building to accommodate future needs. It was that space which was the cause of the problems facing Daniel Ellis.

In 1972 when the company moved to its new facilities the extra space stood idle. Several years later, Travis Harper, maintenance supervisor manager, suggested that the unused facility be devoted to a maintenance and repair facility for the company's service vehicles. The service trucks were large, specially equipped custom vans which enabled almost all of the service work to be performed at the customer's site. The trucks were equipped with special test equipment, and because they were constantly on the road during the harsh local winters, their maintenance requirements were significant.

The unused space was ideal for the truck-repair facility, as it did not require any alterations to the building, and there was virtually no increase in plant maintenance and utilities. The in-house repair operations had been an immediate economic success, saving the company a total of well over $100,000 and providing the company with immediate service for its vehicles. By the end of 1982 the fleet had grown to twenty-five full-service trucks that were on the road from Albany, New York, to Erie, Pennsylvania.

When Harper had been allowed to move the truck-repair operations into the unused space, it was recognized that the initial purpose of the space had been for business expansion, and that the truck service operations would eventually have to find a new home. However, for seven years no opportunity presented itself, until in late 1982 the company found an opportunity to expand its service business to in-plant maintenance and repairs.

The new business opportunity consisted of rebuilding specialized control devices for use in large graphics and printing equipment. The work would consist of purchasing obsolete equipment, removing the electronic control mechanism and reconfiguring it for installation into OEM equipment or to repair existing equipment at the customer's facilities. While the life of this project would be only about six years, the company felt strongly about the project since it would place it in a new and growing part of the market.

Ben Braddock, the director of marketing, had estimated that sales from the new project would be as shown in Exhibit 7-1.

In 1979 the company had adopted a formal capital-budgeting procedure. This procedure required that any project submitted to the Executive Committee for approval have a positive net present value (NPV) and an internal rate of return (IRR) of greater than the company's cost of capital. Currently, the cost was estimated at 10 per cent, and that number was being used in all capital projects. Thus, every project had to be evaluated on its after-tax cash flows, and

Exhibit 7-1   Sales of Rebuilt Control Devices

Year	Sales
1983	$270,000
1984	380,000
1985	350,000
1986	250,000
1987	200,000
1988	185,000
1989 and beyond	Project abandoned

those cash flows had to generate a positive NPV when discounted at 12 per cent and the internal rate of return on the project had to be greater than 12 per cent.

In preparing his analysis of the project, Ellis had gathered the following data:

1. *Capital Costs.*   The test equipment, work stations and other capital improvements would cost the company $375,000. All of this expenditure would be eligible for the investment tax credit (ITC) of 10 per cent. At the end of the sixth year it was estimated that the equipment could be sold in the used test-equipment market for $138,000.

2. *Operating Costs.*   Based on other operations within the company and the cost of purchasing the used equipment for overhaul, Ellis had estimates that direct variable operating costs would be 42 per cent of sales. Variable overhead, such as employee benefits, additional utility expense, etc. were estimated to be 12 per cent of sales. In addition to these costs, company cost-accounting practices required that any project be charged 15 per cent per year of the gross capital cost for allocated corporate overhead. In this way the project would pick up its share of the corporate administrative costs.

3. *Depreciation and Taxes.*   The new equipment necessary for doing the overhaul would be eligible for depreciation under the ACRS method. This depreciation scheme allocated capital investment into a class life and depreciation rates were then applied. Rates for assets in the three-year life and five-year life are shown in Exhibit 7-2.

Exhibit 7-2   ACRS Depreciation Rates (in Per Cent)

Year	3-Year Life	5-Year Life
1	25	15
2	38	22
3	37	21
4		21
5		21

Under ACRS, depreciation was taken with the rates applied against the full cost with no allowance for salvage. If the equipment were eventually salvaged at greater than its net book value, ordinary income-tax rates were applied to the gain so long as the salvage did not exceed the original purchase price. If salvage did exceed the original cost, the excess over the original cost was taxed as a capital gain.

The company expected to take the full 10 per cent investment tax credit for the equipment, and because the company made quarterly tax payments, the savings would be realized immediately. The company expected to use the five-year class life, although if they did use ACRS and the investment tax credit, they would have to subtract half of the credit from the basis. This meant they could only depreciate 95 per cent of the cost of the equipment. In effect, for tax purposes the company would have to pretend they only paid 95 per cent of the original cost of the equipment. The accounting department had estimated the company's marginal state and federal tax rate at 45 per cent.

4. *Working Capital.* In addition to the investment in physical equipment, additional investment in receivables and inventory would be required. This investment would be offset to some degree by increased accruals, but it was felt that new net working-capital requirements would be 16 per cent of sales. The net working-capital requirements for analytical purposes would be at the beginning of each year and would rise or fall as sales rose and fell over the life of the project. Company practices allowed for the recovery of the net working capital under the assumption that the inventory and receivables would be liquidated at the end of the project.

The administrative problems began when Harper learned that his vehicle maintenance and repair operations would no longer have space in the plant. Ellis called a meeting with Harper and Braddock to see if some sort of agreement could be reached among the three of them, because the Executive Committee would be troubled if a proposal of this size did not have the support of the key people in the company. Unfortunately, Harper had not been willing to give up his opposition to the project.

Harper stated in the meeting that although he recognized that the space occupied by vehicle maintenance had been intended for business purposes, he did not think it should be used for the proposed project. He pointed out that the project had only a six-year life, and there was no guarantee that it would permanently expand the company's business base. Customer service support had been a key part of the company's success, and disruption of the vehicle-service department could endanger the success of the base business.

Harper also pointed out that there were economic considerations that had not been taken into account in the proposed change. If vehicle operations were dislodged from its space, there was no other space in either the plant or in the industrial park for them to go. The service would have to be bought from outside contractors at a cost, in 1983, of $23,000 per year more than in-house costs. Furthermore, this cost was expected to grow at 8 per cent per year. Harper also stated that, because of the slower service time, another truck would have to be purchased at a cost of $22,500. Ellis later learned this truck would have a six-year life and no salvage, have a three-year life for ACRS and be eligible for the 6 per cent ITC. The depreciable basis would be reduced by one-half of the ITC taken. Finally, Harper said they would have to lay off seventeen vehicle-repair personnel, skilled craftmen whom they could not easily replace if at the end of the project they wished to put vehicle maintenance back in the space.

Braddock's reaction to this opposition was that the problems of the vehicle-repair operations had no relationship to this project. He stated that it had been known when vehicle repairs started up that they could only have the space temporarily; they should have made contingency plans for moving their operations. He recognized that there might be additional costs of shifting to outside service work, but he did not feel those costs should be taken into account for this project; this investment should stand or fall on its own merits. He didn't see how the cost of a new truck was relevant to the economics of the project.

At the conclusion of the meeting Ellis knew that he would have to decide whether or not to recommend the project, and that the decision would leave at least one person unhappy. He felt he would let the numbers make the decision for him; that is, he would recommend the project if it were profitable. But he still had to wrestle with the problem of how the additional costs associated with moving the vehicle-maintenance operations to outside contractors would impact on the economic analysis of the new business opportunity.

SUGGESTED QUESTIONS

1. Based on the information in the case, determine if the additional costs and investment in the vehicle-repair area should be included in the economic evaluation of the project.

2. Based on your answer to Question 1 and the information in the case, determine the after-tax cash flows for the project. Assume the investment is made in January 1983 and that all subsequent revenues, expenses, and other items that affect cash flows occur at the end of each year.

3. Compute the IRR and the NPV at 12 per cent.

4. Prove that your computed IRR is correct by using it as a discount rate on the cash flows.

5. Make a recommendation on the project. Support your views with both the quantitative results and a qualitative evaluation of the project.

Omega Office Services, Inc.

NPV for a Replacement-Type Project

Omega Office Services, Inc. owed its name to its founder. Susan Charles was a young Stanford University graduate trying to earn a living by typing papers and dissertations for graduate students and professors of the College of Arts and Sciences. She did not particularly like the work, but it paid the bills and it was something she was very good at. However, when people suggested that she make a career of the practice, Charles would always say that typing professionally was the last thing she would ever do. When she finally did decide to make a business of the typing services, she named it Omega, after the last letter of the Greek alphabet. It was going to be the last thing she would do.

Charles' success in university typing was a result of her skill and dedication to the task. The work required strict adherence to certain guidelines—margins, for example, had to be exactly as specified and headings and other features of the manuscript also had to meet exact specifications. A doctoral dissertation was checked by two different people in the office of the graduate school, not for content, which was the responsibility of the academic department, but for compliance with university style regulations. Any deviance from accepted norms, including the kind of paper, would mean automatic rejection regardless of how well qualified the applicant was or how well-written was the document.

Charles quickly developed a reputation of being an expert in the field. Graduate students preparing theses and professors preparing manuscripts for publication knew that they could deliver to her a rough manuscript and would receive a typed version in full compliance with all rules. As a result, within two and one-half years of starting the at-home business, Charles had more work than she could handle. It was at this pont that she decided to commercialize the business, partly in the belief that she would make money and partly because, as owner and manager, she would hire people to work and so do less typing herself.

Omega Office Services set up in a small office near the Stanford campus in late 1969. The business was almost an immediate success because of the ability of the shop to produce quality work on schedule. Within two years, Omega moved to larger quarters, this time closer to the commercial district of the city in order to attract more business and professional projects. This strategy worked as various consulting groups and professional organizations used Omega to prepare proposals and documents where production quality and speed were essential. In 1978 the company moved to its current location, using an entire floor of a large office building in Palo Alto. Charles by this time employed a staff of over twenty-five people, including typists, supervisors, systems-support personnel, and sales personnel. In late 1985 sales approached $2 million and profits, after tax, had broken the $100,000 mark.

Productivity had been a key element in the success of Omega. The company had purchased some of the first generation of electronic typewriters and had been one of the early users of word-processing systems. In January, 1980, the company had purchased an integrated word-processing system known as the APEX 4000. The system was manufactured by Apex Products and had cost $120,000 installed. The system had a depreciable life of ten years, after which it was expected to have a salvage value of $30,000. The equipment was being depreciated on a straight-line basis for the ten-year period, since at the time of purchase earnings were not sufficient to benefit from accelerated depreciation.

Problems with the system began within six months after its installation and were compounded in early 1982 when the manufacturer of the equipment went into Chapter 11 and ceased to support units in the field. Omega found that it was able to obtain parts from independent suppliers but had to develop its own in-house expertise to service the equipment. While this arrangement cut service costs, Omega was never able to fully utilize all the features and potential of the system, and after five years of fighting with the equipment, the manufacturer, the courts, and the other problems, Charles decided to replace the system if it were at all economically feasible.

After reviewing systems, Charles tentatively chose HAL 950 from Coast Computer. A description is shown in Exhibit 8-1. Coast Com-

Exhibit 8-1 Excerpt from the Sales Brochure for the HAL 950 Word-Processing System

The HAL 950 Word-Processing System from Coast Computer is a complete package designed for maximum office productivity whether you are working with a one-page document or a 2000-page manuscript. . . . There are no delays even when all twenty stations are in operation. Each station has its own keyboard, CRT terminal, and a draft-quality printer rated at better than 150 cps. The system supports four letter-quality printers that can be operated remotely from the work stations. If all four are in service, the system will automatically queue each job as it is entered, feed the paper, and go on to the next job.

The HAL 950 is fully supported by a technical staff and a twenty-four hour, seven-day-a-week maintenance agreement. The system is fully warranted for one year when installed by Coast Computer personnel, and the full parts and labor maintenance agreement is available at the cost of $12,500 per year for five years. If the system is installed by Coast Computer, the first year of the maintenance is covered by the warranty at no additional cost.

The HAL 950 has a list price of $75,000 FOB any West Coast city. The system may be purchased with the following options:

1. A fully installed system, guaranteed by Coast for parts and labor for one full year for $20,000.00.
2. Full training program for up to twenty users, total cost of $8,000.00

puter was a San Jose, California, company with over thirty years experience in electronic data processing equipment. The company had been producing the HAL 950 for two years and the system had won rave reviews by users. Equally important, Coast Computer had impeccable financial credentials, and there was little danger that the company would not be around to service and support the system. The nearby location was especially advantageous: Charles was the kind of person who would not hesitate to march into the headquarters of Coast Computer if she had difficulty with the system and refuse to leave until she was satisfied.

The initial cost of the system was $75,000. The price included delivery to the front door, and Omega was given the option of installing the system or having it installed by Coast for an additional cost of $20,000. If Coast did the installation, the system would be covered by a full warranty for the first year, and this would eliminate a $12,500 maintenance contract if Omega did the installation itself. The maintenance agreement covered all parts and labor for one year and was payable at the first of the year. Another option available from Coast was full training for up to twenty users at a cost of $8,000.

Charles had asked her accounting firm to review the proposal and comment on the tax implications of the purchase. The firm reported the following.

1. The new equipment would be depreciated using ACRS rates for a five-year life. Because of factors not associated with this purchase, the investment tax credit would not be applicable to this purchase. The cost of any option selected would be included in the base price of the machine and depreciated along with the cost of the machine.

2. Under ACRS the equipment would be depreciated to a zero base. If it were salvaged, the salvage income would be treated as ordinary income as long as it did not exceed the original cost.

3. If the old machine were sold below tax book value, the loss would be an ordinary loss and would save on taxes. When the current system was purchased it was depreciated on a straight-line basis to a $30,000 salvage value. The current price of the system in the used market is $30,000, and the accounting firm suggested that this value would probably not change over the next five years.

4. If Omega elected to install the machine itself, the first year's maintenance payment, due at the time the machine is purchased, would be a tax-deductible expense. For analysis purposes, Omega could assume the tax reduction would occur at the time the machine is purchased and the maintenance contract costs are paid. Subsequent maintenance contract costs would be paid at the beginning of each of the next four years, but it could be assumed that they are paid on the last day of the year just ended—that is, the maintenance agreement cost for year two is paid at the end of year one, the maintenance agreement for year three is paid at the end of year two, etc.

5. For analytical purposes, the accounting firm suggested that Omega use a tax rate of 45 per cent.

A summary of the data is shown in Exhibits 8-2 and 8-3. In discussing the new system with her operations manager, Charles learned that he felt that the new system would enable the company to attract specialty business that it was then unable to handle. He estimated that this new business would initially be a net gain to the company, after salary and supplies expense, of $25,000 in the first year, and that the gain would increase by $2,000 a year for the following four years. This number did not include depreciation on the

Exhibit 8-2   Data on Existing APEX 4000 System

Initial Cost	$120,000
Estimated life	10 years
Current Age	5 years
Expected Salvage	$30,000
Depreciation	Straight line
Current Salvage	$30,000

Exhibit 8-3   Data on HAL 950 System

Initial Cost	$75,000
Install Option	$20,000
Training Option	$8,000
Depreciation	ACRS 5 Year
Year	Rates
1	0.15
2	0.22
3	0.21
4	0.21
5	0.21
Estimated Salvage	$40,000
Tax Rate	0.45

new equipment nor its service and maintenance. He also felt that given the growth and development of Omega's business, the new equipment would be replaced at the end of five years and that, for purposes of evaluation, it should be assumed that it will be sold at the end of five years for $40,000. No additional working capital requirements were anticipated for the increase in business.

The only controversy over the purchase of the new machine surrounded the question of whether or not to purchase the equipment on an installed basis or on a "just-delivered" basis. Charles was certain that Omega would not purchase the equipment with the training option because, she felt, and rightly so, that her staff's experience with word processing made them better equipped to handle training than the vendor. On the question of whether or not to purchase the installation, Charles was not as certain. Omega employed one full-time technician who was responsible for servicing the existing equipment, and she was so good that on occasion she earned the firm extra money by servicing equipment on the outside. The sales staff had two marketing representatives with strong technical backgrounds, and between the three of them, they could probably install the new system.

If Omega installed the system itself, it would save the $20,000 installation cost, although this savings would be offset to some degree by the payment of the first year's maintenance fee. However, Charles was equally concerned about the quality of the system and its ability to deliver. A major reason for the change in systems was to have the technical expertise of Coast Computer involved with the company, and by installing it herself, Charles would run the risk of delaying implementation of the system and severely harming the ability of Omega to deliver its services. With the Coast installation she knew it would be done right and on time, with in-house installation, she wasn't certain what the outcome would be.

SUGGESTED QUESTIONS

1. Assume the facts in the case, and take account of all tax implications.

    a. Compute the net initial outlay if the system is purchased without the installation option.

    b. Compute the net initial outlay if the system is purchased with the installation option.

2. For the purchase without the installation option, compute the net cash flows for years 1–5 and the NPV at 15 per cent. Assume all cash flows occur at the end of the year.

3. For the purchase with the installation option, compute the net cash flow for years 1–5 and the net present value at 15 per cent. Assume all cash flows occur at the end of the year.

4. Which way should the system be purchased? Base your argument on economic and noneconomic reasons.

Union Plastics, Inc.

UNION PLASTICS, INC.

Risk-Adjusted Discount Rates

By 1981 Union Plastics, Inc., was one of the typical large U.S.–based multinational industrial corporations. The company, headquartered in the pleasant New Jersey suburb of Teaneck, had operations in seven major countries and served markets in almost all of Europe, North America, and South America. In late 1981 the company had 126,000 employees worldwide, sales of $3.2 billion, and net income in U.S. dollars of over $145 million. Its customer base included almost every major industrial firm in Europe and the Western Hemisphere.

For operating purposes, the company organized into three major groups, the North American Group, the European Group, and the Southern Group. The North American Group contained all operations in the United States and Canada, the European Group consisted of the company's operations in the United Kingdom, France, and West Germany, and the Southern Group consisted of operations in Mexico and Brazil. Within each group, the operations were further divided into divisions, organized along country lines. Thus the North American Group consisted of the U.S. and Canadian divisions, the European Group, the West German, French, and British divisions, and the Southern Group, the Mexican and Brazilian divisions. Each division was headed by a general manager, who was also a vice-president of the parent corporation. The division managers reported to three group vice-presidents, who in turn reported to the chairman and chief executive officer in Teaneck. In effect, each division was like a miniature company, similar in size, products, and markets to the other divisions.

The purpose of this organizational arrangement was to provide for strategic management at the corporate level and operational management at the group and division levels. Major policy decisions were made by the Strategy Council, consisting of the chairman, vice-chairman and the three group vice-presidents. These decisions involved major marketing plans, acquisitions, introduction of new products, major capital expenditures, and divestiture or discontinuation of existing operations. Once the overall course of action was decided upon, the group vice-president and his division general managers were given authority to implement the program. Other than having to meet the specified goal, the group and division had a wide range of discretion in terms of what specific actions to take.

One of the areas that the Strategy Council was heavily involved with was the area of major capital-spending projects. Despite its size, the company consistently had more capital projects proposed by the operating divisions than it had internal funding sources and new debt available to support. The process was further complicated by the fact that the risk associated with various projects was different in the various operating divisions. This was because of socio-economic factors unique to each country.

For example, despite their membership in the European Economic Community, France and West Germany were considered significantly different in terms of investment opportunity. Investments in the stable, high-growth German economy were preferred to investments in the relatively more difficult French economic climate, unless the potential profits in France were far greater than those in West Germany. In its meetings on capital spending, the Strategy Council recognized it needed an operational procedure to deal effectively with competing capital projects in different countries and commissioned the Corporate Financial Planning Group to develop such a procedure.

The procedure that was proposed by the Financial Planning Group and ultimately adopted by the council was that of using risk premiums to eliminate the variation in projects due to project type and geographic location. Essentially, the system would use as its base cost of capital the required rate of return on the least risky type of project in the least risky geographic environment. Risk premiums would then be added to this rate as the project type and geographic location of the project changed. In this way, by using the risk-adjusted cost of capital in the capital-project evaluation process, differences in project type and project location would effectively be neutralized. After the risk-adjusted cost of capital was computed for the appropriate project type and location, the project could be evaluated using traditional DCF-IRR methods.

For risk-analysis purposes, capital projects would be classified in one of five categories, shown in Exhibit 9-2. The least risky of the classes was an expense-reduction program. Since these projects typically employed known and proven technology, and since expense savings could be estimated with a high degree of accuracy, this class became the zero risk premium class. The cost of capital for this type of project was assigned a rate of 16 per cent for the least risky country, the United States.

The other four types of projects were each assigned a risk premium based on their degree of risk. These four categories all involved business expansion, and their risk depended upon whether or not it was a new product for Union Plastics or an existing product, and whether or not it would be sold to a new group of customers, considered a new market, or sold to an existing group of customers, an existing market. The four types of expansion projects and their risk premiums are shown in Exhibit 9-1. The risk premiums would be added to the base rate to determine the cost of capital for the particular project. Thus, if the base rate were 16 per cent, that of an expense-reduction project in the United States, an expansion project to sell an existing product in a new market would have a risk premium of 4 per cent, and this 4 per cent would be added to the 16 per cent to obtain a required rate of return of 20 per cent for evaluation of the project.

In analyzing risk associated with the individual countries in which Union operated, the Financial Planning Group broke risk into two major components. They realized that the success or failure of a project depended not only on the economic conditions of the country, but also on the political conditions. A project, and even an entire

Exhibit 9-1   Risk Premium for Project Type

Type	Risk Premium (in Per Cent)
Expense Reduction	0.00
Expansion	
Existing Product	
Existing Market	2.00
Existing Product	
New Market	4.00
New Product	
Existing Market	7.00
New Product	
New Market	10.00

operation could fail despite strong economic factors if the political situation were unstable and ultimately collapsed. Union Plastics had not invested in South Africa, for example, despite the fact that South Africa had the continent's strongest economy, because the company felt the political instability of the country raised the risk of investment beyond a prudent level.

For each of the countries in which Union had operations, a risk premium was assigned for the economic risk and a risk premium was assigned for the political risk. The United States was considered to be the base, so a zero premium was assigned to it. The other countries' risk premiums were shown in Exhibit 9-2. The required rate of return for a project with no project-type risk would be the base rate, plus the economic risk premium, plus the political risk premium. Using the data in Exhibits 9-1 and 9-2, the required rate of return for any country for any project type could be determined by adding the country's risk premiums to the project risk premiums and adding that total risk premium to the base rate.

In late 1981 the Strategy Council was considering whether or not to authorize the manufacture of a new product, Pallents, and if so, in which division or divisions to allow manufacture. Pallents was the trademark given to the name of a new plastic ball bearing developed in the labs of Union Plastics. Plastic ball bearings were superior to steel and other metal ball bearings in terms of cost and weight, but they were not suitable for use where heat and pressure were involved. Until Pallents was developed, plastic ball bearings had only a few uses.

Pallents were developed in the Teaneck labs of Union Plastics. They were cheaper than metal ball bearings and they tended to last longer. Ball bearings themselves were inexpensive to replace when they failed, but the resulting loss of productivity while machinery had to be overhauled put a premium on long-lived bearings. Pallents were of a special design, which allowed heat to dissipate, thus significantly increasing the life of the bearings. As long as the stress did

Exhibit 9-2   Risk Premiums for Various Countries (in Per Cent)

	Base Rate	Economic Risk	Political Risk
United States	16.00	0.00	0.00
Canada	16.00	2.00	1.00
West Germany	16.00	2.00	2.00
United Kingdom	16.00	4.00	0.00
France	16.00	5.00	2.00
Brazil	16.00	8.00	7.00
Mexico	16.00	10.00	5.00

not exceed certain limits, Pallents performed much better than traditional steel bearings.

All three groups at Union Plastics wished to construct facilities to manufacture Pallents. The North American Group planned to renovate a small facility in Athens, Georgia, for production. The European Group planned to build facilities outside of Dusseldorf, and the Southern Group set production for São Paulo, Brazil. All three divisions submitted production plans, summarized in Exhibit 9-3.

The differences in construction costs were the result of local conditions and the location of the proposed facility. Renovation of an existing facility was less expensive than building a new one. Net working-capital requirements represented primarily receivables and inventory that would be associated with the production and sales of the product. The assumption was made that the initial investment in net working capital would be sufficient for the life of the project. For planning purposes, it was assumed that the projects would have a six-year life, and that salvage, on an after-tax basis, would be 10 per cent of the facility's cost. At the end of the project the net working capital would also be salvaged, with no tax effects.

Net cash flows after taxes represented revenues minus expenses and whatever adjustments were necessary for depreciation. All of the flows were adjusted for local taxes and translated into U.S. dollars at the appropriate rate. The estimated net cash flows after taxes are shown in Exhibit 9-3 for each of the three countries involved. All three group vice-presidents felt rather confident in these figures,

Exhibit 9-3 Selected Data on the Manufacture of Pallents by Country

(in U.S. $000)

	United States	West Germany	Brazil
Initial Capital Cost (net)	1,250	1,550	950
Net Working Capital	200	250	100
After Tax Cash Flow			
Year			
1	450	480	410
2	480	520	430
3	550	580	390
4	530	500	440
5	450	450	430
6	380	400	320
Salvage (at end of year 6)			
10% of Investment			
Plus Working Capital			

since 93 per cent of the sales would be to industrial customers who were already purchasing products from the local Union division. Although they felt the project might have a life greater than six years, they also were concerned that by that time innovations may well move Pallents out of the market, and that six years was a reasonable time horizon. For all three plans, the net cash flows peaked in the fourth year and had significantly declined below that peak value by year six.

SUGGESTED QUESTIONS

1. Compute the risk-adjusted discount rates for each country for each project type.

2. Compute the NPV of the project for the United States. Use the appropriate discount rate from Question 1.

3. Compute the NPV of the project for West Germany. Use the appropriate discount rate from Question 1.

4. Compute the NPV of the project for Brazil. Use the appropriate discount rate from Question 1.

5. Evaluate the results of Questions 2–4 and recommend which countries, if any, should be authorized for production.

6. List and explain what reasons there might be for accepting a project in a location even if it did not meet the economic requirements of a positive NPV with the risk-adjusted cost of capital.

Quad Products, Inc. (A)

*Capital Budgeting—Expected
Value and Worst Case*

Risk has always been a factor in the business operations of Quad Products; in fact, the company had been founded on the basis of a large risk. Quad Products, located in Dallas, was just ten years old in late 1983, with sales expected to pass the $500 million and net income just beginning to turn positive after years of losses or near break-even. If starting Quad Products had been a gamble for the four founders, it was a gamble that was finally beginning to pay off.

Quad Products had been founded by four computer engineers from Houston Instruments, a multibillion-dollar computer hardware company. The four, Jerry Harris, Gene Reynolds, Susan Banks, and Vera Mills, were all in their early 30s when they broke away from H.I. to start Quad Products. All four had roughly the same motivation for leaving a secure career with a major computer firm: They wanted to show the industry that, given the time and resources, they could do it better than the major manufacturers. So far, their creation, Quad Products had gotten big, but it did not achieve the profitability that had been hoped for when it was created.

The immediate stimulus for the formation of Quad Products came when Houston Instruments shut down its manufacture of add-on equipment for competing computer brands. Houston Instruments had, until 1970, been a leading manufacturer of plug compatible equipment for the computer industry. However, in a major company reorganization in late 1971, the company sold off or closed its operations in this area, preferring to concentrate on development of its own integrated systems. Harris, Reynolds, Banks, and Mills had all been involved in the add-on area, and because of their overall skills and ability, all had been offered positions with a new product-development group within Houston Instruments. In assessing their situation, however, they felt that manufacture of add-on equipment had a greater future than complete systems, and that, with their talents and concentration, they could make a business of it where the larger manufacturers, such as their current employer, had failed.

With their reputation, their own personal savings and a $10 million investment by a venture capital group, Quad Products began operations in early 1974. Their philosophy was that every product they made would be compatible with every major system; that is, the selling point of the company would be "if Quad Products made it, it will fit your computer system." Their first product line was composed of many of the products that had been abandoned by Houston Instruments. Quad Products purchased the rights to these items, many of which had been originally designed by the management team, and production began in a new industrial park outside Dallas. Reynolds was named president of the company, and the other three principals took over in areas of sales, engineering, and production management.

After nine years of operations, the combined losses totaled close to $20 million, and only a fresh infusion of capital and a new CEO kept the company in business. The business had foundered because of two problems. The first was that the industry was changing so rapidly that the initial product line lost its market eighteen months after its introduction and start of production. Quad had planned for new products to come on line, but the philosophy of making products compatible with all systems held back introduction, and finally some lines were introduced which did not meet this criterion.

For most computer companies, producing items with limited compatibility would not have been a problem, but because of the position that Quad had taken in the marketplace, it confused customers, who were not certain whether or not the Quad add-on products would fit their systems. Although the company had begun to recover from some of its early difficulties by the 1980s, a new strategy had to be developed if the growth in sales that brought the company to a half-billion dollar level was going to be translated into profits.

The new CEO of the company, George Enright, came from outside the computer-manufacturing area. His most recent experience had been supervising the turnaround of a meat-packing company, a turnaround whose success was due more to his management ability than to his knowledge of the industry. Enright was hired at the insistence of the venture-capital company that controlled Quad Products. It felt that Quad had established itself in the marketplace, that its original founders had the technical expertise to develop, market, and product the products, and that what was now needed was sound business judgment about which products to bring to market. It wanted to keep the original concept that each product line would fit all major computer systems, but it wanted a business judgment made as to which products should be brought to market.

After several months in the job. Enright realized that the key element in any decision involving the company was risk. The computer-hardware business was unlike any he had ever been involved with, and possibly unlike any other industry in the country. The meat business, his last assignment, had been characterized by stable products and stable markets. The concept of a steak or ribs did not change.

However, the products in the computer business were constantly changing. One never knew how long any system would be sold and supported by its manufacturer or what the manufacturer planned to do as far as enhancements were concerned. A company could upgrade its basic product line or drop the line altogether and introduce a new product based on entirely different technology. All of this could, and did, happen in a matter of months with two major lines for which Quad had developed compatible add-on equipment.

A second problem lay in competitive analysis. There were a number of other firms in the industry similar to Quad. One never knew what they were working on or what they were planning to introduce. Quad, because of its technical expertise, had been considered to be a leader in the market, but a new company, Allis Enterprises, had recently been formed along similar lines. Enright was uncertain as to exactly what markets Allis would enter, but the consequences for Quad Products would be significant if Allis were to enter into similar markets. If their products were to compete, profit margins for both companies would be reduced, and neither would make a reasonable rate of return.

A final concern for Enright was in the area of production. Cost estimates were notoriously unreliable for products that had never before been produced. It wasn't that the production staff was not competent; but in many cases, it could not be determined how long it would take to produce an item and how much it would cost until full-scale production was underway. At that time, the company would be lucky to sell its product above cost; in some cases, for Quad that had not been the case. The price of the product was generally dictated by what the market was willing to pay and by the price of competing products from the mainframe producer, if he indeed did produce such items. Once a price was set, it was almost impossible to raise, and in many cases prices fell over the life of an item.

Enright's first major decision as head of Quad Products was whether or not to authorize production of a new memory-expansion

Exhibit 10-1   Data on Plug Expansion System

Plant Cost	$60,000
Life	6 years
Tax Rate	0.4%
Salvage	0

system. Data on the system is shown in Exhibit 10-1. This system, as proposed, would expand the memory and capability of a wide range of computers that had just been introduced by the three major manufacturers in mainframe systems. Based on an initial evaluation, it appeared the product would offer significant profits over its expected six-year life. It was known that none of the major manufacturers had plans for development of similar products and, of Quad's competitors, only Allis had the potential for development and marketing of a competing product. If successful, the new line, dubbed PCES for Plug Compatible Expansion System, would lead Quad into a period of sustained profitability.

The initial evaluation of PCES indicated that the investment in specialized mcahinery and other produciton-related areas would cost $60 million after recognition of investment tax credit. Because of the losses in the past, the equipment would be depreciated on a straight-line basis rather than ACRS, and it was estimated that at the end of the project the equipment, while still usable, would have no economic use and be scrapped at a net salvage of zero. The applicable tax rate for the project would be 40 per cent, and Enright had recently decreed that no investment project would be undertaken if it did not produce at least a 16 per cent rate of return on the after-tax cash flows.

In keeping with his concern about risk, Enright had asked for a risk assessment on the project. It turned out that the uncertainty in the project revolved around three areas: market size, market share, and cost of production. Excerpts from the project proposal concerning risk were as follows.

... which means that market size is expected to be either $300 million or $200 million each year for the next six years. The key factor is whether or not GHI, the main manufacturer, brings out its new system or upgrades its existing system. The new system would expand the market for the PCES program while a simple upgrade of the existing product line would not. No information has been obtained about GHI's plans, and the feeling is that the chances of the market being $300 million are 50 per cent, as are the odds of its being $200 million.

In terms of competition, the major uncertainty is whether or not Allis will bring out a competing product at the same time as the introduction of the Quad Products PCES line. Based on the current competition, it would appear that in the absence of Allis coming into the game, our market share would be 30 per cent for each of the next six years. In the event that Allis does introduce a product, that product would take 10 points from our share and leave us with 20 per cent of the market for the next six years. Our estimate is that the probability of this occurring is 50 per cent.

Finally, the production of the PCES will require costly manual assembly process. There is an automated system that can be licensed, but we are not certain it will work for the quantities that we need, and we really won't known until production is underway. In the absence of that system the estimate is that costs, exclusive of depreciation, will be 70 per cent of sales. If the system can be used, our costs will be reduced to 60 per cent of sales. Our estimate is that the probability of the system being applicable is 50 per cent. There are no savings in the initial outlay, because our cost of the new system is based solely on our use of it.

The probabilities in the above report appeared as a direct result of a specific request by Enright. He wanted risk taken into account in all capital projects and had developed the following criteria for any project to be acceptable.

1. The NPV of the expected value of the after-tax cash flows had to be positive at the 16 per cent discount rate.

2. The NPV of the cash flows, using the worst case had to be no less a loss than 20 per cent of the project outlay.

This last criterion was the method by which Enright hoped to measure risk. He realized that while under the worst case scenario, where the cash flows were computed assuming the least favorable events, would likely result in a negative net cash flow, he did not want this cash flow to be worse than 20 per cent of the cost of the project.

SUGGESTED QUESTIONS

1. Compute the net cash flows for years 1–6 using the expected-value concept. (Note: The cash flows are the same for each year, since whatever condition occurs is expected to occur each year.)

2. Compute the NPV on the expected value of the net cash flows.

3. Compute the net cash flows for the worst case scenario.

4. Compute the NPV on the cash flows for the worst case scenario. Does the project meet the risk criteria?

5. Evaluate the risk criteria that Enright uses.

Quad Products, Inc. (B)

Simulation in Capital Budgeting

Gene Reynolds, executive vice-president of Quad Products, learned that the proposal to manufacture Plug Compatible Expansion System for major mainframe computers had been rejected. The rejection was based in part on the risk associated with the project; George Enright, the company president, had argued that the risk was too high to justify the investment in the manufacture and sale of the system.

In a meeting with Reynolds, Enright explained that the project had to pass two tests in order to be acceptable. The first was that the project had to have a positive net present value on its expected cash flows, and that the PCES project did pass this test. The second criterion was a risk measurement, and Enright's requirement was that the project had to be tested under a worst-case scenario. Under this criterion the NPV of the cash flows was computed assuming the least favorable conditions, and the standard was that the project's NPV under this situation could not be less than a loss of 20 per cent of the project cost. Since the project had failed this test, Enright had refused approval of the project.

Reynolds' position in arguing with Enright was that the worst-case scenario was not a realistic test of the risk of the project. He stated that while it was reasonable to assume that some adverse conditions would occur, it was not reasonable to assume that all would occur together. Since the likelihood of the worst case ever appearing was small, Reynolds felt that it should not be used in evaluation of a project.

As an alternative, Reynolds proposed that all possible outcomes be computed for the project. From this set of outcomes, a mean and standard deviation could be constructed, and assuming the mean and standard deviation were estimates of the value of a normal probability distribution, a test could be made to determine the probability that the project would have a positive NPV. Confidence limits could also be constructed which, argued Reynolds, would give a much better picture of the risk than the simple worst-case analysis.

Enright agreed with this approach and agreed that the project should be re-evaluated. He stated that, for the project to be accepted, the expected value of the NPV must be positive, the probability that the NPV was zero or greater must be 60 per cent, and the loss associated with a probability level of 10 per cent or less should not be more than 20 per cent of the cost of the project, which was projected to be $60 million. This last criterion meant that when this value was computed, the probability was 90 per cent that the NPV would be equal to or greater than this number. For the project to be selected, this number could not be less than a negative $12 million, which was 20 per cent of the project cost.

SUGGESTED QUESTIONS

1. Compute the NPV for each of the eight possible sets of conditions for the data from Case 25.

2. Compute the mean and standard deviation of the project NPV's using the eight values.

   3. a. Is the expected value of the NPV's greater than zero?

     b. Is the probability that the NPV is equal to or greater than zero 60 per cent or more?

     c. What is the value such that the probability of the NPV being equal to or greater than this value is 90 per cent? Is this higher than $12 million.

Ork Paper Company

Capital Budgeting—Unequal Lives

In early 1985 the executive management team of Ork Paper Company felt that the worst of the bad times were over, and that if the company could solve an internal conflict its recent poor financial performance would give way to better things. The company had not done well in recent years (see Exhibits 12-1 and 12-2 for financial statements for the past three years), but the senior officials felt that at least a part of the problem was due to circumstances beyond their control. In management's view the problems were due to temporary circumstances, and at the beginning of 1985 there was a universal feeling that better things were ahead.

The two major problems of the past had been environmental-pollution control and the recession that characterized the U.S. economy in the early 1980s. By 1984 the recession had ended with a booming U.S. economy, and though 1985 was expected to be slower, the forecast was for continued growth in demand for the company's products. The company had also made great strides toward solving the worst of its pollution problems, and the attitude of the Environmental Protection Agency (EPA) was definitely more sympathetic than it had been in the past.

Ork Paper was headquartered in Milwaukee, Wisconsin, but its plants were in the northern regions of Wisconsin and Michigan. The removal of its headquarters to Milwaukee a decade before had been a source of problems for the company: Local residents in the north of the state claimed the executives were running away from the pollution created by their mills. The publicity over the move was one

Exhibit 12-1   Ork Paper Company: Statement of Revenues and Expenses (in $000)

	1982	1983	1984
Net Sales	78,943	81,234	94,564
Cost of Sales	61,232	67,432	72,987
Gross Profit	17,711	13,802	21,577
Operating Expenses			
Sales	1,689	1,756	2,345
Administrative Expenses	7,498	8,145	8,659
Other	2,134	2,568	1,760
Total Operating Expenses	11,321	12,469	12,764
Nonoperating Income (Expenses)	(3,456)	(4,322)	(4,765)
Income Before Taxes	2,934	(2,989)	4,048
Taxes	1,262	(1,285)	1,741
Net Income	1,672	(1,704)	2,307

Exhibit 12-2   Ork Paper Company: Statement of Financial Condition

Year Ending Dec. 31 (in $000)

	1982	1983	1984
Assets			
Cash and Marketable Securities	2,345	3,567	10,876
Accounts Receivable	11,456	13,567	18,975
Inventory			
Raw Materials	7,856	7,654	9,876
Work in Progress	2,134	2,256	2,560
Finished Goods	8,760	8,897	9,654
Total Inventory	18,750	18,807	22,090
Other Current Assets	2,450	2,345	2,670
Total Current Assets	35,001	38,286	54,611
Land	2,260	2,260	2,260
Plant and Equipment	135,670	142,500	148,950
Less Accumulated Depreciation	75,450	87,900	96,500
Net Plant and Equipment	60,220	54,600	52,450
Other Assets	11,340	11,780	11,260
Total Assets	108,821	106,926	120,581
Liabilities and Net Worth			
Accounts Payable	12,876	11,245	17,654
Other Payables	11,234	10,987	12,345
Other Current Liabilities	3,456	5,432	6,543
Short Term Debt	2,240	2,560	4,675
Total Current Liabilities	29,806	30,224	41,217
Long Term Debt	34,568	32,467	37,560
Other Liabilities	3,320	3,567	4,534
Total Liabilities	67,694	66,258	83,311
Common Stock	5,500	5,500	5,500
Earned Surplus	35,627	35,168	31,770
Total Equity	41,127	40,668	37,270
Total Liabilities and Equity	108,821	106,926	120,581

factor in causing a detailed investigation of company practices by the EPA, and the result was that in 1976, the company in an out-of-court settlement agreed to an extensive abatement plan.

Because of the difficulty of the program, its overall cost and the relatively small size of Ork, the program consumed almost all of the company's capital budget in the following eight years. Ork financed much of the project with tax-exempt, pollution-control revenue bonds, and had this financing vehicle not been available it is doubtful the company could have survived. Barry Bahnsen, company president, argued strongly in favor of the program, stating that modernization and capacity growth could wait, because without a successful pollution-control program the company would not be allowed to operate.

Because other capital projects were delayed by the pollution-control program, the company saw its costs of production rise above that of the competition because its aging plant could not operate as efficiently as the newer, more modern facilities that were being built by other companies. The main products of Ork were high-quality, specialty printing papers, and while the company was able to pass on some of the higher costs to its customers, it was forced to absorb much of the rise in the form of lower margins. The recession of 1981–1982 also hurt the company substantially, and after years of flat earnings, 1983 saw the first loss for the company since the 1930s.

In late 1983 management developed and began to implement a long-term strategic plan that would enable the company to return aggressively to its main markets. The last of the pollution-control expenditures were to be made in mid-1984, and current practices at EPA indicated that the company would not be forced into any additional programs for at least several years. Bahnsen felt that by 1985, for the first time in almost a decade, the economic environment and the company's financial position would both be ready for a major commitment to growth and improved profitability.

The first phase of the plan was to restore the liquidity and profitability of the company so that financing would be available to support the capital budget necessary to implement growth. Through a major sales and marketing effort, the company significantly increased sales in 1984, and the cash account by year end gave the company about $6 million in excess funds. After showing the preliminary 1984 financial statements to its investment bankers, Bahnsen was advised that the results would support a new debt issue of $25 million to $30 million, albeit at a rather high interest rate. Based on this information, Bahnsen gave the approval to the Corporate Development Group to produce a capital budget which would enable the company to (1) expand its capacity and (2) reduce production costs so that the company would become once again the low- to medium-cost supplier of the market.

Disagreement within the Corporate Development Group led to two different, mutually exclusive, proposals being presented to the Capital Appropriations Executive Committee. This was very unusual, for the Corporate Development Group had been established within the company to provide independent analysis of capital projects. The difficulties arose when the group had requested the general manager of operations to produce a capital plan that would implement the strategic plan. The new capital plan called for a complete renovation and rebuilding of the process facilities. The project would cost $17 million and produce substantial cost savings, along with some capacity gains. It was estimated that the life of the project would be five years, at which time it could be repeated.

The engineers within the Research and Development Group rejected this proposal as not fully meeting the strategic goals of the company. After reviewing several new technologies, they presented a proposal to the Corporate Development Group for a new production process built around new, dryer technology. While this proposal would cost $24 million, it provided for substantially greater savings and would last eight years instead of the five years of the rebuilding project. After-tax cash flows for the two projects are shown in Exhibit 12-3.

Exhibit 12-3   Summary of Project Cash Costs and Cash Flows

	Automated Dryer	Rebuilt Production Line
	(in $000)	
Initial Cash Cost	24,000	17,000
Cash Inflows		
Years		
0	(24,000)	(17,000)
1	4,250	3,900
2	4,500	4,400
3	5,900	5,300
4	6,320	7,800
5	7,700	8,400
6	8,100	
7	6,200	
8	5,900	
Discount Rate 15.00%		
Tax Rate 40%		

Surprisingly, the operations group rejected the Research and Development Group proposal. They felt basically uncomfortable with the newer technology. The rebuilding project, they felt, would allow the company to continue manufacturing paper with the same process as in the past, would achieve significant cost reductions, and would give the company the benefits of the new technology without the risk of implementing a new process.

Normally, the economic evaluation would decide the issue between two competing projects. However, with these projects, with their different lives and different outlays, the Corporate Development Group felt uncertain about the economic evaluation. They wondered if they might not be comparing apples and oranges. The more expensive project would certainly have higher gross dollar profits even if its rate of return were no better than the smaller project, because the bigger project involved more dollars. Unless they found a way to account for the fact that one project was bigger than the other and had benefits over a longer period of time, any evaluation would be biased in favor of the bigger project.

In conducting the economic evaluation, the Corporate Development Group found that one project had a higher rate of return than the other, but the other had a higher net present value. Uncertain over which project to recommend for approval, they sent both projects to President Bahnsen and the Capital Appropriations Executive Committee.

SUGGESTED QUESTIONS

1. Compute the internal rate of return for each project.
2. Compute the NPV for each project.
3. Compute the equivalent annual annuity for each project. Write a short analysis explaining exactly what this method is, the logic behind it, and why it is applicable in this case.
4. Make a recommendation to the company as to which project should be selected. Use both the economic analysis conducted above and noneconomic issues in the case.

Bod Products, Inc.

Pricing Using NPV Concepts

To Jack Brodie, president of Bod Products, Inc., the invitation to bid on a contract with a large regional retailer represented a break through of unexpected proportions. The Sausalito, California, manufacturer of health foods and health products had just managed to earn a small profit in the last fiscal year, after seven years of losses and breaking even since the start of the business. Prospects were not much better for the coming fiscal year.

However, if the company could obtain a contract from Orlens of California to exclusively supply that company with the vitamin supplements and health-related products sold under the Orlens brand name, Bod Products could reasonably expect a record profit in the coming year and a base for building on that profit in the next five years. Not only would winning this contract put the company solidly in the black, but demonstrating an ability to deliver the product might well open up other possibilities with mass retailers. The future of the company might well hinge on whether or not it was successful in its bid for the contract with Orlens.

Brodie founded Bod Products in 1976 after a short but brilliant career as a football player at the University of California. A knee injury had ended Brodie's career in his senior year, and since his only plans had been to play professional football with the Los Angeles Rams, he had no immediate plans after graduation. A roommate had suggested that Brodie capitalize on his health food and vitamin knowledge and somehow turn his hobby and obsession into a business venture. Brodie had developed a knowledge of health food and

63

nutrition while in athletic training. Although many athletes subscribe to special diets and vitamin supplements, Brodie had made a careful study of nutrition and taken several courses while in school. Unlike many athletes who accepted the regimen that was put in front of him, Brodie developed his own diet and nutrition plan and stuck to it. The results were good, at least as far as his own health was concerned, and it certainly wasn't the diet's fault that a blind side tackle had left him unable to run faster than a slow trot.

With the help of several wealthy alumni, Brodie started his company in late summer, 1976. He originally wanted to call his product line Jack Brodie's Health Supplements, but was talked out of it by two of his backers who argued that by the time somebody told a store clerk what he wanted, he would have forgotten why he wanted it in the first place. Instead the name was shortened to Body Products, but after several months, when it became apparent that everyone would call the stuff "Bod Products," Brodie adopted that term as the official name of his company. By 1983 Bod Products manufactured or sold under its own label about seventy-five different health foods and health supplements. The product had built a market based in part on Brodie's own personal fame and in part on the public's demand for food supplements which would have a positive affect on its health and wellbeing.

Brodie started the company in a small warehouse outside San Francisco. The production facilities consisted of equipment for mixing various supplements and packaging them under the Bod Products label. The company would purchase raw ingredients, mix them according to accepted industry standards or, in some cases, Brodie's own formula, and package them for sale. Brodie spent most of his time in two functions: devising and refining the formulas for the products and setting up a distribution network. Fortunately his fame on the football field opened many doors for him and in five years his distribution network stretched over much of the Pacific Northwest and northern California. In 1979 the company started selling products manufactured by other companies under the Bod Products name, and while this increased the size of the product line, the margins on these re-sold products were very low and the overall profitability of the company remained approximately at the break-even level.

At the end of 1980 the company turned a small profit and in 1982 the company had earnings of about $150,000 on annual sales of nearly $4 million. Brodie had been able to pay back some of the initial capital, and the expectations were that the company was on solid footing. However, profit improvement would be extremely difficult because of the degree of competition in the field. There were over

152 competing brands in the west coast area, and while the gross margins on the products were relatively high, as bulk ingredients were inexpensive, gross margins were quickly eroded by marketing and distribution expenses. It was clear to Brodie that unless the direction of the company changed, it would always be a marginal operation. Profits were sufficient to allow Brodie to make a decent living but not much better; in its current business arrangements the company was unlikely to ever achieve the growth and stature envisioned by Brodie and the investors at its inception.

Orlens of California was an up-scale department store chain that operated stores in five western states. The mainstay of the stores was high-priced fashions for both men and women, but in the last several years the stores had installed various "in store departments," and one of these was a health-foods and vitamins operation. Initially, Orlens sold a variety of brands, and Brodie had managed to place a small display with Bod Products items in the stores. The success of the in-store health-foods units led Orlens management to consider selling products under their own brand name, and the company requested bids from several producers to supply the items.

To his surprise, Brodie received a letter from the Director of Purchasing for Orlen's with a specific request that he bid on supplying a nutritional supplement. If Bod Products won the contract with the most favorable bid, Bod Products would manufacture the item and label with the Orlens trademark, but the label would clearly state that the item had been produced by Bod Products and was an official Bod Products item. The store's strategy was to capitalize on the brand-name recognition of Bod Products and also obtain the higher markup associated with the Orlens label.

The potential profits plus future growth from similar activities led Brodie to feel that he must obtain this contract. The details of the project were that Orlens would purchase 50,000 cases a year for six years. However Orlens was only willing to sign a fixed-price contract, and while Orlens would have the option to extend the contract for an additional three years, there would be no guarantees beyond six years. Consequently, Brodie had to base his bid price to Orlens on the assumption that the project would last only six years.

A review of the project with Calvin Hiller, production supervisor, and Rory Tindle, sales and marketing manager, indicated that the company's current facilities had plenty of room to handle the increased production. Data on the contract is presented in Exhibit 13-1. New equipment costing $650,000 installed would have to be purchased in order to produce the product, and an additional $40,000 investment in inventories would be required. The equipment could be used indefinitely, but Hiller estimated that if it had

Exhibit 13-1   Data on Orlens Contract

Investment Required	$650,000.00
ITC	10%
Cases Per Year	50,000
Fixed Costs/Year	$82,000.00
ACRS Life	5 years
Project Life	6 years
Salvage Equipment	$47,000.00
Variable Cost per Case	$12.00
Working Capital	$40,000.00
Tax Rate	45.00%
Discount Rate	15.00%

to be sold at the end of the project it would bring about $47,000 in salvage. The equipment would have an ACRS life of five years and be eligible for the 10 per cent investment tax credit. The applicable tax rate of 45 per cent could be applied to all taxable income generated by the project.

Tindle indicated that the variable costs per case would be $12.00 in labor and materials, and that while inflation might take some toll on this figure, operating efficiencies that could be achieved once production was underway and long-term contracts signed with major suppliers would likely keep this cost at the $12.00 level for the six-year life of the project. With respect to setting a price, Tindle suggested that the company should use at least a 75 per cent markup on variable costs, which would make the price $21.00 a case. Tindle argued that this 75 per cent figure was the minimum that Bod Products had enjoyed in the past, and that if the company could not do this well, it shouldn't enter into the project at all.

Brodie had serious reservations about this strategy. First of all, he knew that the company had enjoyed a 75 per cent markup in the past, but he wasn't sure that was necessary in this case because the fixed costs were covered by existing sales, except for $82,000 a year in maintenance, insurance, and other costs related to this specific operation. He knew the bidding on the contract would be extremely competitive and that if other companies did not try to make their average markup, he would not be the low bidder. He agreed with Tindle that the company was in no position to be a loss leader on this, that the project had to carry its own weight and earn a decent return. The minimum rate of return that he was willing to accept was 15 per cent, but he was not certain how much to charge for each case in order to generate the 15 per cent return per year over the life of the contract.

SUGGESTED QUESTIONS

1. a. Based on the data in the case and in Exhibit 13-1, calculate the cash outlay required for the project.

    b. Calculate the basis for depreciation under five-year ACRS.

2. Assuming zero revenues, compute the annual after tax-cash flow of the project for the six-year life. Assume the salvage of the working capital and the equipment takes place at the end of the sixth year.

3. Compute the NPV of the cash flows at Brodie's required rate of return.

4. a. Given the answer in Question 3, compute the six-year annuity necessary for a zero NPV on an after-tax basis.

    b. Recompute **a** on a before-tax basis.

5. From your answer in Question 4b, what is the price per case necessary to earn a 15 per cent internal rate of return.

6. Compare your answer in Question 5 with the policy of a 75 per cent markup on variable costs that Brodie traditionally enjoys. Which pricing policy should he adopt, and why?

PART III

Long-Term Financing

Duffy Photographic Equipment

Cost of Capital Using Dividend Growth Model

Duffy Photographic Equipment could trace its roots back to George Eastman and the development of modern photography, but that common heritage was about all the small, OTC company had in common with the giant, billion-dollar New York Stock Exchange firm of Eastman Kodak. While Eastman Kodak dominated the photography field in almost every aspect, Duffy Photographic was content to dominate only a very small segment of the industry. And while Duffy was small compared to others in the industry, its profits and growth had made it an institutional favorite among the heavily traded OTC stocks. The management of Duffy Photographic liked to feel that in their own small way they were just as successful as the larger companies in the field.

The company's founder, Frank Duffy, had not only been a contemporary of George Eastman but had worked closely with that business pioneer in the development of photography equipment and film. It had been Eastman's view that photography could be brought to the mass market if the equipment and film were developed so that large bulky cameras, expensive chemicals, and extensive training and experience in the art of photography could be replaced by products that the amateur and home photographer could use. Duffy had been a chemist and inventor who had worked with Eastman on technical development. After several years Duffy came to the conclusion that photography was just too complicated to ever bring to the mass market. Duffy felt that the future of the industry belonged solely to professionals, and that it made sense to develop products for that

71

group. When Eastman could not be convinced of this idea, Duffy left, relocated to Chicago and took what was left of a small inheritance to start his own company.

Despite the fact that Duffy was somewhat in error in his assessment, he was correct in perceiving a market for high-quality, professional-level photographic equipment. Duffy Photographic Equipment started in a Chicago warehouse to manufacture and sell camera accessories and dark room equipment to professional photographers. Duffy reasoned that this market would pay a premium price for a high-quality product, and the company's dedication to quality quickly established it as a force in the marketplace. In over seventy years of business operations, the philosophy of the company never changed, and while its product line expanded as the technology grew, it continued to serve the professional market. Several times in the last twenty years the company had been approached about licensing its name to a line of consumer products, but the current managers of the company were fearful of destroying the existing market and the mystique that had built up around the product, and so refused.

Following the economic recovery after World War II, the company made its initial public offering, two million shares. Since that time the company had gone to the market twice again, and in late 1983 there were 4.5 million shares outstanding, trading on the over-the-counter market. The company had begun regular dividend payments in the mid-1950s and had a record of twenty-seven straight years of a cash dividend. The company's rate of growth had been relatively steady, as its products were not all that sensitive to the business cycle. In the last three years the net income and dividends had grown at close to the historical rate, and the management of the company saw no reason why this growth should not continue into the future. Financial statements for the company for the last three years are shown in Exhibits 14-1 and 14-2.

While the company had been able to maintain its rate of growth with relative ease, the growth rate had required significant outlays on capital projects. Shaun Duffy, a distant descendant of the founder of the company and vice-president of finance, had been concerned that the company was not making proper decisions concerning the expenditures on capital equipment. The traditional method for authorizing capital expenditures was for the sales engineering department to propose a new product or an upgrade of an existing product. If the marketing department considered the product feasible from a sales point of view, the production and operations-engineering staff was directed to prepare cost estimates for production. If the product met company guidelines in terms of gross margins on variable costs, then at 45 per cent, then production was authorized

Exhibit 14.1 Duffy Photographic Equipment: Income Statement

Year Ending Sept. 31 (in $000)

	1981	1982	1983	1984 (fcst)
Net Sales	$67,845	$73,254	$77,432	$84,564
Cost of Goods Sold	43,212	46,413	48,953	53,240
Gross Profit	24,633	26,841	28,479	31,324
Operating Expenses	13,455	14,765	15,230	16,854
Interest Expense	2,245	2,567	2,890	3,120
Income Before Taxes	8,933	9,509	10,359	11,350
Taxes	3,752	3,994	4,351	4,767
Net Income	5,181	5,515	6,008	6,583
EPS	$1.15	1.23	$1.34	$1.46
Dividends per Share	$0.75	$0.80	$0.87	$0.95
P/E Ratio	11	12	11	11

Exhibit 14-2 Duffy Photographic Equipment: Balance Sheet

Year Ending Sept. 31 (in $000)

	1981	1982	1983	1984 (fcst)
Assets				
Cash	1,245	1,345	1,456	1,567
Accounts Receivable	22,654	24,879	27,134	29,756
Inventory	29,770	32,145	34,578	37,980
Other Current Assets	1,345	1,567	1,765	1,810
Total Current Assets	55,014	59,936	64,933	71,113
Net Plant and Equipment	38,976	41,298	44,019	48,908
Other Assets	12,340	13,654	14,011	14,511
Total Assets	106,330	114,888	122,963	134,532
Liabilities and Net Worth				
Accounts Payable	12,455	17,654	20,897	24,560
Accruals	7,865	8,733	9,213	9,873
Short-Term Debt	5,477	5,898	6,021	6,890
Current Portion	2,000	2,000	2,000	2,000
Total Current Liabilities	27,797	34,285	38,131	43,323
Long-Term Debt	21,000	19,000	20,927	25,000
Other Liabilities	6,790	8,930	9,129	9,129
Total Liabilities	55,587	62,215	68,187	77,452
Equity				
Common Stock (6,000,000 authorized; 4,500,000 outstanding)	4,500	4,500	4,500	4,500
Retained Earnings	46,243	48,173	50,276	52,580
Total Equity	50,743	52,673	54,776	57,080
Total Liability and Equity	106,330	114,888	122,963	134,532

and the capital investment necessary to produce the product was made.

Shaun Duffy was concerned that this method did not adequately consider the question of return on the capital-investment aspect of the product. While depreciation on the equipment necessary to produce the product was taken into consideration as a cost, no requirement was made with respect to earning a rate of return on the total capital cost. If the project met the margin requirements, then it was considered an acceptable project. There was no further tracking of the total profits from the project on any measurement of the return to capital employed in the project.

While funding had been easily available through internal sources and debt issues to support these expenditures, Duffy was worried that the fixed assets of the company were rising faster than they should be, and that fixed assets as a per cent of total assets was higher than it should be in companies of the size and nature of Duffy. In Shaun Duffy's opinion, a part of this problem was the failure to adequately evaluate the capital expenditures in terms of rate of return on investments. Duffy was convinced that the company was making uneconomical investments, and he resolved to implement procedures to improve the capital-budgeting decision-making system.

As a first step in this process, Duffy requested a thorough analysis of all projects scheduled for 1984. While the capital budget contained over twenty-four projects in all, most were small, maintenance items. Five major projects were included, representing substantial new business ventures for the company. Duffy had requested that the project analyses contain a discounted cash flow rate of return.

The five major projects and their estimated rates of return were as follows.

	Return	Outlay ($000)
Production of SuperFast (Trademark) darkroom Chemicals	17.8%	$4,500
Auto Focus Attachment for Enlarger	14.5%	2,850
Print Dryer	11.2%	1,670
Automatic Chemical Mixer	9.5%	2,130
Sepia Toning Paper	8.5%	3,320

After reviewing the project proposals, their costs and rates of return, Duffy became concerned as to whether or not all of the projects would have a high enough rate of return for adoption. He was particularly concerned about the last three projects, for although they represented major technical breakthroughs for the company, with current investment in research and development close to $5 million for all three, he was not certain the payoff was sufficient to justify production. Duffy did not know what the cutoff should be in using a rate of return criteria, but he did feel that projects below 10 per cent were highly doubtful.

The strongest advocate for the approval of the entire capital budget as presented was Harold Downs, vice-president of marketing and sales. Downs pointed out that all of the projects met the company's previous criteria with respect to margins and that, more importantly, all three were necessary for the continued growth of the company. As Downs saw it, the industry that Duffy Photographic Equipment was in was highly competitive, and growth was achieved only with a vigorous capital spending program to develop and introduce new products. Duffy had always been a high-quality, innovative company and enjoyed a strong reputation with customers and shareholders alike because of its growth and innovations.

Based on his personal assessment of the industry, Downs felt that adoption of a decision scheme that excluded most of the projects shown above would ultimately result in a no-growth position for the company. The current rate of growth had been relatively steady and was projected to remain so for a long time. Given Duffy's size and its ability to develop innovative products, the current rate of growth could be maintained indefinitely. If, however, the capital program were curtailed below what was proposed, Downs estimated that the company would continue at its rate of growth for only six more years and that, after that, sales and earnings would remain essentially flat.

Downs went on to argue that the rates of return were more than adequate for the company. The rates of return were computed on an after-tax basis, and given the company's cost of borrowed funds before tax of 14 per cent, the cost of funds was slightly over 8 per cent on an after-tax basis. Even the weakest of the projects would earn, according to Downs, more than the after-tax cost of debt.

Turning to the equity markets, Downs stated that the company's stock was selling at a multiple of eleven times earnings, far above the average of companies its size in the OTC market. Down's attributed this strong stock performance to the company's demonstrated ability to grow and to increase the dividend, and the expectation of the market that the rate of growth for the past three years would continue unabated into the future. That growth would be achievable, he thought, only with adoption of the capital budget as proposed.

Duffy agreed that the growth of the company was critical to its current valuation by the market, but that other factors were also involved here. He was particularly concerned about the increasing debt ratio of the company, and pointed out to Downs that the company would not be financing all of the future growth by debt only.

The Board of Directors had recently approved a policy whereby the company would raise all future capital in a ratio of 45 per cent debt and 55 per cent equity through retained earnings, as the board was opposed to any new issue of common stock. While the board did not adopt a specific dividend policy, it was widely assumed that the prevailing opinion was to continue with a relatively constant payout ratio, and that dividends would continue to grow at their recent historical rate.

The error that Duffy felt was being made by Downs in his analysis was that the rate of return on the projects must include a rate of return on this new equity capital, that is, the portion of the project that was being financed by retained earnings. Downs had left the cost of equity out of his analysis on the argument that there was no cost to the new retained earnings as there was no obligation incurred on the part of the company to obtain those funds. Duffy, however, said that the new equity capital, in the form of retained earnings, would be agreeable to the shareholders because they expected a return on that capital, and the company could retain the earnings only if it could provide a rate of return expected by the shareholders. Otherwise, according to Duffy, the money should be distributed to the shareholders.

The meeting broke up on this note, and Duffy was left with the task of determining the minimum rate of return that should be used in evaluating the projects proposed by the marketing and productions groups.

SUGGESTED QUESTIONS

1. Based on the data in Exhibits 14-1 and 14-2, compute the
   a. average annual compound growth rate in earnings between 1984 and 1981.
   b. Compute the average annual compound growth rate in dividends for the same period.
   c. Compute the price per share at the end of 1983.
   d. Compute the tax rate for 1983.

2. Based on the data in the case and the answers in Question 1, compute the cost of equity capital using the dividend/growth model.

3. Based on the data in the case and the answer to Questions 1 and 2, compute the marginal after-tax weighted cost of capital.

4. Using the value from Question 3, determine which projects would be acceptable.

5. Assume that Downs is correct, and that, based on actions taken, growth would continue at the same rate for the next 6 years, and then remain flat. Compute the new price of the stock.

Thoreau Landscaping Service

Cost of Capital Using CAPM

In January, 1983, Jack Nakamima, the president and chief executive officer of Thoreau Landscaping Service, was wrestling with a familiar problem in financial decision making. The question involved the minimum expected rate of return on new equity capital. Thoreau's policy, since it had become a public company in 1971, had been to invest all of the company's net income back into the company, thus increasing the retained earnings account and providing for the growth that made the company one of the leaders in lawn and garden services in the Southwest and Far West. When the company had been a private company, Thoreau had not had problems with investors questioning its decisions, but as a public company that did not pay dividends, concern had been voiced by investment bankers and prominent shareholders over the growth and dividend policy.

The company operated on a calendar fiscal year and generally held its annual shareholders meeting in Los Angeles during February. In the 1982 meeting the company had been questioned as to its dividend policy and the rate of return on investments that were financed with retained earnings. The company had never paid a cash common-stock dividend, although stock dividends had been regularly declared, and several groups of shareholders raised the question of whether or not cash dividends would be declared in the near future. The company had expected these questions, since a presentation to investment bankers the previous week had brought out the same concern.

Nakamima had answered that the company's future growth would

77

probably prohibit a cash dividend for the foreseeable future, but that growth would ultimately allow for dividends and that the stock dividend would continue. This failed to satisfy another group of shareholders who pressed the point that the retention of earnings was new equity capital provided by the current owners, and that if the company continued to retain the net income for investment purposes, they and the other shareholders were entitled to a reasonable return on that investment.

Nakamima had replied to those comments that the company would continue to retain net income only for as long as proper investment opportunities existed, and that if those opportunities were to cease, the company would adopt a policy of cash dividends. His final point, which seemed to satisfy the dissident group, was that the stock price of the company had risen in three of the last four years and had exceeded the rise of the stock market as a whole. In 1981, the year preceding that meeting, the stock price had gone down, but Thoreau shareholders had lost less than the market as a whole. This claim was backed up by data in Exhibit 15-1, subsequently released to the shareholders. The data that Nakimima used, the market returns and the returns to investors in the stock of Thoreau, is updated for 1982.

In getting ready for the 1983 shareholders meeting, scheduled for February 17 at the company auditorium, Nakamima wanted to preempt the concerns over dividends and the rate of return on retained earnings by presenting his own data and assurances to the shareholders. As a highly visible company in a major consumer market, Thoreau Landscaping was able to benefit from favorable press and shareholder reaction to its financial situation, in effect gaining free publicity and strong word-of-mouth advertising. The company was in the top three in market share in every geographic area in which it participated and was planning an expansion in the spring into the Louisiana and Arkansas areas from its Southwest base in Dallas. As

Exhibit 15-1   Market Returns vs. Company Returns

Year	Market	Thoreau
1974	0.33	0.42
1975	0.15	0.19
1976	−0.02	−0.13
1977	−0.04	−0.05
1978	0.12	0.31
1979	0.26	0.22
1980	0.11	0.06
1981	−0.08	−0.07
1982	0.29	0.38

Expected Risk-Free Return   0.085

with all expansions, the more favorable the publicity that preceded it, the easier it would be to penetrate the market.

Jack Nakamima was the second president of the company, the first having been his maternal uncle, Joe Matasi. Matasi had founded the company in the mid-1930s as a expansion of his gardening services to Orange County, California. The company was initially set up to provide landscaping of newly developed areas, areas that until the advent of suburban Los Angeles had been orange groves. Matasi Landscaping provided contractors and developers with a complete job, taking the land that was almost barren of vegetation and turning it into the flowered neighborhoods that the area is now famous for.

While Matasi Landscaping was originally set up for commercial work, Joe Matasi soon found that those who ultimately purchased the homesites and commercial areas were eager to contract with his firm to maintain the area. Thus, the company expanded into residential services, doing lawn mowing, weed control, gardening, landscaping, and other services for the affluent inhabitants of the suburbs surrounding Los Angeles County. This work was more trouble than the commercial work but generally carried a higher profit margin and helped the company during times when commercial opportunities were reduced.

By 1941 Matasi Landscaping had a commercial division and a residential division, each grossing about $250,000 in sales and each employing about forty-five workers. However, the bombing of Pearl Harbor effectively ended the company's operations. Through his standing in the community, Matasi was able to avoid internment in a camp, but only by volunteering for military service in Europe. While serving in Italy his entire family was forcibly relocated to an internment camp, resulting in the complete shutdown of the company. When Matasi returned to Southern California after the war he regained his family but found the business in total ruin. Instinct also told him that business under the name of Matasi Landscaping was impossible until much of the anti-Japanese feeling from the war had dissipated.

In 1946 the old Matasi Landscaping Service was reborn under the name of Thoreau Landscaping Service. Joe Matasi was not ignorant of American literature and was content to hide the nationality of the company, at least until times were more suitable. The success of the company in the postwar prosperity made the name change back to its original impossibly expensive. By the time anti-Japanese sentiment had disappeared, the company had too much invested in its current name and trademark to make any change. Thoreau Landscaping Service it was, and Thoreau Landscaping Service it would remain.

In the mid-1950s the company extended its market into the San Diego area and caught the growth of that city as it was just beginning to boom. By the 1960s the company was moving toward Arizona and Texas, but its ability to grow was limited at that time by its financial resources, or rather the lack of them. In order to gain more capital, the company went public in 1966, and with that funding its market territory was expanded into Houston and Dallas. At the end of 1982, sales had reached $300 million profits, a healthy 8 per cent of sales, and assets exceeded $85 million.

The company's success was primarily due to high productivity, which kept costs down. Its policy was to employ and utilize all of the known technology as soon as it was available. In addition, the company maintained a small research and development staff, which was making constant improvements to trucks, tractors, grading equipment, and the like so as to maximize the productivity of its highly trained staff. In almost all cases the company was able to do a job, either industrial, commercial, or residential, at a lower price and higher profitability than its competitors. As the work itself required relatively little skill and training (many of the competitors were unskilled laborers), Nakamima felt that the company must be dedicated to this price strategy if it were to preserve its place in the market.

One result of all of this investment had been a dividend policy that precluded the issuing of cash dividends. The company had attempted to mollify shareholders by continually issuing stock dividends. While shareholders generally liked increasing the number of shares they held at no cash cost to themselves, concern over the lack of a cash dividend was beginning to surface and become a major investor-relations problem. Shareholders felt that a company of this size and profitability should be distributing a cash dividend.

Nakamima had succeeded his uncle in the presidency of the company in the late 1960s, after extensive training in both horticulture and business, and after working his way up through the company ranks from day laborer. With this experience, Nakamima had seen firsthand the success of the high-tech, high-productivity policy and he was determined to continue that policy. He recognized, however, that as a public company, Thoreau owed it to the shareholders to invest their money wisely, or else distribute it to them. His objective for the upcoming shareholders meeting was to prove that Thoreau did indeed take into account the rate of return on the shareholders' investment and to demonstrate how the company's investment policy allowed for at least a minimum return to capital.

The company's capital-investment policy was to rely on payback as the acceptance criterion for a capital project. Almost all of the capital budget went into replacement or new machinery. For the most part this equipment had a life of four to five years, and consequently Thoreau required a payback of three years or less before any project was approved. While this policy served the company well, Nakamima was aware that the payback criterion did not in any way measure profitability and could not be presented as evidence that the company was making investments which provided for a reasonable return on common equity.

In reviewing the company's position, Nakamima examined the balance sheet in Exhibit 15-2. The company had issued preferred stock several years before, and the composition of the balance sheet at the end of 1982 appeared to have the exact proportions that the company desired. Over the immediate future, the company expected to raise capital according to the ratio of components shown in the balance sheet at the end of 1982. The preferred stock was straight preferred, and discussions with the company's investment-banking firm indicated that a rate of 11 per cent could be used for the future. The company expected to pay an average of 13 per cent for debt and was currently in the 48 per cent marginal state and federal tax bracket.

Nakamima knew he could use the above data for computing the cost of debt and preferred capital but was uncertain as how to proceed with the cost of equity. One of the traditional models, dividend yield plus growth rate did not seem appropriate, due to the lack of dividend payment by the company. After reviewing the data in Exhibit 15-1, Nakamima felt that the capital asset pricing model (CAPM) might be appropriate. That model allowed for the computation of a beta coefficient for the company and then used that information in estimating the cost of equity capital. Nakamima felt that the use of this system to compute the cost of equity capital could then be combined with the cost of debt and preferred to give the company an overall cost of capital. By setting his criteria for investments to have an internal rate of return at least this great, Nakamima would then be able to assure his shareholders that an adequate return was being earned on their investments, and that

Exhibit 15-2 Thoreau Landscaping Service: Condensed Balance Sheet (in $000)

	1981	1982
Current Assets	23,893	30,787
Fixed Assets	47,854	54,690
Total Assets	71,747	85,477
Debt	33,600	44,780
Preferred Stock	11,400	11,400
Equity	26,747	29,297
Total Liability and Equity	71,747	85,477

dividends would be paid as soon as the available funds exceeded the available opportunities that gave rates of return higher than this rate.

SUGGESTED QUESTIONS

1. Of what value, if any, is the issuing of a stock dividend in increasing the value of the equity or in providing a return to the common stockholders.

2. a. Given the data in Exhibit 15-1, compute the mean return on the market as a whole and Thoreau over the time period listed.

b. Compute the variance for the rate of return for the market as a whole and for Thoreau over the time period listed.

c. Compute the covariance between the returns to the market as a whole and the returns to Thoreau shareholders.

d. Compute the beta coefficient for Thoreau.

e. Compute the cost of equity capital for Thoreau based on the above data and the CAPM.

3. Given the information above, and the information in this case, compute the weighted after tax cost of capital for Thoreau.

4. Write a short report summarizing the information that Naka-mima might present to the shareholders.

Aaron's Automotive Supplies

Cost of Capital—Break Points

In early 1985, Aaron Praline, vice-president of administration and finance for Aaron's Automotive Supplies, reflected upon the unexpected problems that the recovery in the automotive industry had wrought for his company. In 1983 and 1984 the auto industry in the United States, with the help of a general economic recovery and, in particular, import restrictions, posted large sales increases and record profits. This recovery pulled companies like Aaron's Automotive Supplies with it, and in looking over the past two years Praline was pleased to see record profits and record sales. He did not, however, like the fact that the company faced 1985 spending plans that greatly exceeded its ability to fund them without issuing new debt and common stock.

Praline had joined the company fresh out of Ohio State's M.B.A. program in 1973, and in eight years he had worked himself up from the position of manager of financial planning to vice-president. Praline was not certain if his having the same first name as the name of the company had made him choose his employer, but he had never regretted the decision. The Cleveland based manufacturer of OEM and replacement auto supplies had been a tightly managed, somewhat profitable OTC company in 1973. By 1980, with Praline's help it had passed the $25 million mark in sales, and a conservative financial position had allowed it to withstand the oil embargo, the inflation of 1978–1981 and the 1981–1982 recession. Looking forward to 1985 (Exhibit 16-1), Praline saw the year filled with a record increase

Exhibit 16-1   Aaron's Automotive Supplies: Pro Forma Income Statement

	1985 (in $000)
Income	32,566
Cost of Goods Sold	17,899
Gross Profit	14,667
Overhead	3,555
Interest Expense	2,550
Income Before Tax	8,562
Tax	4,090
Net Income	4,472

in sales and profits. Yet that very success was now giving him the biggest problems he had faced with the company.

Aaron's Automotive Supplies was one of a number of companies that operated on the edge of the automotive industry. Very small by General Motors or Ford standards, Aaron's nevertheless participated in the same markets and enjoyed the same market problems as the larger companies. Whereas GM and Ford made complete cars, Aaron's made the smaller components that make up the cars. About 15 per cent of its sales were to the auto manufacturers, the remainder was in replacement parts. This remaining 85 per cent was split between 45 per cent in the wholesale or repair market and 40 per cent in the retail market. The repair market consisted of sales to distributors who sold to service chains and independent garages. The retail market was serviced by Aaron's through hundreds of small, independent retail stores and a lesser number of larger chain stores.

Aaron's products were primarily priced under fifty dollars and many sold for less than ten dollars. The company manufactured a full line of filters, ignition parts, engine and transmission parts, and selected auto-care products. The items were sold under Aaron's brand name except for a small program in which Aaron's manufactured items that were packaged under auto-service company names. The industry was highly competitive, and survivors were those who delivered on both price and quality. Aaron's was well known for meeting both of these criteria, and that was one of the reasons why the company was one of the more successful in its field.

Aaron's management had stressed productivity and control, and as a result the company enjoyed a good market share, high margins, and a reputation as a well-run company. The stock had been trading on the OTC for over seven years and the price reflected a rather high multiple for a company of its size and type. Current data on Aaron's financial position is shown in Exhibit 16-2. Relative to other companies of similiar size in the same industry, Aaron's had less debt higher margins. It had also established a relationship with both com-

Exhibit 16-2   Financial Data

Shares Outstanding	2,500,000
Current Share Price	$7.88
Projected Dividends	$0.75
Expected Growth Rate	11.00%
Projected Tax Rate	42.00%
Cost of Short-Term Funds	14.00%
Cost of Long-Term Funds	16.50%
Rate on New Preferred (after Issuing Costs)	11.50%
Estimated Cost of Issuing new Common Stock	7.00%
Available Short-Term Debt	$2,000

and higher margins. It had also established a relationship with both commercial banks and investment bankers that enabled it to obtain funds on an as-needed basis.

The company's recent growth and success had led to a situation that, in Praline's mind, could possibly be the undoing of the company. For the past several years the company had deferred capital expenditures in order to consolidate its markets and to protect it against the adverse movement in the automotive industry. While its replacement segment had not been bothered by the auto-sales weakness in 1980–1982, the sales to auto producers were down sharply. At 15 per cent of total sales, this part of the business was the lowest it had been in the history of the company. Now that sales and profits were above target levels, several senior executives in the company felt that the time was ripe to expand significantly and to reduce further dependence on the OEM market. Two of the members of the executive management team wanted to reduce sales to the OEM market to zero, because of the high volatility and competitiveness of that market.

Accordingly, the marketing department had hired a consulting firm for a market survey that identified new markets for the company. Based on this information, a capital budget was submitted for 1985 that in addition to normal projects that would be funded from depreciation, contained eight expansion projects. The only trouble was that the outlay for these projects far exceeded the ability of the company to fund them with internal financing and new debt.

The proposed projects are summarized in Exhibit 16-3. A brief description is as follows.

Automated Filter Inserter.   This system would replace the current technique of inserting filter media into cartridges by hand, by replacing the entire manufacturing process with an automated system. Significant savings would result from lower labor costs, and with the lower costs Aaron's could move aggressively in the market by lowering prices. This cost improvement might

Exhibit 16-3 1985 Proposed Capital Budget

Project	Cost (in $000)	Return (in Per Cent)
Automated Filter Inserter	1,760	23.00
Ring Calibrator	2,350	21.00
In-House Printing	960	19.50
Engine Block Rebuild	2,240	17.50
Private Brand Program	1,250	15.20
Production Line Productivity	1,970	14.50
New Tool Line	3,890	13.30
Oil and Lube Products	2,780	12.90

allow the company to expand its private-brand label program to several large discount store chains.

Ring Calibrator. Aaron's sold a complete line of piston rings, whose tolerances were to thousanths of an inch. The calibration of machinery was done by hand, which was both time consuming and expensive. A new computerized system was available which would produce considerable cost savings.

In-House Printing. Aaron currently had all of its packaging printed by outside companies. Purchase of printing equipment and hiring of personnel would result in considerable savings. In addition, it was possible that Aaron's could then do this type of work for other companies, diversifying its businesses and reducing its reliance on the highly cyclical automotive market.

Engine Block Rebuild. Several large distributors had approached Aaron's about supplying them with rebuilt engines. This would be a new business for Aaron's.

Private Brand Program. The marketing department had identified four potential customers for Aaron's. These customers would purchase current Aaron's products labeled under their own in-house brand.

Production Line Productivity. This project consisted of installing computer controls which would speed up the production line and reduce defects.

New Tool Line. The marketing department felt that a hand-tool line imprinted with Aaron's name could be sold through the existing retail and distributor network. This business would draw upon the brand-name recognition already established by Aaron's, which the consulting firm had learned was very strong among consumers.

Oil and Lube Products. Aaron's did not currently produce products in these areas. If it entered the business, it would purchase in bulk from independent oil refiners and package and label under the Aaron's brand name.

As Praline reviewed the list shown in Exhibit 16-3, he knew that the company would have to go to the capital markets in order to finance many of the projects. In strategy meetings earlier in the year the company had adopted a target capital structure, shown in Exhibit 16-4. Any future financing would have to be in approximately the proportion shown in that Exhibit. In looking at Exhibit 16-4 and the information shown in Exhibit 16-2, Praline knew that some of the equity financing could come from retained earnings, but that if the capital budget exceeded the amount that could be supported by retained earnings, a new stock issue would have to be made. Underwriting and other costs were estimated to be 7 per cent.

As far as debt was concerned, the company had a short-term line of credit with a local bank. It had been Aaron's policy to continually role over this line, and Praline felt that the bank would continue to allow this policy, thus making the short-term debt a permanent part of the company's capital structure. However, the additional funds from this source was only about $2 million. In financing the new projects it would be the company's policy first to use this source for new debt. After this short-term debt was used up, the company would have to go into the long-term debt markets, most likely through a private placement. Praline recognized that this policy would change the proportion of short-term debt to long-term debt in the overall capital structure, but that total debt would still be kept to the desired proportion shown in Exhibit 16-4.

While the short-term funds would cost 14 per cent, the long-term funds were expected to cost 16 per cent. Given the relatively small needs, new preferred stock could be sold at any level for a net cost to the company of 11.5 per cent. All of these costs were on a before-tax basis. The combined state, local, and federal tax rate applicable to the decision on new project and new capital is shown in Exhibit 16-2.

Exhibit 16-4 Aaron's Automotive Supplies: Target Balance Sheet Composition (in Per Cent)

Debt	45
Preferred Stock	9
Common Equity	46
Total	100

The company had historically computed its required rate of return on the assumption that no new common stock would be issued. In examining the list of proposals, Praline knew that if the majority of them were to be funded, a new issue of common stock would be required, and that use of long-term debt would also be necessary. The increase in retained earnings expected in 1985 would be based on a dividend of $.75 a share, but without even calculating how much in new equity capital this would bring in, Praline knew it would not be enough. In view of the fact that new long-term debt and new common stock would raise the cost of capital, he was concerned as to whether or not the higher cost of capital should cause the firm to reject any of the proposals.

SUGGESTED QUESTIONS

1. How large can the capital budget be without requiring a new issue of common stock?

2. How large can the capital budget be without requiring use of the long-term debt?

3. Compute the cost of capital, assuming the short-term debt is used and no new stock is issued.

4. Compute the cost of capital, assuming that new common stock is issued but no long term debt is used.

5. Compute the cost of capital, assuming new common stock is issued and new long-term debt is used after the short-term capacity is exhausted.

6. Based on your answers, which projects should be chosen?

Ellettsville Steel Corporation

Zero Coupon Bonds

The president of the Ellettsville Steel Corporation was wrong. Jack Decker, controller of Ellettsville Steel knew he was wrong. Linda Simpson, treasurer of Ellettsville Steel knew he was wrong. The problem, though, was that in the recently concluded meeting involving exactly how Elletsville Steel would fund a $20 million requirement neither Decker nor Simpson had been able to show the president why he was wrong. The result was the proposal that Simpson and Decker had so carefully prepared was on hold until they could come up with a more convincing argument.

Ellettsville Steel Corporation was a medium-sized foundry and fabricating shop located in south-central Indiana. The company's major businesses were the manufacture of steel components for large industrial machinery and the custom design and casting of specialized steel components for almost any type of industrial application. Despite the fact that the steel industry in general had undergone several difficult years in the early 1980s, the company had prospered in recent years because low-cost steel imports, which had hurt the large steel producers, had been a benefit to Ellettsville Steel. Ellettsville Steel used a mixture of low-cost imports and domestic steel in their products. The company had grown from sales of less than $50 million in 1972 to the expected level of $50 million in 1982.

The growth of Ellettsville Steel had put significant strains on the cash flow of the company. The company's stock was actively traded in the OTC market, but because of the general depressed level of the stock market in 1982 and the even more depressed level of any stock with "steel" in its name, Ellettsville had adopted a policy of not issuing common stock. To conserve funds the company paid no dividends and funded the cash shortfall by a short-term credit line. When the credit line reached its upper limit, the company refunded by issuing long-term debt, most frequently with a private placement.

The problem facing Ellettsville Steel in late 1982 was the future requirements for $20 million. The proceeds of this loan would be used to pay off the line of credit, which had reached its upper limit during the year, to fund growth in 1983 and 1984, and to pay for state-mandated pollution-control devices. There was no question that somehow or other the $20 million would have to be raised.

Complicating things was the fact that the five-year business plan that had been put together under the supervision of Simpson and Decker showed significant cash deficits in the next few years. At current interest rates for the company of 14.5 per cent to 15 per cent, Simpson, in particular, was concerned that the company would be in the position of having to borrow money just to make interest payments on existing debt in 1983, 1984, and possibly into 1985. She had asked the company's investment-banking firm of Brillig and Gyre to explore alternative ways to traditional financing to see if there was some financing vehicle that could better fit Ellettsville's needs.

After studying Ellettsville's current position and business plan, Jack Daniels of Brillig and Gyre had suggested that the company consider issuing zero-coupon bonds. Zero-coupon bonds were medium-term debt that made no periodic interest payments. Instead the bonds sold at a discount from their par, or mature, value, and the investor received his return when the bonds came due. In effect, the bonds sold at the present value of the par value discounted at the current rate of interest.

Daniels explained that the advantage to investors of such bonds is that they are assured a reinvestment rate of the intermediate funds that is generated by the investment, as opposed to traditional bonds where as the intermediate interest is paid in cash and has to be reinvested at the prevailing interest rates. Interest rates at this time were considered to be at abnormally high levels, and many investors felt that, in the long term, interest rates would average considerably lower than their current levels. He said there was considerable demand for such bonds by IRA investors and pension funds, so much so that the bonds often sold at a cost below that of the interest rate on conventional debt. He saw no difficulty in selling enough bonds to generate $20 million for Ellettsville.

The attraction of such bonds to Simpson and to Decker was their effect on the cash flow of Ellettsville. In effect, the bonds allowed deferral of the cash interest payments until maturity. Not only that, the IRS allowed the company to accrue interest payments and deduct those payments from the taxable income. In effect, during the life of the bond not only did the company not have to make interest payments but it also received a positive cash benefit from the income-tax shelter resulting from the interest accrual. In effect it was able to take a deduction for interest costs that were accrued and not paid until the maturity date of the bond.

Simpson and Decker knew they would have to convince the conservative president of Ellettsville Steel in order to proceed with their issuing of zero-coupon bonds. They asked Daniels to help prepare a presentation that outlined the advantages of the bonds. Simpson and Decker made their proposal based on the two major advantages they saw to the bonds of Ellettsville, the fact that interest was deferred until the maturity of the bond, and the fact that a positive inflow of cash from the tax shelter would reduce the actual interest cost during the life of the bond.

Daniels also prepared Exhibit 17-1, which showed the proceeds from a hypothetical one thousand dollar zero-coupon bond at various interest rates and maturities.

Simpson and Decker decided to ask for authorization to issue enough bonds to raise $20 million. They proposed issuing the bonds for ten years and 14 per cent interest and based their argument on the savings in interest payments from the lower interest cost, the deferral of the payment of interest until the maturity of the bond, and the reduction in taxes for Ellettsville Steel during the life of the bond.

The president of the company rejected the proposal as being far more costly than ordinary borrowing. He pointed out, for example, that based on Exhibit 17-1, to borrow $385.50 the company would have to issue a 10 per cent zero coupon bond for ten years. With an ordinary bond, the company would pay $38.55 in interest each year for a period of ten years. The total interest cost before tax considerations would be $385.50. However, with the zero-coupon bond the company would pay $1,000 at the end of the tenth year. The total interest payment would be $614.45 over the ten years or an average of $61.44 per year. This meant the effective cost to Ellettsville was $61.44/$385.50 or approximately 16 per cent a year.

Exhibit 17-1 Proceeds of Zero-Coupon Bonds

| Rate | Maturity (years) | |
	8	10
10%	$466.50	$385.50
12%	403.90	322.00

The president said he had not computed the tax effects, but he didn't see how any tax benefit could make it more desirable to pay a total of $614.45 in interest when he could get the same money for a total of $385.50 in interest. He also admitted that he was certain there was something wrong with his reasoning, because based on his computations no firm would issue zero-coupon bonds, when in fact their popularity was growing. He told Simpson and Decker to go back to their offices and either demonstrate how the zero-coupon bond would save the company money or come up with some other proposal.

Simpson and Decker knew there was faulty reasoning in the president's arguments. However, they didn't know exactly how to go about the process of demonstrating that the zero-coupon bonds were good for the company.

SUGGESTED QUESTIONS

1. Demonstrate how the computations in Exhibit 17-1 are done.

2. Determine how much in par, or mature, value would have to be issued for Ellettsville Steel to have proceeds of $20 million in 14 per cent, ten-year zero-coupon bonds.

3. Construct an amortization table for the 14 per cent ten-year zero-coupon bonds.

4. Using the fact that the true interest on the bonds is the internal rate of return, show what the rate of interest is on a before-tax and after-tax basis. Assume a tax rate of 48 per cent.

5. Reconcile your answers in Question 4 with the argument of the president of Ellettsville Steel. If the cost is the same as a traditional 14 per cent bond sold at par, why is the total interest paid on the zero-coupon bonds so much more than that paid on the traditional bond?

6. Why do zero-coupon bonds appeal to IRA investments and pension funds in particular, as opposed to ordinary investors?

Major Medic Services

Stock Sale Through Rights Offering

Major Medic Services was one of the glamour companies of the 1970s. The business was founded in 1968 by two physicians, Alan Ginsburg and Everett Hilton, to provide a unique type of medical service for the general public. From a beginning of one office and three physicians in 1968, the company grew to have operations in twenty-four states with sales in excess of $230 million by the end of 1982.

Along the way, the company became the darling of Wall Street. With Americans spending larger and larger amounts on health care, Major Medic Services found that the limits of its growth were only the ability of its managers and the amount of capital it could raise. At one time the company found itself on the recommended list of almost every major stock advisory service and brokerage operation. Given its humble beginnings in the office of a general practitioner group, the company had come a long way in a short period of time.

The phenomenal success of Major Medic Services had a lot to do with being in the right place at the right time, a somewhat trite adage but never more applicable than in this situation. Ginsburg and Hilton had been partners along with a third doctor in a practice in a suburb of St. Louis, and one day Hilton remarked on the large number of new patients they were attracting. Reliance on the old family physician was rapidly disappearing, because families no longer settled down in the towns in which they were raised, and when they did settle in a community, were often gone again five years later. The movement in and out of the prosperous suburb that

Ginsburg and Hilton lived in meant patient turnover of 15 per cent to 20 per cent a year. Ginsburg also noted that they were treating a large number of transient patients, people who needed medical care while on a visit to friends and relatives, or in many cases businessmen who were away from their home and needed some type of immediate, though nonemergency, medical care or medical prescription.

Discussion between the two doctors brought out another interesting point. Although much of the medical advice they gave was health related, a large portion of it was physician related. Newcomers to the area wanted to know all about the local practitioners, who was good at what, and who was recommended. Ginsburg and Hilton attempted to answer these questions, within the bounds of medical ethics, but both noticed a severe concern in their patients about doctors of whom they had little or no knowledge. The comfort index of patients with new, untried doctors was very low, and some even traveled thousands of miles to utilize a specialist in whom they had gained confidence.

Out of this discussion came the concept of Major Medic Services. The idea was to develop a chain of physicians' offices as similar as possible in physical layout and services offered. The expectation was that the offices would attract two types of customers. One would be the newcomer to the area who, having little knowledge of the area and no reliable way of obtaining information, would naturally gravitate toward a situation with which he or she was familiar. The second type of patient would be the individual temporarily away from home who needed special attention and would be likely to go to a service he knew something about. Furthermore, patients at one office could easily be referred to the office in the new area in which they relocated, so that once a patient was serviced by Major Medic Services, he would remain a patient or customer of the organization as long as he lived in a community where a Major Medic Services office was also located.

The company was organized without any capital investment whatsoever on the part of Ginsburg and Hilton. They started by incorporating and then selling stock to ten physician groups in suburban locations. In exchange for the stock, these physician groups agreed to redo their offices into Major Medic Centers, and the attraction to them was that they would keep their current patients, but also participate in growth as the service expanded. Furthermore, as shareholders in the company they would participate in the profits that were generated by the entire operation, not just their own practice.

This method of organization led to the creation of twenty-two offices in nine midwestern suburban locations by 1973. By that time, Ginsburg and Hilton had left medical practice to participate in full-time management of the company they had started, and the business had grown sufficiently that each became a specialist. Ginsburg took responsibility for existing operations, and his major function was to see that all participants were meeting the company standards, as standarization of medical services was the key to the success of the concept. All offices were staffed by a general practitioner, a pediatric specialist, and an ear, nose, and throat specialist. Patient attrition was carefully measured and any corrective action in the area of quality of services was addressed by Ginsburg in consultation with the physicians involved. Ginsburg liked to argue that for the first time modern management practices had been brought to the physician's office without sacrifice in the quality of care.

Hilton took over responsibility for the growth of the company, setting up new operations and providing them with enough guidance until they could operate freely on their own, at which time they fell under the direct control of Ginsburg. Hilton also assumed the responsibility for financing the growth. Capital requirements were extensive, since facilities that conformed exactly to company requirements frequently had to be constructed from scratch, and a major marketing program was necessary before the opening of any office in order to educate consumers to the concept and gain acceptance in the community. Not only was the program expensive, but all marketing programs had to conform to medical ethics and restrictions, thus making the planning of a program time consuming and expensive.

The company used debt extensively in its financing, because its shareholders did not have the liquidity to make large equity investments in the business. However, even with a high debt ratio the company found that growth requirements required the periodic issuing of common stock. Thus, as the company developed it took on more and more of the look of any other public company.

In 1974 the company made its first issue of common stock. The reasons were twofold, one to raise capital and the other to provide a ready market for those early participants in the company who had subscribed to common stock in order to join the organization. By going public the company created a secondary market for the stock, and the early investor-physicians were able to take substantial capital-gains profits by selling their stock, and yet retain their income as a participant in the company. The initial issue was successful, and the growth aspects of the company soon caught the attention of major Wall Street advisory services and money managers. By 1980, adjusting for splits and stock dividends six million shares were outstanding. At one time the company's stock traded as high as $57.00 a share, but as growth slowed and as the novelty of the company wore off, the stock price slipped back to its level at the end of 1982

Exhibit 18-1   Data on Common Stock
January 1, 1983

Shares Outstanding	6,000,000	
EPS 1982	$3.25	
Price/Earnings Ratio	12	
New Equity Required	$12,000,000	
Proposed Rights Offering Prices	Plan A	Plan B
	$30.00	$10.00

of just under $40 per share. Current market information on Major Medic Services is shown in Exhibit 18-1.

In early 1983 the company faced two financial problems. One problem was the need to raise additional equity capital, the second was to do something about the falling stock price. The company had never paid a cash dividend, as growth consumed all of the earnings that were available, and more besides. In discussions with various investment bankers and brokerage firms, this lack of dividend payment was cited as a reason why the stock had not performed as well recently as the market as a whole. Hilton felt that something should be done to make the stock more attractive, and he knew that cash dividends could not be paid given the near-term requirement of about $12 million in new equity capital.

In early January, 1983, Hilton set up a meeting with the investment bank of Morgan, Black, Inc., one of the leading firms on Wall Street. Jamie Regers, a partner of the firm, had done extensive research on the company prior to that meeting. During the meeting Regers indicated that Morgan, Black was prepared to underwrite a new issue of common stock to raise the $12 million in new equity. Regers also told Hilton that the sum was a rather small one as far as Morgan, Black was concerned, and that the issuing costs were likely to be substantial. Regers estimated that for a new issue of that size, the issuing costs including fees and commissions to Morgan, Black would be in the area of $800,000 to $1 million.

Hilton's response to this information was that while Major Medic would be willing to go this route if there was no other alternative, the costs of issuing new stock were almost prohibitive, and asked Regers what alternatives existed. Regers answered that Morgan, Black would be prepared to assist Major Medic with either a private placement of new stock, provided the company would commit to paying a cash dividend at some time in the future or a rights offering for a relatively modest fee. With the rights offering, each shareholder would be issued one right for each share of stock owned. The shareholders could then tender a fixed number of rights plus the subscription price of a new share of stock to the company in order to purchase a share of stock.

Regers explained that the number of rights needed to buy a share of stock would depend upon the subscription price of the new stock, and that the lower the subscription price, the more shares that would have to be issued and the less the number of rights needed to buy a new share. Regers also told Hilton that the subscription price would have to be set well below the current market price of the stock in order to make the rights offering succeed. She indicated that the benefit to Major Medic of a rights offering would be substantial savings in the issuing costs. The shareholders would benefit because they could choose either to exercise the rights or to sell them in the secondary market. Thus, a shareholder with, say, one hundred shares could sell the rights and still have one hundred shares of stock. Hilton was attracted to this plan because of the savings and because the rights offering might be viewed by some shareholders as a cash return on their investment, and hence the pressure on the company to pay dividends might be lessened.

Hilton's immediate concern was how low a subscription price would have to be set, because he recognized that the lower the subscription price, the greater the downward pressure on the stock as a result of the new offering. Regers replied that Morgan, Black would recommend one of two plans, a mild discount and a deep discount. Based on the information in Exhibit 18-1, Regers said that Plan A would be to issue the stock at a price of $30.00 a share, plus the appropriate number of rights. Plan B would be to issue the stock at $10.00 per share plus the appropriate number of rights. Regers stated that the issue was likely to be successful under either plan; that is, the issue would be fully subscribed under either Plan A or Plan B, and it was up to Major Medic to decide which they would like to do.

Hilton thought that Plan B might be better, for it gave the current stockholders a much better deal if they could purchase the stock for $10 a share as opposed to its current price. He did, however, want a complete analysis of the program before proceeding.

SUGGESTED QUESTIONS

1. For each plan, how many shares would have to be issued?

2. For each plan, how many rights would have to be tendered to buy a share of stock?

3. For each plan, what is the theoretical value of a right?

4. For each plan, what is the value of the stock selling rights on? Rights off?

5. For each plan, assume ownership of one hundred shares. Assume that the rights are sold at their theoretical value. Show that the value of the holdings of cash and stock after the sale, when the stock is selling "rights off," is the same as before the rights offering.

6. Evaluate the plans and a rights offering in general. In what ways are the company and the shareholders really better off?

Great Bear Motels

Refunding a Debt Issue

At corporate headquarters of Great Bear Motels it was always referred to as the Great Bear mistake, the $56 million dollar boner, or Finance's Doom and Gloom. It was really no laughing matter, though. It cost two executives their jobs, a third was forced into retirement, and a major investment-banking firm lost a trusted and valuable client. Finally, in early 1985, it appeared possible that Great Bear Motels had the opportunity to wipe the mistake off its books, but not without some cost and not without dredging up memories that many of the company's top management would rather be forgotten.

In January, 1985, Great Bear Motels was one of the ten largest motel chains in North America. The company had units in place in almost every urban area in the United States and Canada, and current plans were to open one unit every seven days for the coming two years. While this rate of growth might seem high, it was down from the pace of the previous ten years when the company had grown from a regional, midwestern chain into a national and international concern. That growth had led to significant profitability (see Exhibits 19-1 and 19-2) but had also produced a balance sheet that was heavily tilted toward the debt side. If the company was to continue its recent trend, several financial advisers had recommended a "cleaning up" of the balance sheet, beginning with the company's $56 million long-term debt issue.

Great Bear Motels ran primarily family businessmen's motels in the midwestern area, with most of its units in the Ohio River Valley,

Exhibit 19-1 Great Bear Motels: Income Statement for Calendar Year (in $000)

	1983	1984
Revenues	876,543	1,034,876
Cost of Products and Services Sold	433,678	498,766
Gross Profit	442,865	536,110
Operating Expenses	185,670	220,560
Operating Income	257,195	315,550
Other Income	53,444	67,890
Interest Expense	66,789	75,678
Income Before Taxes	243,850	307,762
Taxes	87,865	115,876
Net Income	155,985	191,886

Exhibit 19-2 Great Bear Motels: Balance Sheet as of December 31 (in $000)

	1983	1984
Assets		
Cash and Marketable Securities	56,780	76,450
Accounts Receivable	167,890	204,874
Inventory	56,789	78,904
Other Current Assets	23,876	30,876
Total Current Assets	305,335	391,104
Land	43,850	49,780
Buildings and other Depreciable Assets	416,750	440,675
Less Accumulated Depreciation	87,659	101,340
Net Building and Other	329,091	339,335
Other Assets	43,560	54,322
Total Assets	721,836	834,541
Liabilities and Net Worth		
Accounts Payable	76,899	102,340
Other Accruals	23,457	29,870
Short-Term Debt	54,367	66,433
Total Current Liabilities	154,723	198,643
Mortgages	307,560	330,568
Long-Term Debt	56,000	56,000
Other Liabilities	27,777	29,374
Total Liabilities	546,060	614,585
Common Stock	30,900	30,900
Retained Earnings	144,876	189,056
Total Equity	175,776	219,956
Total Liabilities and Net Worth	721,836	834,541

and in Michigan, Illinois, and Indiana. The units were located along major highways just outside downtown areas of such cities as Cincinnati, Cleveland, Detroit, Chicago, and Indianapolis. Most units were standard, two hundred–room buildings with a small restaurant. The company was steady but relatively unexciting. All of that changed in 1973 when Alvin Stevenson took over as president and chief operating officer. Stevenson had been brought in by the Board of Directors to change the direction of the company. The directors felt that a major opportunity was available in the motel business by upgrading to semiluxury units that sold rooms at popular prices. The board reasoned that both business and private travelers were becoming more particular and wanted more than just a roof over their heads and a coffee shop to eat. Stevenson was hired to institute the change.

Stevenson realized that the company could not grow solely through company-owned units and began an aggressive program of franchising motels in areas where the company did not operate directly. In order to encourage franchising, the company would grant exclusive rights to a large territory in exchange for an agreement by the franchisee that he or she would construct motels at a given rate. The process was very successful, and by 1985 several of the franchisees were as big as Great Bear itself. Some had become public companies and even franchised out part of their territory to other companies. In January, 1985, it was almost impossible to travel in a large Canadian or U.S. city and not be able to spend the night in a Great Bear Motel.

The parent company had reserved the highest end of the luxury market for itself. Stevenson developed the concept of the Great Bear Lodge—a small, luxury motel in the heart of major cities, catering to the business customer during the week and the affluent traveler during the weekend. This concept proved very successful, but company plans to build the units outstripped its ability to finance the construction with internal funds. Because most of the investment was real estate and buildings, Great Bear did the majority of its financing with commercial mortgages. During construction, a construction mortgage was obtained that paid for the construction of the facility and was due when construction was completed. This type of mortgage was usually charged on a floating-rate basis. At completion the construction mortgage was rolled over into a fixed-rate commercial mortgage, leaving the company with a large amount of debt on its balance sheet.

By 1979 the program had been so successful that the company was strapped for funds. It had relied heavily on a short-term line of credit for financing working capital, which was largely receivables from its franchisees, but as short-term rates rose, the cost of this debt began to eat into profits. Furthermore, the consortium of banks that had been providing this credit had indicated that they were not likely to increase the total limit, which Great Bear had reached in late 1979, and that they rather looked forward to the company repaying at least a part of the line. They suggested either an equity issue or a subordinated debt issue with the proceeds dedicated to reducing the line of credit outstanding as a way of reducing reliance on the line of credit.

In late 1979 the company was approached by Frederick Rose and Company, a Wall Street investment firm about the possibility of issuing long-term debt. Rose indicated that it felt a $60 million issue would be feasible and pointed out several advantages to Great Bear from the issue. The proceeds would be used to pay down the line of credit, thus freeing up the line for emergency use. By issuing long-term debt at fixed rates, the company would be protecting itself against rises in the short-term rate of interest, since the line of credit was a prime-tied loan. Finally, by issuing a subordinated debenture, the company would actually be improving its debt position with respect to the senior debt, and thus increasing its ability to borrow in the future.

With respect to the rate of interest, Rose's general partner, Cyril Manley, indicated that a rate of 17 per cent would be necessary, a high rate historically, but one that the company should expect as reasonable. The reasons for this high rate were that a recent change in Federal Reserve policy was expected to drive rates dramatically higher in 1980, and the company's high debt ratio and the fact that the issue would be subordinated put a rather large risk premium on the issue. When C. J. Alexis, vice-president of finance of Great Bear, and George Dervis, the treasurer, objected to the high rate, Manley showed the two executives a confidential report by his firm's chief economist. That report indicated that the prime rate would likely rise to 22 per cent in the next twelve months, and that long-term rates for the best credit risk debt would be in the 16 per cent to 18 per cent range. Furthermore, the higher rates would be built into the economy along with high rates of inflation, and real-rate relief would not come until 1986 at the earliest.

Alexis and Dervis were in general agreement with the forecast and saw the debt issue as a way to avoid paying short-term rates in the 20 per cent range. They were concerned about one aspect of the issue, the fact that the debentures would not be callable for five years, and then at a price of 105. However, Manley pointed out that given the interest-rate scenario, it was highly unlikely that the issue could be refunded by the end of the decade, and that the call protection probably saved the company about seventy-five basis points

Exhibit 19-3 Data on $56 million 25-Year Subordinated Debentures

Issue Date	March 15, 1980
Call Protection	5 Years
Call Price	106
Maturity	March 15, 2005
Coupon Rate	17%
Issuing Cost	2,375,000
Sold at Par	$1000/Bond

in higher interest that otherwise would have to be paid. With Alexis' and Dervis' cooperation, Manley made a presentation to the Board of Directors, and in early 1980 the issue was approved. Details on the issue and its cost are shown in Exhibit 19-3.

For the first several years of its life, the $56 million debt issue looked like a winner. But in 1981 interest rates peaked, and by 1983 both short-term and long-term rates were substantially below the levels they had been when the debt was issued. In early 1984 Great Bear found itself with a 17 per cent debt issue that could not be called, when comparable rates were below 13 per cent. Alexis and Dervis were asked to resign their positions, and the company sought out a new investment-banking firm. Ultimately, Haber and Knowles were retained with the express orders from Stevenson to "do something about that damn 17 per cent issue." However, as the call protection prohibited calling the bonds before 1985, there was little that could be done.

In late 1984 Jerry Harper of Haber and Knowles made the proposal to Stevenson that the issue be refunded. His proposal was for the issuing of $56 million in new debt the proceeds of which would be used to retire the old 17 per cent debt. The details of the new issue are shown in Exhibit 19-4. Harper explained that the debt could be called on March 15, 1985, and that it would take approximately one month to pay off all of the holders. The new issue would

Exhibit 19-4 Data on Proposed New $56 million Issue

Issue Date	April 15, 1985
Amount	$56,000,000
Life	20 years
Issuing Cost	$2,650,000
Coupon Rate	13.00%
Call Date of Old Issue	March 15, 1985
Bridge Loan Per Cent	12.50%
Applicable Tax Rate	46.00%

be sold on April 15, 1985, and the one-month gap would be covered by a bridge loan arranged by Harper with one of the large New York commercial banks. Harper explained that the issuing costs would have to be paid for the new issue, but that the unamortized costs of the old issue could be written off immediately, thus giving the company a sizeable tax reduction. The new issuing costs would be amortized on a straight-line basis over the life of the issue.

Stevenson was irritated enough that he would have to spend $2.65 million in issuing costs just five years after he had issued a twenty-five–year bond, in effect paying issuing costs twice for the same debt. Obviously, replacing 17 per cent debt with 13 per cent debt would produce substantial savings, but he wondered whether or not they justified the additional expense.

SUGGESTED QUESTIONS

1. Assuming the refunding is done, what is the unamortized issuing costs of the old issue before tax? After tax?

2. What are the annual interest rates savings on the new versus the old before tax? After tax?

3. What is the differential in annual amortization of the issuing costs before tax? After tax?

4. What is the amount of the call premium before tax? After tax?

5. Using the after-tax cost of new debt as a discount rate, determine the present value of the proposed refunding.

6. Should Alexis and Dervis have been forced out of the company for this mistake; that is, did they act improperly in approving the first issue?

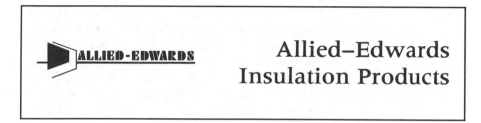

Allied–Edwards Insulation Products

EPS—EBIT Indifference Points

The Allied–Edwards Insulation Products Company did not exist in 1985, yet the company was projected to have sales of over $20 million in its first year of operation, 1986, and by 1990 revenues were expected to triple to more than $60 million. Based on this optimistic forecast, the two creators of the project might be expected to easily reach agreement on how to organize and finance the new company, but in late 1985 about the only thing that Allied Building Products and Edwards Construction Supplies could agree on was the name for the new company. Allied was providing the technology, so their name could go first, but the new company would not be born unless a financing plan was agreed to also.

Allied–Edwards Insulation Products was the product of a new insulation technology developed by Allied Building Products. Allied Building Products was a 118-year-old company that specialized in the manufacture of residential and commercial building supplies. The main products of the company were its line of asphalt shingles and related roofing and siding materials, but its product line was fully diversified and it produced a large number of building-related products. In 1985 the company earned over $160 million on sales of $1.4 billion, and it could boast that at least one of its products was found in almost every American home or commercial building constructed in the last twenty years. Because the company sold products used in repair and replacement, in addition to new construction, its business was a strong, steady profit producer year after year.

The strength of Allied Building Products lay in production. The company's promotional literature stated every product they manufactured was better, less expensive, and more widely available than any competitive product. The better and less expensive part was possibly true, but the availability of Allied Products was substantially less than the company would have liked to admit. Unlike many other companies in the same field, Allied had no retail stores of its own. It sold to the public through a chain of distributors who in turn sold to selected retail and wholesale outlets for the do-it-yourselfer and for the professional builder. Because of this arrangement, Allied products had to compete with a long list of similar products from other companies that were carried by each distributor.

Many competitors were companies of similar size whose marketing and sales efforts were at least equal to Allied's. Several times in the last ten years the company had considered proposals to strengthen its distribution and marketing activities, but in all cases the funding had gone into modernizing and expanding production facilities. Allied's philosophy was that the company would be most successful competing through lower prices and higher quality, rather than expensive and extensive sales and marketing.

Edwards Construction Supplies was just the opposite of Allied. Despite their name and brand, which was seen on several thousand building products, Edwards did not manufacture so much as a single nail. The company was exclusively in the wholesale and retail distribution business. The products that bore the Edwards label were all manufactured by other companies. Edward's philosophy had been that they would excel in sales and marketing and leave the work of manufacturing to someone else.

The Edwards–Allied connection began some seventeen years before, when Edwards contracted with Allied to manufacture roofing cement under the Edwards Trademark. In 1984 Allied manufactured over fifty products that were labeled with the Edwards trademark, and the total sales by Allied from Edwards was in the area of $22 million.

Edwards operated with seventeen central distribution outlets in the major metropolitan areas. The central units serviced the wholesale market in the area and provided a distribution network for the 187 Edwards Building Products stores nationwide. Using a computer link, the company was able to keep inventory costs at a minimum while providing excellent service to all its wholesale and retail customers. Any Edwards store manager or wholesale center could access the inventory of any other store or any of the wholesale distribution centers. Since the distribution centers were constantly supplying the stores using Edwards own trucking fleet, managers could restock almost instantly and fill a special customer order in substantially less time than the competition. Edwards was not the largest of its kind, but it certainly had one of the highest profit margins in the business.

In late 1981 the Research and Development Group of Allied demonstrated a new product possibility to senior management. The new product involved a ceramics process that made thin strands of material that had excellent insulating properties. A proposal was made to start commercial production of the product with the idea of competing with fiber glass in residential and commercial areas. The new product was more expensive than fiber glass, but its much greater insulating capability suggested that it could significantly dent the fiber-glass market in areas of high utility bills where energy savings were important. In late 1981 Allied management authorized construction of production facilities with an eye toward introducing the product into the market in early 1983.

Construction delays and problems with equipment design delayed production for over a year. During that time Allied began to critically review all operations to focus on the company's lack of marketing ability and expertise as a major problem. It became particularly concerned with the marketing program of new products. With over $50 million invested in research and production in the insulation project, that project came under increased scrutiny. The key to success, Allied realized, was not the technical superiority of the project, which already existed, but the ability of the company to displace a very popular form of insulation, fiber glass, with the new product.

By spring, 1985, the product was being test-marketed by several large wholesale distributors, and the results were at best mixed. Those customers who purchased the product generally expressed satisfaction, but it was very difficult to get the large construction firms to try the product in the first place. They were not dissatisfied with their existing insulation products, and it was clear that a major marketing campaign would be necessary to educate builders and consumers about the desirability of the product and to encourage them to use it as a substitute for fiber glass.

At Allied's monthly strategy conference in May, 1985, Nathan Soames, vice-president of corporate development, addressed the problem of marketing the new insulation material. He noted that the company had not developed a marketing plan, had not planned an extensive dealer program, and in general was relying on word-of-mouth advertising to get the message across to the buying public. No efforts were being made to introduce the product into the retail distribution network, and it seemed to him that Allied's attitude had been that "here was a good product, the public was required to buy it." As Soames pointed out, that attitude would surely lead to failure.

During the meeting Soames was appointed head of a committee to propose a strategic plan to penetrate the market with the new product. During the meeting the company rejected any major in-house effort, saying that this one product did not justify adding staff resources, and that the company could not change its basic way of doing business just for the sake of one new product. This attitude, while economically sound, had left Soames with very little leeway in developing a program. In late June, though, he was approached by Edwards Building Supply about the possibility of selling the product under the Edwards label. Edwards had been one of the distributors used in the test market, and it indicated that it had been very pleased with the product. Edwards was willing to contract for up to 15 per cent of the plant capacity, provided suitable concessions were made in price. Edwards also expressed interest in any future developments of the material in other industrial uses.

Following up on this interest, Soames inquired if Edwards might be interested in some type of joint venture, with Allied on the technical and production side, Edwards on the sales and marketing side. When Edwards expressed an interest in such an arrangement, meetings were set up between the top management at both companies to work out an agreement. After several sessions, it was agreed that a new company would be formed to produce and market the new insulation material and related products. The new company would be called Allied–Edwards Insulation and would be a public company with two equal blocks of stock owned by Allied and Edwards. The company would be capitalized at $50 million, and the funds were to be used to purchase the factory, inventory, and other related assets from Allied. All technical knowledge, patents, and rights to the product would be owned by the new company. Edwards would supply the marketing and sales expertise and, in effect, be responsible for sales and distribution of the new company.

After agreement in principle was reached, a financial staff was formed for the new company to set policy. Its first task was to structure the balance sheet, that is, determine exactly how the $50 million would be raised. As a beginning, the group produced a forecast of sales and costs for the period 1986 to 1990. That forecast for the years 1986 and 1990 is shown in Exhibit 20-1. Based on that forecast,

**Exhibit 20-1 Allied-Edwards Insulation Products:
Forecast of Income and Expenses**
Year Ending Dec. 31 (in $000)

	1986	1990
Net Sales	22,000	67,000
Total Costs	17,500	52,000
Income Before Interest and Taxes	4,500	15,000
Applicable Tax Rate	0.4500	0.4500

Exhibit 20-2   Allied-Edwards Insulation Products: Proposed Balance Sheet Structure January 1, 1986
Assets, Liabilities, and Net Worth

$50,000,000 Debt:	Plan A	Plan B	Plan C
Amount	$10,000,000	$30,000,000	$20,000,000
Rate	13.00%	16.00%	15.00%
Preferred Stock			
Amount	0	7,500,000	5,000,000
Rate		12.00%	11.00%
Common Stock			
Value	$40,000,000	$12,500,000	$25,000,000
# of Shares	4,000,000	1,250,000	2,500,000

the group set out to determine alternatives for capitalizing the company. After much analysis and disagreement, the group settled on three proposals, which they were to present to Allied and Edwards management. The three proposals are shown in Exhibit 20-2.

Plan A represented the most conservative proposal and was favored by the Allied side. It would raise $50 million by selling 4 million shares of stock at $10 each and a private placement of a $10 million long-term 13 per cent debt issue. Plan B was the most aggressive of the three plans and favored by the Edwards group. It would sell only 1,250,000 shares at $10 each and would raise the rest of the capital with a $30 million 16 per cent long-term debt issue and a $7.5 million 12 per cent straight preferred stock issue. Plan C, which neither side liked, had been presented as a compromise. It had $20 million in long-term debt, $5 million in preferred stock and $25 million in equity from the sale of 2,500,000 shares at $10 each.

The different attitudes toward the plans reflected the experiences of the two companies with the product thus far. Allied had had only limited success in selling the product and felt that the conservative financing scheme would be the safest for the new company. Edwards, on the other hand, had experienced strong customer acceptance and was confident of its ability to successfully market the product. Edwards believed that as long as Allied could produce the material at the same quality and cost as it had in the past, the sales forecast of 1990 was easily attainable.

SUGGESTED QUESTIONS

1. Compute the EPS and the degree of financial leverage under plan A for 1986 and 1990.

2. Compute the EPS and the degree of financial leverage under Plan C for 1986 and 1990.

3. Compute the EPS and the degree of financial leverage under Plan B for 1986 and 1990.

4. What level of income before interest and taxes produces the same EPS for Plan A and Plan C? Plan B and Plan C? Plan A and Plan B?

5. Evaluate your results and make a recommendation for the capital structure.

PART IV

Financial Analysis and Short-Term Management Topics

James River Bank

Ratio Analysis

Following a meeting with the president and the vice-president of finance of the Wilson Manufacturing Company, Beth Anderson realized that she would have to make one of the more important decisions in her relatively short career as a loan officer for the James River National Bank. Adam Wilson, president of Wilson Manufacturing, had just left her office after giving her a proposal that requested over $1 million in loans from the bank. This represented the largest transaction with which she had yet been involved, and the way in which she would handle it could be crucial not only to the future of Wilson Manufacturing but to her as well.

The James River National Bank was located in the scenic city of Lynchburg, Virginia, and the bank derived its name from the river which flowed through the community. Lynchburg had grown and prospered as a manufacturing town in the Post–Civil War period, and unlike other cities had kept its growth alive by diversifying its manufacturing base into high technology. Wilson Manufacturing was one company that had changed into the high-tech area success fully, and as a result of that success it was now seeking expanded bank financing.

James River Bank was somewhat different from most of its competitors. The State of Virginia had authorized statewide banking many years ago, and as a result a few of the large banks had merged with most of the smaller banks to form a state-banking structure that was dominated by those few large banks. James River Bank was one of the holdouts from the merger mania and remained independent. Though small in relation to the state banks, it had maintained its market share and even grown in the past several years. Its management liked to point to the growth and prosperity of the bank as evidence that one did not have to be large and statewide in order to compete effectively.

James River Bank had achieved its success by providing services to small and medium-sized businesses in the greater Lynchburg area. It competed in service, since it could not compete in size. It had been able to compete by taking on customers who needed and appreciated the more personal attention they were given by the local bank. However, because of its size and the constant competition, the bank had been forced to take on commercial customers whose risk was greater than those customers of the larger banks. Companies such as Wilson sought out James River because they knew their chances of getting loan approvals were greater.

Beth Anderson had joined James River after a career as a lending officer with a competing bank. She had taken the position because of the opportunity of advancing was greater than with her previous employer, and she knew that her promotions would be based on the way in which she managed accounts. After less than a year with the bank she had been promoted to vice-president and given broad responsibilities in commercial lending. She had personal approval authority for $400,000 in borrowings to any single customer.

Anderson had been told that her job would be difficult, in that there were competing pressures placed upon her. On one hand, she would be expected to keep exisiting customers and to recruit new customers as well. At the same time, the bank was concerned that the quality of its loans were less than other banks, and Anderson was told that the credit worthiness of any customer should be carefully analyzed before loans are made. It was this dilemma, the goal of new commercial customers versus the problems of credit risk, that faced Anderson in her negotiations with Wilson Manufacturing.

Wilson Manufacturing was an old firm that had recently taken on new life. It began soon after the end of the Civil War, making valves and fittings for industrial machinery. It remained unchanged except for normal growth until the mid-1970s, when a new generation of Wilsons took over management and sought to expand the product base of the company. Through small acquisitions the company had acquired specialized technology in industrial valves, and its growth in the last five years took the company from $500,000 in sales to close to $3 million.

To finance this growth the company had sold a package of long-term debt and new common stock to a group of local investors. This package of $350,000 in debt and $400,000 in new stock had given the company $750,000 in new capital in late 1982. The new capital allowed the company to expand its line of credit with its existing bank, Shenandoah National Bank, from just over $500,000 to approximately $630,000. Wilson had felt that the new long-term capital and the expanded credit would be sufficient to maintain its existing level of operations and support growth.

As the capital goods sector of the economy began to expand in 1983, the company found demand for its product at a record-high level. As a result, sales in 1983 reached $2.8 million, and the prospects for growth in 1984 seemed just as great. However, the company found that its financial structure posed difficulties in expanding to meet this opportunity. It had reached the limit of $630,000 of short-term borrowings from Shenandoah and, as a result, had fallen behind in its payments to suppliers. Accounts payable had risen about $350,000 during the year, and in some cases the company was 120 days late in payments. Key suppliers had threatened to put the company on a C.O.D. basis unless payments were rapidly forthcoming.

Wilson had first approached Shenandoah with a request for additional short-term borrowings. Shenandoah had responded that the position of the company and its high debt ratio precluded any additional borrowings. Shenandoah suggested that the company seek additional long-term capital in the form of subordinated debentures or new common stock, and that if it were to do so, Shenandoah would consider extending the line of credit to $1 million. However, even this extension would have been less than Wilson was seeking.

Wilson's reaction to the rather cool response to its needs by its bankers had been to seek funds from another financial institution. The company felt that having recently secured funds from investors, it would be difficult to go back and ask for more money. Moreover, the company strongly believed that the increased profitability of its projected 1984 sales would provide it with additional equity capital, since no dividends were contemplated, and that these funds along with an additional $500,000 in bank credit would be sufficient to finance the expansion. It was for these reasons that the company approached Ms. Anderson, to determine if James River would be interested in taking over as the company's bank and providing it with $500,000 in new funding.

Adam Wilson and Beth Anderson had held several meetings to discuss Wilson Manufacturing's current position and its future needs. The company's fiscal year had just ended and Adam Wilson had provided Anderson with the company's financial statements. These statements are given in Exhibit 21-1 and show a prosperous company in need of additional financing, a fact which both Anderson

Exhibit 21-1 Wilson Manufacturing Company: Financial Statements

Year Ending, Dec. 31 (in $000)

	1982	1983
Net Sales	$2,036	$2,844
Cost Goods Sold	1,022	1,460
Gross Profit	1,014	1,384
Operating Expenses	860	1,071
Operating Income	154	313
Interest Expenses	32	124
Income Before Taxes	122	189
Income Tax	55	85
Net Income	67	104

Balance Sheet—Actual, As of Dec. 31 (in $000)

	1982	1983		1982	1983
Cash	134	169	Notes Payable	224	632
Accounts Receivable	342	684	Accts. Payable	165	512
Inventory	564	755	Taxes Payable	24	74
Prepaid Items	18	31	Cur. Port. LTD	70	70
Total Current Assets	1,058	1,639	Total Current Liabilities	483	1,288
			Long-Term Debt	350	280
			Total Liabilities	833	1,568
Plant and Equipment	640	911			
Accumulated Depreciation	87	103	Common Stock	680	680
Net Plant	553	808	Retained Earnings	317	421
Other Assets	152	158			
Goodwill	67	64	Total Equity	997	1,101
			Total Liabilities and		
Total Assets	1,830	2,669	Equity	1,830	2,669

and Wilson already knew. Based on the financial statements, Wilson had asked the James River Bank for funding of a $1,132,000 loan. The proceeds of this loan would be as follows.

$632,000	Pay off line of credit with Shenandoah
300,000	Reduce accounts payable
219,000	Purchase fixed assets
81,000	Increase cash balances

Adam Wilson knew that the current ratio of the company had been one reason why Shenandoah had turned down the company's request for additional credit. Consequently, his proposal to James River was for the $1,132,000 to be divided into a $632,000 line of credit and a $500,000 five-year loan. The $500,000 component would come due in a lump sum at the end of five years, but the company would make monthly interest payments, equal to the prime rate plus two percentage points during the next sixty months.

The total size of the loan request by Wilson far exceeded the lending authority of Beth Anderson. In cases like this, Anderson would be required to prepare an extensive report on the loan applicant, including a detailed financial analysis, and make a recommendation to the Loan Committee. The Loan Committee was made up of senior bank managers and had final approval on all major loans. Anderson knew that it would be a major step forward in her career if she were to recommend and the Loan Committee were to accept her proposals for funding Wilson Manufacturing.

As a first step toward making her decision whether or not to support Wilson's request, Anderson began work on her financial analysis of the company. In order to analyze the financial statements that Adam Wilson had provided, she requested her assistant to produce a set of financial ratios against which Wilson could be measured. The financial ratios came from a data base of companies similar in size and products to Wilson; these were companies the bank had previously made loans to, and the ratios would indicate the bank's standards in making credit available to such customers. The ratios produced are shown in Exhibit 21-2. Notes provided with the ratios indicated that they were made on end-of-year data, that inventory turnover was based on cost of goods sold, and that intangible assets were not taken into account in preparing the ratios.

A second problem facing Anderson was that even if the financial analysis showed that Wilson qualified for the loan, it was not certain if the loan should be made according to the terms that Adam Wilson

Exhibit 21-2 Selected Industry Ratios

	1983
Current Ratio	1.75
Quick Ratio	0.85
Av. Coll. Period	64.35
Inventory Turnover	1.42
Fixed Asset Turnover	3.01
Total Asset Turnover	1.08
Cost of Sales %	53.42%
Operating Exp. %	44.61%
Net Income as Per Cent of Sales	2.80%
Total Debt/Assets	63.59%
Interest Coverage	2.11
Return on Assets	3.35%
Return on Equity	7.85%

requested. Anderson knew the Loan Committee would be reluctant to approve the $500,000 if no principal were to be paid for five years. Two alternatives were possible, one was to have the $500,000 paid off in equal monthly installments, and the other was to have the entire line of new credit as a short-term loan to Wilson.

As Anderson started to prepare her analysis, she realized she had two major decisions. She must decide first of all whether or not Wilson would qualify for the loan, and, if it did, what form of loan should she recommend to the Loan Committee.

SUGGESTED QUESTIONS

1. Using the date in Exhibit 21-1, prepare a set of ratios for 1982 and 1983 for Wilson.

2. Based on your evaluation and interpretation of the ratios, make a recommendation as to whether or not Wilson should get the loan from James River.

3. Assuming the loan is approved, construct a proform balance sheet for each of the three possible loan structures. For each balance sheet compute the current ratio, quick ratio, and debt ratio.

4. Evaluate each of the three proposed loan structures. Based on that evaluation and the information in the case, make a recommendation as to how the loan should be structured.

5. Assuming the bank was not willing to lend more than $632,000 to replace the existing loan, what other sources of funding might be available to Wilson?

Hemingway Fence, Inc.

Financial Forecasting

The Financial Planning Group, known throughout Hemingway Fence as FPG, had been one of the first creations of the firm's new vice-president of finance and administration. J. S. Trantor joined Hemingway at the request of the firm's president, Marcus Alden, to bring some new direction and new ideas to the old-line firm's management style. Trantor's first decision was to establish a three-member team to provide the company with some financial-planning tools. The existence of the three-member FPG was the result of that decision.

Hemingway Fence, Inc., had been in existence in Greenville, South Carolina, for over one hundred years. The firm had started soon after the Civil War, making fencing materials for the new farms that were created by the breakup of the large plantations after the war. The firm began by purchasing wire and lumber, and with the advent of automated machinery, it began producing a variety of wire-mesh agricultural fencing. Ultimately it became one of the country's leading producers of a type of fencing known as "chicken wire," a fine mesh fencing suitable for chicken pens and other animal areas.

Until the 1930s the company prospered by producing fencing products for farming, including the "chicken wire," barbed wire, and other wire-fence products. The firm expanded into fence posts and fencing equipment, and its third president, E. H. Hemingway, liked to boast that a farmer could do any kind of fencing using only Hemingway products for the materials and the installation work. In 1929 sales reached $5 million, and the company did its selling through a large distribution network that covered most of the southeast United States.

During the depression, the company saw its major market, small and medium farms, decline significantly. It survived by cutting wages and easing its credit terms to dealers; but these actions were not sufficient, and the company was sold to a private group of investors who were looking to diversify the product line of single product companies. Before these investors could put their strategy into effect, however, World War II and the demand for all products, including fencing for military bases, brought the company back on its feet.

Following World War II the new owners were able to implement their strategy of diversification. Anticipating the suburban boom that would follow the war, the company diversified into home-fencing products, including manufacture of all components of chain-link fences. In the 1960s, taking its clue from California, the company further diversified into decorative wood fences. By 1980, the company manufactured almost all types of residential fencing materials, while maintaining a core business of agricultural fencing. The company was proud of the quality of its product. Its major sales outlets were national chain stores, with whom the company had non-exclusive agreements for periods into the 1990s.

The conservative management of the compnay had been on a "pay as you go" policy that avoided debt financing for anything other than temporary short-term needs. However, the rapid sales growth in the early 1980s (see Exhibit 22-1) and the need for automated equipment to compete in a highly competitive market had forced the company to take on a term loan. (See Exhibit 22-2 for balance sheet information.) Also, in 1979 the company had made a cash acquisition

Exhibit 22-1   Hemingway Fence, Inc.: Income Statement

| | Year Ending, June 30 (in $000) | | |
	1981	1982	(Fcst) 1983
Revenues	122,987	138,987	161,939
Cost of Goods Sold	65,432	73,454	95,432
Gross Margin	57,555	65,533	66,507
Operating Expenses	23,876	28,939	34,673
Interest Expense	4,323	4,675	4,965
Income Before Taxes	19,553	24,264	29,708
Taxes	8,799	10,919	13,369
Net Income	10,754	13,345	16,339

Exhibit 22-2 Hemingway Fence, Inc.: Balance Sheet
As of June 30 (in $000)

	1981	1982	1983 (fcst)
Assets			
Cash	2,934	3,214	8,000
Accounts Receivable, Net	17,893	24,565	32,132
Inventory	23,543	24,317	33,765
Prepaid Items	970	1,211	1,439
Total Current Assets	45,340	53,307	75,336
Land	2,176	2,176	2,176
Plant and Equipment, Net	26,754	36,833	37,053
Other Assets	1,322	1,329	1,496
Goodwill	5,800	5,650	5,500
Total Assets	81,392	99,295	121,561
Liabilities and Capital			
Accounts Payable	17,654	23,454	26,543
Other Payables	7,865	8,745	9,765
Short-Term Debt	6,754	7,632	8,122
Current Portion, Long-Term Debt	3,000	3,000	3,000
Total Current Liabilities	35,273	42,831	47,430
Long-Term Debt	33,000	30,000	27,000
Total Liabilities	68,273	72,831	74,430
Common Stock	10,000	10,000	14,327
Retained Earnings	3,119	16,464	32,804
Total Equity	13,119	26,464	47,131
Total Liabilities and Capital	81,392	99,295	121,561

of a competitive firm and this resulted in liquidity problems for the company, leading to the addition of long-term debt.

The company's fiscal year ended on June 30. This normally coincided with the ending of the summer sales season and the date was chosen for that reason. In mid-May of 1983 the FPG had been started, and its first charge was to get a handle on the coming year, fiscal 1984. The concern was whether or not the firm would be able to grow without taking on additional financing; that is, would internally generated funds provide all the necessary funding for fiscal 1984.

The FPG held its first working meeting on May 22. It was decided to produce a preliminary forecast of the balance sheet and income statement for 1984, which would indicate if new funding would be needed. The pro-forma balance sheet would be balanced by either having excess cash or by needing additional funds. It was agreed that all information on the activities for the coming year relevant to balance sheet and income statement accounts would be collected for the next working session.

On June 1, when the FPG met for the second time, it had the preliminary forecast for the balance sheet and income statements as they would appear at the end of June and detailed information on each of the relevant activities. The forecast for 1983 is shown in Exhibits 22-1 and 22-2. Specific information about fiscal 1984 was as follows:

Sales. The rapid growth in sales that the company had experienced in the last several years was expected to slow. Sales in fiscal 1984 were expected to be in the $180 million range.

Cost of Goods Sold. The company had experienced relatively stable cost patterns, and it was expected that these costs would remain the same per cent of sales in the coming year as they had been in the past year.

Operating Expenses. The company had experienced difficulty in controlling expenses in the past year, due primarily to competitive pressures, which produced higher than expected marketing and sales expenses. In 1984 the company expected these costs to rise by at least the rate of sales increase.

Interest Expense. Interest costs came from the company's short-term borrowings and long-term debt. The treasurer indicated he did not believe that short-term debt would be reduced: and the reduction in long-term debt, as the term loan was paid off, would not have a great impact on interest costs, as interest rates were expected to rise during the coming year. Consequently, the treasurer estimated interest expense at $5,500 for 1984.

Taxes. For planning purposes, the company used a combined Federal, state, and local tax rate of 45 per cent.

Dividends. The company had not paid any dividends in several years because the demands of growth left little cash. However, the last several Board of Directors meetings had raised the question that some dividend payments might be required in the next several years.

On the asset side of the balance sheet, the FPG learned from studying historical data that working cash was necessary for transaction purposes at a minimum of 2 per cent of sales. However, the treasurer operated very conservatively and expected the cash account to show a balance of $8 million at the end of the next fiscal year. The other items in the current asset accounts were expected to be the same per cent of sales in the coming year as they had been in the past year.

With respect to fixed assets, the company did not expect to add new buildings, but replacement of worn out wire-twisting equipment was scheduled. As a result the net plant and equipment account was expected to have a balance of $55 million at the end of the next year. The FPG had found no one who was willing to forecast other assets and after a short discussion agreed that the best assumption was to assume the balance in this account would not change.

Goodwill resulted from an acquisition that had produced just under $6 million. The acquisition was accounted for under purchase accounting, which required that the excess over the fair-market value of the assets be recorded as goodwill, and that the goodwill be amortized over time. No acquisition plans existed for 1984 and FPG assumed the goodwill amortization would continue.

On the liabilities side, the accruals in current liabilities were expected to remain the same per cent of sales in 1984 as they had been in 1983. The short-term debt was, however, difficult to predict and the FPG felt the best starting point was to assume the ending balance in 1984 would be the same as the ending balance in 1983. The current portion of long-term debt reflected the equal annual installments on the term loan, a portion of which came due every year.

The company had no plans to issue additional long-term debt, at least not until the forecast for 1984 had been prepared. The company had sold common stock in 1983 to help finance some of its growth, but the current investors had indicated they did not wish to invest additional money into the company but were looking to get some cash return on their investment. The company had no plans to make a public offering of stock.

Given this information, the FPG now felt it was in a position to take the first step toward estimating 1984's financing requirements.

SUGGESTED QUESTIONS

1. Based on the information in the case, and assuming no dividends are declared, construct a pro-forma income statement for fiscal 1984 and a pro-forma balance sheet for June 30, 1984 for Hemingway Fence.

Use additional funds required or excess cash to balance the entries on the liabilities side of the balance sheet.

2. Based on the results of Question 1, how much additional funding, if any, is required.

3. List all possible methods by which the additional funding can be obtained and indicate the advantages and disadvantages of each one. Do not be limited by the attitudes of managers and shareholders.

4. How does your answer to Question 2 change if the cash account is allowed to fall to 2 per cent of sales. Does this eliminate the need for additional outside financing?

5. How does your answer to Question 2 change if dividends are paid in the amount of $2 million? Should the company pay dividends? Why and why not?

6. What are the risks inherent in this method of forecasting, that is, where could errors be made? List each possible error and estimate the amount the forecast could be in error for each item.

7. Based on all of the information, recommend and support a financing plan for the company based on what you think is the best solution. Assume any one of the above events could occur in making your recommendation.

Video Seminar Systems, Inc.

Financial Forecasting Under Constraints

The cofounders of Video Seminar Systems had been very satisfied with the term loan that had been arranged several years before to finance the expansion of the company, but current and future financial requirements brought into question the many limitations and restrictions the company had accepted. The covenants in that loan agreement were threatening to severely limit the ability of the company to raise new capital in the manner in which it wanted.

Video Seminar Systems represented a rare case of an academic project that had turned into a business success. Video Seminar Systems had been the outgrowth of a senior project by two young business-school graduates, Sandy Franklin and Karen Carts. The two young women had worked together on an independent study project when they were seniors at Indiana University in Bloomington. They realized that their theoretical project had a chance of succeeding in the real world.

The project had been conceived by Management Professor George Hettens to illustrate how various courses in the Business School curriculum could be brought together in a total management environment. The students, working in pairs, had to develop and outline the start-up of a business and demonstrate how that business might grow and prosper. Franklin and Carts had become friends from experiences in several classes and felt they would work well together. As a result, they teamed up and ultimately Video Seminar Systems was born.

The two students wanted to capitalize on the growing technology in electronics and focused their attention on video. In the mid-1970s the Sony Corporation of Japan had developed inexpensive home and industrial video-taping and playback equipment. By 1980 there was a growing market for home and business video-taping applications. The home market primarily consisted of prerecorded movies, but Franklin and Carts felt that other home-video products would soon capture a large share of that market. They felt that video training tapes, inexpensively produced, would have a positive reception in the corporate arena.

For a class project, the two students developed a detailed business plan that set forth the organization and operations of a company called Video Seminar Systems, Inc. This company had as its major business lines the production of video training films for industry and business-teaching tapes for home viewing. The home tapes were each devoted to a single topic, such as finance, management, marketing, personal motivation. They were designed to provide help and training for technical managers who did not have a business education. The business climate of the 1980s found many technically skilled individuals in management positions with no previous management training.

The concept looked so successful on paper that, in late 1978, the two students decided to implement the company. They obtained seed money from several relatives and purchased sufficient equipment to begin operations. The concept proved an immediate success and in 1980 they expanded into full-scale production. By 1981 they had a staff of over one hundred, sales of over $17 million and were a growing and profitable company.

The initial capitalization of the company had proven to be inadequate to finance the growth of the company, and in 1980 the young owners had been forced to negotiate permanent financing. After many meetings, the choice had come down to selling stock to a venture capital firm or obtaining a term loan from a small insurance firm. The decision was difficult, because the sale of stock would mean potential loss of control of the company, while the term loan would mean restrictions on financial policy that might later hinder the growth of the company.

After several weeks of negotiating, the two deals facing the owners were a term loan of $3.5 million with significant restrictive convenants and the sale of 40 per cent of the common stock at a price of $4.00 per share. If the stock financing were accepted, one million shares would be issued. As a part of the stock deal, the purchasers requested warrants to buy an additional one million shares at $5.00 per share. They allowed a buy-back clause whereby the company could repurchase the shares at a price of $6.00 per share any time before January 1, 1984.

Because the founders were unwilling to give up control of the company, they felt a subordinated debt issue might better suit the needs of the firm. However, with little historical financials, the only debt issue proposal forthcoming was a term loan from a local insurance company. The term loan would be for $3.5 million, at a rate of prime plus two points for ten years. For the first five years of the loan only interest payments were required, and in the second five years interest and principal would be paid on a monthly basis.

The term loan would also allow the lenders an option to purchase 60 per cent of the common stock of the company for $3 million, but the insurance company stated that it would probably not exercise this option as long as the company performed well. To prevent the lenders from later taking over a highly successful company, the loan provided that Video Seminar Systems could pay off the term loan anytime within thirty days after notification by the lender.

The term loan would have been easily preferable to the stock sale except for restrictive covenants in the loan agreement. These covenants were typical of such loans and were intended to ensure that the managers of the company followed sound business practices. There were seven such covenants in this particular loan, but the three important ones were as follows:

1. The company would maintain a current ratio at least equal to 2.0.

2. The company would not allow the debt ratio to exceed 60 per cent of total assets.

3. Consolidated net working capital would not be below $5 million.

Violation of any of these covenants would give the lenders the right to call for immediate payment of the outstanding balance. While this provision made Carts and Franklin nervous, they were assured that such a call would be unlikely and that the company could negotiate a change in these standards if future conditions warranted.

Based on the desire to keep close control of the company, Carts and Franklin decided to go with the term loan. With this additional boost in financial resources, along with a short-term line of credit, internal funding, and other current liabilities, the company added significantly to its line of tapes. By the end of 1981, it had a large inventory of prerecorded tapes for sale and a large list of receivables.

In 1981 sales and profitability were very high for Video Seminar, and the prospects for 1982 looked equally strong. The sales of home-video equipment were zooming, based on declining prices and the emergence of VHS technology. The company's reputation for quality training programs led more and more Fortune 500 companies to seek its services, and the future of the company seemed unlimited.

Exhibit 23-1   Video Seminar Systems, Inc.: Income Statement

Year Ending	Actual 1981	fcst 1982
Revenue	$17,872	$19,862
Cost of Sales	8,345	9,792
Gross Profit	9,527	10,070
Selling Expenses	4,321	4,970
Fixed Administration Expenses	2,121	2,234
Income Before Interest and Taxes	3,085	2,866
Interest Expense	864	917
Income Before Taxes	2,221	1,949
Taxes	1,066	975
Net Income	1,155	975

The only problem facing the two owners was whether or not sufficient capital could be raised to finance the growth.

In late 1981 the company prepared a forecast for 1982. Results of that forecast, along with the financial statements for 1981, are shown in Exhibits 23-1 and 23-2. The key elements of the forecasts were as follows:

1. Sales would increase to approximately $19.8 million. However

Exhibit 23-2   Video Seminar Systems, Inc.: Balance Sheet

As of Dec. 31	Actual 1981	Fcst 1982
Cash	342	431
Accounts Receivable	5,678	7,896
Inventory	4,367	6,532
Other Current Assets	543	613
Total Current Assets	10,930	15,472
Net Fixed Assets	3,478	4,322
Total Assets	14,408	19,794
Accounts Payable	2,124	2,543
Other Payables	1,176	1,233
Short-Term Debt	1,876	1,945
Total Current Liabilities	5,176	5,721
Long-Term Debt	3,817	3,817
Total Liabilities	8,993	9,538
Common Stock	2,500	2,500
Retained Earnings	2,915	3,890
Total Equity	5,415	6,390
Total Liabilities and Equity	14,408	15,928
Additional Financing Required		3,867

lower product prices due to competition and the recessionary economy would lower net income to $975,000.

2. Assets were forecast to grow from $14.4 million to $19.8 million. This growth was due to a build-up in inventory and receivables to support higher growth, along with capital investments in video equipment necessary for the production of an expanded tape library.

3. Short-term bank funding would max out as $1.95 million, while long-term debt would remain unchanged as no debt repayments were scheduled.

The growth in assets produced a funding shortfall that was estimated to reach $3,867,000 at the end of 1982. The problem facing Carts and Franklin was not to finance this deficit. They were limited in options because of the restrictive covenants placed on them by the term loan.

As a starting point, Exhibit 23-3 was constructed. This showed the position of the company with respect to the three restrictive covenants at the end of 1981 and for the forecasted 1982 before financing. For purposes of analysis, the $3.9 million shortfall was simply listed as "additional financing needed." Exhibit 23-3 showed the company would be in compliance with the covenants under this scenario, that is, if the additional financing were not allocated to a specific debt category. Whether or not that would still be the case after a financing plan was developed was not certain.

Franklin and Carts also had begun discussions with the insurance company whose term loan provided for the covenants. The lenders indicated that if Video Seminar could make a case for financing that violated the covenants, the insurance company would waive the covenants and allow that financing to take place. The lenders emphasized, however, that the burden would be on Video Seminar to show that the company would have a prudent fiscal policy under a financing scheme that violated one or more of the covenants.

Carts and Franklin now had to make a decision about future financing. Their choices were to secure short-term debt that could be rolled over; to secure another term loan similar in maturity to the existing loan; or to sell additional shares of stock. They also had the question of whether or not the company's desired plan would violate the covenants and, if so, could a case be made to get the lenders to

Exhibit 23-3   Key Ratios

	1981	Fcst 1982 Before Financing
Current Ratio	2.11	2.70
Debt Ratio	0.62	0.48
Net Working Capital	$5,754	$9,751

waive the restrictive provisions of the loan. Their concerns remained as they had in the past: They wanted to keep control, but they realized that as the company grew this might not be possible.

SUGGESTED QUESTIONS

1. Was the company correct in choosing the term loan over the stock sale for its original financing?

2. Based on Exhibit 23-2, and without violating the covenants, what is the maximum amount the company can issue of short-term debt? Long-term debt? Common stock? (Assume no change in interest expense or any other income statement item.)

3. Assuming there were no restrictive covenants, what financing plan would you recommend?

4. List and support arguments that the restrictions are too severe and should be relaxed.

South Manhattan
Savings Bank

Source and Use of Funds

The difficulty facing the South Manhattan Savings Bank was not the past but the future. The financial institution had already survived some of the worst economic times for savings banks since the Civil War, and the question before the Asset/Liability Management Committee was whether or not the bank was equipped to survive another crisis. High interest rates forecast for 1985 posed a potential threat to the future of the bank.

Savings banks, like other financial institutions, were vitally dependent upon the level and stability of interest rates. Contrary to public opinion, the banks did not prosper during periods of high interest rates; in fact, they had the strongest financial performance during periods of falling interest rates. The reason for this was that as interest rates went up, so did funding costs, and the return on assets lagged behind, since many loans were made at fixed rates. Twice in the past five years short-term interest rates had spiked upward, and twice it had meant hardship for various financial institutions. Many had not survived and were either merged into stronger banks or allowed to liquidate themselves and go out of business. South Manhattan had been one of the survivors, and it was committed to strategies to stay that way.

Savings banks are institutions unique to the northeastern United States and their descendants, savings and loan associations, are found throughout the country. Savings banks differ from savings and loans primarily in their legal form and in the agencies that regulate them; from an operations point of view they are almost iden-

131

tical. South Manhattan Savings Bank historically had performed the same financial function as savings and loans, providing long-term, fixed-rate residential and commercial mortgages, although in recent years the company had moved aggressively in the area of diversified financial services.

South Manhattan had been started by a group of wealthy New Yorkers in 1856. Their initial goal had not been profits, but to provide a safe, secure repository of savings and encourage thrift among blue-collar workers. Prior to legislation of the 1860s, the U.S. banking system was a jumble of highly stable, legitimate banks along with a large number of poorly run, highly unstable banks. Placing money in a bank could at that time be considered a risky business.

The history of South Manhattan was uneventful until after World War II when the bank aggressively expanded into residential mortgages on Staten Island. In the late 1940s and early 1950s the Federal government encouraged savings banks and savings and loans to make long-term, fixed-rate home mortgages through its FHA and VA insurance programs. These programs insured the lending institution against default and were spectacularly successful in promoting home construction and home ownership. South Manhattan soon found that the default rate in home mortgages was sufficiently low that it could make conventional (uninsured) loans as safely as FHA and VA loans, and by the mid-1970s the bank had a large portfolio of home mortgages.

Problems for South Manhattan and the industry as a whole developed in the 1970s when rising short-term interest rates caused deposit outflows as the institutions were unable to compete with high-yielding nonbank accounts such as money-market funds. While a secondary market had grown up for mortgages, mostly involving the private FNMA and government agencies GNMA and FHMC, high interest rates meant that existing mortgages could only be sold at a loss or discount from their face or book value. After a rather painful period of trying to maintain the industry, Federal legislation was passed which effectively deregulated the banking industry on a phased in basis. In the mid-1980s banks were fairly free to set their own rates on deposits and, within limits, to lend money as they saw fit.

Unfortunately, deregulation did not immediately solve the pressing problems of savings institutions. Because of past practices, these institutions had a large portfolio of long-term, low-yielding mortgages on their books, some with rates as low as 6 per cent, and in South Manhattan's case, an average yield of 9.2 per cent. As long as deposit and borrowings costs were near or just slightly above this number, the bank would be financially sound, because returns on other loans and investments would make the institution profitable. However, in the periods when interest rates were rising, the cost of funds would be substantially above what could be earned on the portfolio, and the bank would suffer huge operating losses. This had already happened in 1979 and 1981.

In order to deal effectively with this problem, the bank had created an Asset/Liability Management Committee to oversee and manage its interest rate exposure. It was the committee's job to develop and implement strategies which would lessen the risk of a substantial negative impact in the event that interest rates would rise sharply. The committee consisted of the executive vice-president for finance and the group vice-presidents of lending and portfolio management.

The group met the third Wednesday of every month to review the current status of the balance sheet and the economic forecast for the coming twenty-four months. At their August, 1984, meeting the group heard a report from the chief economist that the bank's major economic forecasting service was predicting significantly higher interest rates in 1985 and the first half of the 1986. While the chief economist cautioned that no forecast could be one hundred percent accurate, it was indeed possible that interest rates could be one to three percentage points higher in twelve months.

Following this report, the committee asked the controller to review the balance sheet of the bank. The bank's fiscal year had just ended, and the controller went over the preliminary balance sheet and income statement shown in Exhibit 24-1. Here are excerpts from that report:

Our major securities categories are Fed funds, money-market investments, government securities, and municipal bonds. Fed funds represent bank reserves we have loaned overnight to other institutions, and consequently their yield is the current market yield. Money-market investments are primarily T bills and commercial paper, all of less than one year maturity, and are kept for liquidity purposes. Government securities are long-term government bonds whose interest rates are mostly below current yields. As a result their current prices are below par.

In the mortgage area we have tried to move to adjustable mortgages whose yield changes every twelve months, and whose interest rates is 2 to 3 points below that of fixed-rate mortgages. Still, some customers want fixed-rate mortgages and we have added some in the last year. Our major emphasis is on consumer and commercial loans. Consumer loans currently yield about three to four points above prime and have an average maturity of three years. Our commercial loans are floating rate, and on the average are tied to prime plus one percentage point.

On the liability side, our lowest cost of funds is in the demand accounts, NOW/time accounts, and money-market accounts. Demand deposits are

Exhibit 24-1   South Manhattan Savings Bank: Statement of Financial Condition
As of Dec. 31 (in $000)

	1983	1984
Assets		
Cash and Due From Banks	4,367	5,984
Fed Funds	16,876	19,543
Money-Market Investments	31,212	35,438
Government Securities	6,879	4,912
Municipal Bonds	2,156	1,156
Mortgages		
Fixed Rate	325,983	345,612
Adjustable Rate	54,329	89,735
Consumer Loans	122,245	145,322
Commercial Loans	43,267	87,452
Other Loans	17,623	21,564
Total Financial Assets	624,937	756,718
Fixed Assets	32,541	36,935
Other Assets	11,736	11,982
Total Assets	669,214	805,635
Liabilities and Net Worth		
Deposits		
Demand Deposits	24,587	27,698
NOW Accounts	43,292	44,212
Money-Market Accounts	67,897	43,565
Time Deposits		
6-Month Accounts	103,567	134,786
1 Year	216,820	234,569
2 Year	29,765	76,542
5 Year	43,212	66,049
7 Year	21,343	34,232
FHLB Borrowings	34,545	47,654
Other Liabilities	68,543	77,654
Total Liabilities	653,571	786,961
Net Worth	15,643	18,674
Total Liabilities and Net Worth	669,214	805,635

Income Statement
Year Ending Dec. 31 (in $000)

	1983	1984
Interest Income	73,456	96,543
Interest Expense	61,245	79,654
Net Interest Margin	12,211	16,889
Other Income	2,143	2,519
Operating Expenses	11,654	14,312
Nonoperating Income (Expense)	(324)	(517)
Income Before Taxes	3,024	5,613
Taxes	1,391	2,582
New Income	1,633	3,031

Exhibit 24-2 Summary of Fixed Asset Account

Balance, December 31, 1983	$32,541
Gross Additions, 1984	7,481
Depreciation Expense, 1984	3,087
Balance, December 31, 1984	36,935

noninterest bearing checking accounts, while the NOW/time accounts pay only 5.5 per cent. The money-market accounts were set up to compete with money-market funds and allow immediate access to the account by check-writing privileges. We are currently paying 9.25 per cent, which is about 150 basis points below the current rate paid by money-market funds.

The major source of borrowings of the bank in the event that deposits were not sufficient was from the Federal Home Loan Bank of New York. Current borrowings were on a ninety-day basis, although loans for one hundred and eighty days were available at the same rates. The FHLB discouraged borrowings except for liquidity purposes; that is, the FHLB did not want the bank to borrow funds at the artificially low rate and then loan them at the higher rate. The FHLB was also concerned about the capital adequacy of the banks it regulated and required a minimum of 3 per cent ratio of net worth to total assets. While it would not take punitive action against banks that were below that rate, it closely monitored bank performance for those institutions whose net-worth ratio dropped below 3 per cent.

Given the current net-worth position of South Manhattan, the committee was obviously worried about whether the regulatory agencies would allow the bank to continue as an independent entity, try to merge it into another institution. The controller presented the income statement for 1984 (Exhibit 24-2), which showed that net income had increased substantially from the previous year. However, the critical question was, was the bank in a better position than it had been in one year before to withstand an increase in interest rates in the coming year.

SUGGESTED QUESTIONS

1. Compute the net worth to asset ratio for 1983 and 1984. Analyze the change and why it occurred.

2. Construct a Source and Use of Funds Statement for fiscal 1984. Show the statement in both a dollar form and also each item as a per cent of total sources.

3. Analyze the Source and Use of Funds Statement to determine if the bank had reduced its exposure to a short-term increase in interest rates.

4. Based on the information in the case, what actions would you recommend for the committee to take to further insulate the bank against a rise in interest rates.

King Components Corporation

Break-Even Analysis—Operating Leverage

General Manager Bert Samuels of King Components Corporation had the idea to bring in an economist as part of the company's annual planning exercise. Afterward, he remembered all the jokes about economists and realized that there was some basis for the stories. While Dr. Erin Davis of nearby Seatac University had been helpful in analyzing the trends in the economy and specific industries that affected King Components, she had been unable to solve the specific problem facing Samuels at the time she had been brought on board.

Samuels had been concerned with the level of sales that King Components could expect in the coming year, fiscal 1983, which began on January 1. It was mid-December of 1982 and Samuels was still not ready to submit the corporation's business plan to the parent company. That business plan was due in less than one week, and Samuels knew he would be forced to choose between three different sales scenarios. Dr. Davis had been brought in to help with that choice. But after her report Samuels felt no closer to a decision than he had been when the planning process started.

King Components Corporation was essentially a single-product company, manufacturing an electronic control device that was a part of many heavy industrial machine tools. The product, whose trade name was King Controller, was sold in both the OEM and replacement markets, with sales split approximately 80 per cent to 20 per cent between the two categories. The device had a large market share, as it performed various control and diagnostic tasks for a large variety of machine-tool applications. However, since it was a component and not a stand-alone product, its sales were vitally dependent upon the sales of new machine tools.

The machine-tool industry itself is highly dependent upon the level of economic activity and the overall health of the economy. Essentially, a strong economy means significant investment outlays by business and the purchase of machine tools. This in turn would mean increased demand for the King Controller and higher sales. On the other hand, a weak economy means reduced investment and lower demand. In effect the health and well-being of the company was almost totally controlled by an external force over which the company had no control, the strength or weakness of the U.S. economy.

In late 1982 it appeared that economic conditions were at a turning point. In 1981 and early 1982 the economy had gone through a serious recession, and total results for 1982 for King Components were expected to be down significantly from the company's record high profits of $1.7 million in 1980. Samuels had asked that a preliminary income statement be prepared on a contribution basis for 1982, and that statement, shown as Exhibit 25-1, showed income before tax of $950,000. King Components was a division of Drone Electronics, all taxes were paid on a consolidated basis by the parent corporation. Each division was responsible for profits only for the income before-tax line.

The economist Davis had been brought in to assess the markets in which the machine tools that used King Controllers are sold in and to help develop a sales forecast for 1983. Unfortunately, Davis had not been able to provide a definitive forecast for the coming year. In her report she pointed out that the economy had suffered a deep recession and that while signs pointed to recovery, it was not certain that the recovery would take place, or if it did, how strong it would be. The economy was reacting to the stimulus of the Reagan tax cuts, but interest rates were still very high and large government

Exhibit 25-1 King Components Corporation: Income Statement—Contribution Method
Pro Forma
Year Ending December 31, 1982

Price/Unit	$475.00
Sales (units)	17,500
Gross Income	$8,312,500
Variable Cost/Unit	$315.00
Total Variable Cost	$5,512,500
Contribution	$2,800,000
Fixed Costs	$1,850,000
Income Before Taxes	$950,000

deficits were expected to push them even higher. In any event, Davis said that consumer spending was likely to be the initial force in an economic recovery, and that the recovery in investment spending might be one to two years down the road.

As a result of this analysis and studies of markets, Samuels felt the company should restrict its analysis to three sales scenarios of 1983. The first scenario was based on a modest recovery of the economy, primarily in the consumer sector. This would result in King Components experiencing the same level of sales in units in 1983 as it had in 1982. The second scenario called for a robust recovery in the area of business investments, this would result in sales growing to about 22,400 units in 1983. The third scenario had high interest rates aborting the recovery; if this happened, OEM sales would be reduced, and replacement sales would be higher as older machine tools were rehabilitated. The net effect would be a drop in sales to 13,250 units. The best that Samuels could do was to assign about an equal probability to each of the three scenarios.

King Components was a relatively young company. It was begun by three engineers who had been unable to interest their employer, Drone Electronics, in an integrated control device for industrial machine tools. With permission of Drone, they took the idea to several venture capitalists, and with the help of a consultant they developed a business plan that showed the product could be profitable in several years. With a loan guaranteed by the venture capital company and the proceeds from a second mortgage on their homes, the three engineers formed King Components, and began manufacturing in a former Boeing hanger near downtown Seattle.

By 1976 the company had sales of over $3 million and net income was positive. Their former employer, Drone started to realize the potential of electronic controls in machine tools, controls that performed a variety of tasks, and in 1977 approached the founders about selling the company and staying on to run it. This was accomplished, and by early 1978 Samuels found himself working for the company he had left a few years ago.

Drone required each of its divisions to submit a detailed business plan for the coming fiscal year. After review and approval by the senior management of Drone, the business plan became a commitment for which each division was measured. A division which equaled or exceeded the profit goal received a substantial bonus. In order to prevent "sandbagging," the corporate staff reviewed each plan and made its own recommendations as to profit goals. Thus, any plan presented had to be reasonable and be supported by underlying market trends and conditions.

In its initial planning efforts in late 1982, Samuels had made the decision to go with a new production process which would have the effect of reducing variable costs per unit from $315.00 to $250.00.

Because more sophisticated manufacturing equipment would be used, fixed costs under this arrangement would rise from $1,850,000 to an estimated level of $2,950,000. While this was not expected to raise income before tax substantially at current sales levels, it was thought that the lower variable costs would better position the company if increases in volume were to occur.

There were, however, two other proposals for changes in the production process. The first was the introduction of a highly automated production system, whose savings would lower variable cost per unit to $185.00 per unit. This would, however, result in a further increase of fixed costs to $3,650,000. Since this high level of fixed costs would leave the company vulnerable to a recession, this alternative was rejected despite its favorable economics.

The third alternative was to cease production altogether and to subcontract for the components from an outside manufacturer. This alternative had been seriously explored in 1982 because of the recession and the desire to reduce exposure of the company to a significant downturn in the economy. Bids had been solicited and an acceptable bid had come from a reliable source to supply King with as many units as it needed at a cost to King of $390.00 per unit. This arrangement would allow King to eliminate its production facilities, and fixed costs would be reduced to administrative costs and be only $545,000.

The question facing Samuels was, then, which alternative made the most sense under the expected sales scenario.

SUGGESTED QUESTIONS

1. Assess the current risk status of the company by computing the break-even level of units and degree of operating leverage for 1982 using the data in Exhibit 25-1.

2. What is the expected percentage increase in income before tax with a 20 per cent increase in sales, based on your answer to Question 1. Prove your answer is correct by constructing an income statement with a 20 per cent increase in sales.

3. For a sales level of 17,500 units in 1983, compute the income before tax, break-even point, and degree of operating leverage for each production alternative. Do the same with a sales forecast for 22,400 units. A sales forecast for 13,250 units.

4. Which is the riskiest production alternative? Support your answer with the results from previous questions.

5. Make and support a recommendation on production alternatives to Samuels.

Singleton Hardware, Inc.

Cash Budgets

In early January, 1984, F. J. Ross, vice-president and controller of the Singleton Hardware Company, called a meeting of his two assistant controllers for the purpose of discussing the problems of cash flow and the line of credit the company currently had with its bank. The meeting was a direct result of Ross's conversation earlier that morning with the company's loan officer, Frank Peterson, of the Wake County National Bank.

Peterson had called Ross to inform him that the company had overdrawn by $50,000 the line of credit that the company had at the bank and to alert Ross to the fact that the company's bank balance was $30,000, the minimum cash balance that the company could carry. Peterson indicated that while the bank was cognizant of its customer's needs to occasionally borrow more than had been originally approved, the bank needed assurances that this was a temporary situation that would be corrected.

Ross had negotiated the line of credit in early 1983, and its key provisions were that Singleton could draw upon it up to a maximum of $150,000, and that there would be at least a thirty-day period during which the company completely paid off the balance in the credit line. The line had been set up to support Singleton through its seasonal cash requirements, but it had proved inadequate in December of 1983 and the company currently had $200,000 outstanding. Ross had obtained the extra credit by demonstrating that fourth quarter sales had been stronger than forecast. Based on preliminary year-end numbers and a projection of the income and expenses for the year, the bank was willing to go along with the company at least for a short period of time.

During the most recent conversation with Peterson, Ross told the bank officer that the compnay would soon be collecting the accounts receivable generated by the high fourth-quarter sales, and that the proceeds would not only allow the company to reduce the line of credit to its previously approved level but would enable it to comply with the other provisions of the loan agreement. Among other things this meant Singleton would completely pay off the line for a period of thirty days. Ross also assured Peterson that the company would stay within the credit limit of $150,000 for at least the next six months.

Singleton Hardware, Inc., was a hardware distributing company, operating in Raleigh, North Carolina, and surrounding communities. The company purchased a wide variety of hardware items and resold them to retail hardware stores and chains. It was in a very competitive business but maintained a large customer base through its large inventory, quick service for special orders, and its easy credit terms. The company sold on the basis of net thirty to most customers, although small customers with a poor credit history were required to pay cash. Many customers took over sixty days to pay, and because some customers were small businesses the bad debt expense ran to approximately 4 per cent of sales.

Although Ross had assured Peterson that the company would repay the line and not need more than the $150,000 that the bank had granted, he did not know if this could actually be done. Accordingly he has asked his two assistants to obtain all information regarding cash collections and disbursements for the January to June, 1984, period and to meet with him. Peterson knew that the situation was critical because dividend payments, tax deposits, and interest on a term loan were to be made in March. If the company was going to pay off its line of credit, it would have to do so before then.

Jack Wilson presented information on sales and collections. The actual sales for the last three months of the quarter and the projected sales for the first six months are shown in Exhibit 26-1. The credit and collections people had told Wilson that, based on historical patterns, the company could expect that 8 per cent of the sales would be cash or collected in the month they were sold, 38 per cent collected one month later, 24 per cent two months later, and 26 per cent three months later.

The warehouse manager told Bill Hackett, the other assistant, that purchases included in the cost of sales generally ran around 43 per cent. The orders to the manufacturers were placed two months

Exhibit 26-1 Sales, Wages, Advertising

Month	Sales	Direct Labor	Wages and Salaries Administration	Advertising
Oct.	$248,500			
Nov.	311,250			
Dec.	298,450			
1984				
Jan.	72,000	28,000	12,000	4,000
Feb.	93,000	32,000	12,000	4,650
Mar.	167,500	35,000	12,000	8,400
Apr.	254,000	38,000	15,000	9,700
May	201,000	38,000	15,000	10,050
June	155,000	33,000	12,000	7,750

in advance, received one month in advance, and were generally on terms of net thirty. This meant that the cost of sales were paid for in the month that the sales were incurred. The warehouse manager also told Hackett that the company could probably defer payment for sixty days, but that this might damage relationships with some suppliers and reduce the company's ability to get quick service. He recommended that the company keep current with its suppliers if this was financially feasible.

The payroll department had estimated direct labor costs and wages and salaries for the six months as shown in Exhibit 26-1. It also indicated that nontax related fringe benefits generally amounted to 9 per cent of the wages paid. FICA and income taxes would be paid in quarterly installments in March and June, with an estimated payment of $25,000 for each quarter. The president of Singleton had recently approved the 1984 business plan, which called for rent and utilities at $4,000 a month, other administrative expenses at $24,000 a month, and advertising as shown in Exhibit 26-1. Dividend payments of $50,000 to members of the Singleton family were planned for March and June. Finally, the company had recently sold some land for $136,000 with payments coming in four equal installments of 34,000 during the March–June period.

The agreement with the bank provided for interest payments on the outstanding line of credit at a rate of 15 per cent a year. These payments were made on a monthly basis; that is, the interest payment on the outstanding $200,000 line in December would be made in January, and the interest payment on January's balance would be made in February. The company also had a large term loan, and although it was not currently paying on principal, it did have scheduled interest payments of $74,000 in March and June.

Because of the company's liberal credit policy, Ross did not think that it would be able to fulfill his commitment to the bank to pay off the line of credit for at least thirty days and to keep borrowings under $150,000 unless changes were made. He solicited recommendations from his two assistants as to what changes could be made in management of cash flow that would reduce the borrowing requirements but not seriously affect the overall operations of the firm.

Wilson indicated that the easiest thing to do would be to eliminate the March dividend payment. This, he indicated would save the company more than the $50,000 in cash flow. Ross admitted that this would have the least affect on operations, but members of the Singleton family depended upon that payment for much of their income and would not be pleased to see the loss of a quarterly payment.

Hackett said that he thought the company could defer payment to the suppliers for another thirty days, beginning in February. This would still keep the company on an average payment of 60 days, and most suppliers would be willing to go along with the arrangement in order to keep Singleton's business. Hackett felt that there would be only minimal disruption in service, and that the company could still provide the high quality of service it always had to its customers.

In looking at the expense categories Ross noted that advertising was the one area with the least direct relationship to operations. The advertising was primarily institutional and for public relations. Although the marketing department would be upset, Ross felt that the advertising could be eliminated with minimal impact on sales.

As the meeting broke up, Ross asked his assistants to determine whether or not he could keep his commitment to the bank and, if not, what would be the impact on cash flow of the recommendations they had discussed. He placed the highest priority on meeting the promises to the bank but realized that any disruption to operations would have more serious long-run consequences than failure to meet line-of-credit obligations. He assumed the bank would not call the line if Singleton was unable to pay it off for thirty days or reduce requirements to $150,000.

SUGGESTED QUESTIONS

1. Compute a cash budget for January to June, 1984, based on the information in the case. Determine if the existing $200,000 line could be paid off during the period. If the company would need more than $150,000 during the period.

2. Compute the cash budget assuming the elimination of the March, 1984 dividend payment of $50,000.

    a. Does this alleviate the problems?

    b. Why are the savings in borrowings more than $50,000?

3. Compute the cash budget, assuming the payments for purchases are pushed forward to sixty days, starting in February. Does this alleviate the problems?

4. Compute the cash budget, assuming the advertising budget is eliminated. Does this alleviate the problems?

5. Make a recommendation with respect to what changes, if any, should be made in the initial cash-flow budget in terms of bringing down required borrowings.

Lone Pine Inns, Inc.

Investing in Marketable Securities

Lone Pine Inns was a very successful company consisting of company-owned and franchised restaurants throughout the southeastern United States. The company had grown from humble beginnings in 1945 to a chain with over 250 eating facilities in seven southern states. As an indication of success, in late 1984, one of the problems facing the company was the proper management of the excess cash generated from the highly profitable food and beverage operations.

Like many other franchise food operations, Lone Pine Inns had started as a single facility, the Lone Pine Inn of Augusta, Georgia. The business was begun by two brothers, Corey and Alvin Payton, who had learned to cook during service in World War II. After their discharge, they returned home and opened the Lone Pine Inns. It had a menu of medium-priced family meals using regional cooking, such as ham and biscuits and southern fried chicken. Because of the economic growth of the area fueled by the post-war economy and the golfing boom, the restaurant prospered beyond all expectations. By 1954 the Augusta unit had seating for over four hundred people, and the brothers had opened other units in nearby cities and towns. In 1958 the chain consisted of seven company-owned-and-operated restaurants in northern Georgia and South Carolina.

Company growth stopped in late 1958 after the brothers realized that the current level of operations was at the limit of their capacity to manage. The company remained static until 1967, when a second generation of Paytons took over management. In 1968 the first franchise was sold to a group of investors in Ocala, Florida. The investor purchased the right to open as many as seven inns in central Florida using the Lone Pine Inn name and trademark, and agreed to follow the decor and menu of the existing Lone Pine Inns. In return, the parent company received a right to impose operating standards on the franchisees, sell services and supplies to them, and to collect a royalty on sales.

The franchise agreement worked well for both parties, and when the tourist business in central Florida boomed in the 1970s, the new franchised operations boomed as well. The success of the expansion led the company to expand its franchise operations, as well as to open new company-owned restaurants. The strategy was to select medium-sized cities where the simple country atmosphere of the Lone Pine Inn would appeal to the local population and also to locate near tourist attractions where the family-oriented business could attract restaurant goers who wanted a break from hamburgers and fries.

Cash flow was continually a problem for the company in the 1970s as expansion used up more cash than was generated by operations. The company paid no dividends and retained 100 per cent of the income supplemented with borrowings. But even this was not sufficient to fund the expansion. In late 1979 the company approached an investment-banking group in Atlanta about a public offering of common stock, and in February, 1980, one million shares of stock were sold, bringing the company $3.5 million in cash and some much needed equity to its balance sheet.

In late 1983, with over fifty company-owned restaurants and about two hundred franchised operations, the company entered a period of consolidation and control. A decision was made not to expand out of the geographic market in which the company operated and, instead, to concentrate on improving profit margins. As a result of this policy decision, an experienced financial staff was brought on board, including for the first time a full-time corporate treasurer to manage cash for the company.

By December of 1984 the new treasurer, Jean Rabin, had installed a planning and forecasting system that enabled the company to produce a three-year business plan and a one-year detailed cash-flow forecast. In looking at 1985 it appeared that for the first time the company would have a small amount of excess cash in each month of that operating year. A by-product of the forecasting process was Exhibit 27-1, which showed the excess of cash over what was needed for operations for each month. It appeared that even in the "worst" month of 1985 in excess of $200,000 would be available.

As a part of the planning process Rabin had been asked to come up with a recommendation for the management of the excess cash in 1985. One possibility was the payment of dividends, but in an

Exhibit 27-1 Estimated Excess Cash, January–December, 1985
Excess Cash at the Beginning of the Month

Jan.	$345,000
Feb.	223,000
Mar.	326,000
April	267,000
May	312,000
June	432,000
July	380,000
Aug.	312,000
Sept.	214,000
Oct.	267,000
Nov.	365,000
Dec.	412,000

executive meeting this option was eliminated for several reasons. One concern was that the forecasting process itself was not a sure thing. There was no assurance that some of the excess cash might not be needed to fund operations. A second, more compelling reason for not declaring a dividend was that the funds would be needed for possible expansion in 1986. Thus, any payment in 1985 might not be continued in 1986; and in order to avoid interruption of a dividend payment, it was decided that no dividend payment at all would be made.

The options facing Rabin were how to invest the excess cash by maturity and whether or not to invest in fully taxable securities or in tax-exempt or preferred-stock issues, which gave some relief from taxation. Rabin had discussed the situation with the investment-banking firm that had handled the stock sale for the company and found that the following options were available.

Overnight Funds. The brokerage house would invest as much as Lone Pine Inns wanted in overnight or twenty-four-hour money. The advantage of this type of investment was that it was the most liquid available to the company. If the funds were needed they were available immediately; if not, they could be rolled over for another twenty-four hours. The rate, as shown in Exhibit 27-2 was 11.3 per cent.

Time Deposits. A local financial institution offered various maturities in time deposits for accounts such as Lone Pine. The maturities could be 30 day, 60 day, 90 day, 180 day, or one year. The higher rates were associated with the longer maturities, as shown in Exhibit 27-2. In the event that the company would need the funds before the maturity of the account, the bank was

Exhibit 27-2 Interest Rates, January 1, 1985 (in Per Cent)

Overnight	11.30
30 Day	10.80
60 Day	11.10
90 Day	11.30
180 Day	11.80
1 Year	12.30 Fully Taxable
	7.10 Tax Exempt
	10.50 Preferred Stock

willing to loan up to the full amount of the CD at a floating rate, currently 13.5 per cent

Other Issues.   As a profitable company, Lone Pine Inns was in the 45 per cent marginal tax rate. All of the above issues would be fully taxable. Also available to the company was a one-year tax-exempt issue which was rated single A and paid 7.1 per cent. The brokerage firm indicated that investment quality preferred stock was available with a current yield of 10.5 per cent. As a corporation, Lone Pine Inns would qualify for the dividend exclusion associated with holding preferred or common stock. The stock could be liquidated in the secondary market at any time, but the company would have to take the current market price, which could be higher or lower than the initial purchase price.

SUGGESTED QUESTIONS

1. Based on Exhibit 27-1, and assuming the excess cash balances move uniformly from one month to the next, what is the maximum amount Lone Pine Inns should invest in one-year securities?

2. Since the overnight rate is equal to the 90-day rate and higher than the 30- and 60-day rate, Rabin decided to invest funds not needed for 90 days or shorter in the overnight market. What arguments can you give against such a strategy.

3. For each of the one-year rates in Exhibit 27-2, compute the effective after tax yield based on Lone Pine's rate of 45 per cent.

4. For each of the one-year rates in Exhibit 27-2, compute the effective before-tax yield based on Lone Pine's rate of 45 per cent—that is, what is the fully taxable equivalent rate for each investment.

5. Based on your results should the company invest in the preferred stock? Give at least one argument for and one argument against.

Uptown Apparel, Inc. ***Uptown*** apparel

Cash Management with Lock Box

In early January, 1981, Ken Casey, president and chief executive of Uptown Apparel, Inc., was reviewing the preliminary financial statement of the company for the just-concluded fiscal year. Casey did not know whether or not to be pleased or concerned. It seems the company improved its operating performance all across the board, yet at the botton-line net income was down about one-third over the previous year. Casey was not certain what steps to take for 1981; he was certain he had about exhausted all of his operating efficiencies and opportunities in 1980.

The treasurer and chief financial officer, Murry Samuels, reviewed the income statement, shown as Exhibit 28-1 and noted the positive aspects of increased margins. In late 1979 a new cost-control program had been put into effect at Uptown, and the results were clearly successful. Both operating costs and overhead declined as a per cent of sales, and the result was that while sales were up less than 10 per cent in 1980, operating income increased by better than 30 per cent. Still, the year could not be counted as a success because net income dropped below $1 million for the first time since 1975, and Samuels could only console Casey with the thought that without the economies from the cost-control program there might not have been any income at all.

Uptown Apparel, a New York–based designer and manufacturer of medium- to high-priced women's clothing, derived its name for its location in the uptown end of the garment district of New York. There had been two Casey clothes companies, and this one was con-

Exhibit 28-1   Uptown Apparel, Inc.: Income Statement
Year Ending Dec. 31

	1979	1980
Sales	$23,765,000	$25,872,000
Cost of Goods Sold	$16,732,000	$17,432,000
	70.41%	67.38%
Gross Margin	$7,033,000	$8,440,000
	29.59%	32.62%
Selling, General and Administration Expenses	$3,343,000	$3,561,000
	14.07%	13.76%
Operating Income	$3,690,000	$4,879,000
Interest Expense	$1,456,000	$3,289,000
Income Before Tax	$2,234,000	$1,590,000
Taxes	$1,017,000	$784,000
Net Income	$1,217,000	$806,000
	5.12%	3.12%

stantly being referred to as the "uptown" one. Julius Casey, father of the current president, liked the name and in 1955 made the change official.

Ken Casey succeeded his father in 1967, and in 1970 he had made a significant change in the strategic position of the company. Prior to 1970 the company had been a supplier to small, family-owned low- and medium-priced women's clothing stores. The company primarily manufactured under private labels, so that almost any store could sell its own brand of clothes. Casey, however, felt that the trend in the 1970s would be away from the smaller dress shops and toward the larger, more up-scale department stores that were then beginning to invade the suburbs with stand-alone stores and large complexes in shopping malls.

In 1970 the Company introduced its new line of designer clothes under the Uptown label. Using the motto "Go Downtown with Uptown," it secured accounts with high-quality, high-priced department stores in Chicago, Dallas, Houston, San Francisco, and other prosperous cities. Based on slick advertising graphics and an appeal to the fashion-conscious shoppers in these cities, along with a generous markup for the store, the new line gradually became the dominant business for Uptown. By 1978 the Uptown label accounted for 72 per cent of total sales. The company was gradually phasing out its other lines.

In 1978 the company made a second strategic decision. In order to expand its line, it purchased a small sportswear manufacturer and renamed it the Uptown Leisurewear Division. In 1979 this operation was completely integrated into the Uptown operations and began

producing a complete line of sportswear under the Uptown label.
Casey reasoned, correctly as it turned out, that with the economies
of scale in production and the brand name recognition of the
Uptown label, the new line should be very profitable. While sales
were good in 1979, the profits were below expectations, and the company put in very stringent operating controls in 1980. It was the
tighter control that produced better margins in 1980, but the company's profits were substantially below that of 1979.

The cause of the decline in profits in 1980 could be traced directly
to interest expense. The acquisition in 1978 had completely
exhausted the cash reserves of Uptown, and the expansion required
large funding for inventory and receivables. In late 1979, the company negotiated a $22 million package, consisting of a $15 million
term loan and a $7 million line of credit. The proceeds were used to
pay off existing debt and to provide working capital. Unexpectedly
large cash requirements led, in mid-1980, to the entire $7 million line
being taken down. Unless there was some action soon, additional
funding would be needed for 1981.

The two loans were made on a floating basis and tied to the prime
rate. Because of its relatively large amount of debt, Uptown's best
offer from any bank was a prime plus two, meaning that the interest
rate would be equal to the bank's prime rate plus two percentage
points. On the line of credit the monthly payment consisted entirely
of interest, while the term loan was being paid in sixty equal installments with a balloon of $5 million at the end, plus interest
payments.

The interest rate in late 1979 increased sharply due to the change
in Federal Reserve policy. In an attempt to bring down the rate of
inflation, the Fed had adopted a policy which led to a fixed rate of
growth in the money supply. This policy led to a dramatic increase
in rates in early 1980, and even after a decline in rates in mid-1980,
end-of-year rates remained at or near record levels. Prospects for
1981 were more of the same, and Uptown was faced with interest
rates in the coming year in excess of 20 per cent.

Because of these difficulties, Samuels had met with Alvin Kapp,
vice-president of cash management services for New York Bank, the
company's commercial bank. Kapp had indicated that one solution
for Uptown would be to implement procedures which would significantly increase the case-collection process of the company. Kapp
noted that based on information Uptown had provided during the
loan negotiations, it appeared that on the average it took four days
from the time that customers mailed checks until they reached
Uptown's offices, and another full day before the checks were pro-
cessed at Uptown and submitted to New York Bank for deposit. By
decreasing the time it took for the money to be deposited, Uptown

would, in effect, be getting an interest-free loan. Based on 270 working days during the year, for each day saved Uptown would get an interest free loan of ½₇₀ of the 1981 collections. This money could be used to pay off borrowings that on the average were estimated to cost Uptown about 19 per cent in 1981.

Kapp indicated that he felt four lock boxes should be set up for Uptown (data is shown in Exhibit 28-2). The lock boxes would consist of post office boxes in Chicago, Houston, and San Francisco, along with one in New York. Customers would be instructed to send their payment to a post office box address instead of the company headquarters in New York. Kapp estimated that two of the four mail days would thereby be eliminated.

In New York, New York Bank would collect the checks from the lock box twice each day, deposit the checks in the account for Uptown, and then send the paperwork to Uptown for processing. In the three outlying cities, Uptown would set up accounts with a major bank in each city. These accounts would be "zero balance" accounts. The bank in each city would make collections at the lock box twice a day, deposit the funds, and then by electronic funds transfer send the funds to the New York Bank. The transfers would take place twice each day on every business day.

The effect of this direct deposit would be to eliminate one day of check processing and would result in a total saving of three days from the time the customer mailed the money. While the checks would still take their usual time to go through the clearing process and the funds would not be available until they cleared, Kapp felt that this three-day savings would make the arrangement worthwhile.

The cost of the service would be in three parts. New York Bank would charge a flat fee of $5,000 per year for setting up the system, and twenty-five cents for each check it processed from the New York lock box. Kapp estimated that the other banks would also charge twenty-five cents per check, and that the depository transfer checks through the electronic funds system would cost twenty-five dollars per check.

Exhibit 28-2   Lock-box Data

Annual Collections, fcst 1981	$27,362,000
Business Days	270
Average Check Size	$7,700.00
Depository Transfer Check Cost Per Check	$25.00
Check Processing Cost Per Check	0.25
Lock-Box Service Cost Per Year	$5,000.00
Estimated Borrowing Costs, 1981	19%

In discussion with Casey, Samuels felt that the cost of the service was too high to be of much benefit, but with expected borrowing costs at 19 per cent any action should be profitable. Casey said that he had just returned from an economic conference, and based on the forecast there, he felt that company should require a 15 per cent return on any excess funds that were freed up from the system. Samuels said he wasn't too certain the lock-box arrangement would be profitable based on 15 per cent investment opportunities for the excess funds.

SUGGESTED QUESTIONS

1. Why is a lock-box arrangement more desirable the higher the rate of interest?

2. If Uptown goes with the lock-box arrangement, what are its annual interest savings in 1981 if interest rates are 19 per cent?

3. What is the total cost of operating the lock-box system in 1981?

4. a. Is the lock box system as proposed by New York Bank profitable?

b. Is it profitable if the return on the funds saved is 15 per cent?

Phillips Valve Division

Accounts Receivable—
Change in Credit Standards

In conclusion, if the company wishes to expand sales beyond what normal growth will produce we must have greater flexibility in the granting of open-accounts status to new customers. Our present policies mean that almost all of our lost sales are the result of credit denials.

—from a memo to Sandy Marvis
from Tom Willis, Sales Manager

In preparing for the operating plan for fiscal 1981, we must recognize that the company will face increased bad-debt expense and longer collection periods unless our credit policy is tightened significantly. We must be more selective in granting credit.

—from a memo to Sandy Marvis
from Sarah Dixon, Credit Manager

Sandy Marvis, vice-president and general manager of the Phillips Valve Division of the Ramjack Corporation, had underlined the two passages in the above memos when he had first read them. He knew he would have to come back to the issues they raised, and in late April, 1980, as the planning process was about to begin for the next fiscal year, he had pulled them from his file.

Phillips Valve Division was a small part of a conglomerate known as the Ramjack Corporation. Ramjack had purchased Phillips seventeen years ago as part of a diversification plan. The merger had been beneficial for Phillips, which had been allowed to grow by using Ramjack capital, and for the most part Phillips had been left alone, free to manage its affairs as it saw fit, so long as cash flow was positive and earnings performance met the business plan.

The business plan was one of the few areas where Ramjack made active demands on Phillips. Ramjack required that each of its divisions submit a detailed business plan including projections of revenues, expenses, assets, and capital requirements for approval by the parent corporation. The plan was to be submitted by May 15 of the current year, and approval could be expected in time for the Division's start of its fiscal 1981 year on July 1, 1980.

The plan was important because Phillips would be judged by its performance relative to the plan. Each year, the planning guidelines from Ramjack would emphasize different aspects of the business, depending upon who was in the executive suite at Ramjack and what his areas of concern were. In past years the division had concentrated on new-product development, market share, cost control, and asset management. This year the emphasis was on growth. The planning guidelines that came from Ramjack indicated that in addition to normal growth, Ramjack would expect a business plan that showed sales growth expanding higher than the market rate.

Marvis knew that the objective of above average sales growth would be difficult to meet. Phillips operated out of a single plant in an industrial section of Fort Wayne, Indiana. The location gave it geographical access to the industrial midwest, principally Chicago, Detroit, and Cleveland. Its products were standard-size industrial valves, and although Phillips liked to boast of its quality, its valves performed about as well as those of its competitors. Sales and growth were the result of the rapid delivery time from its centrally located plant and its competitive pricing policy. Because of product similarity, Phillips prices would fall or rise to meet competitive conditions, and so the firm had few lost sales on price differentials.

Unfortunately, the prospects for growth were limited. The industrial base that Phillips served had been declining in recent years, and it had not found a cost effective way to market outside its geographic region. Recent cost-cutting actions had allowed Phillips to lower the price of some items, but it found whenever it did this the competitors would match the lower prices. The competitors would rather accept lower margins than lose market share.

The memos excerpted above were the result of preplanning meetings Marvis had set up with the key managers. He had told them of Ramjack's request and asked each of them to submit his own thoughts on the problems of sales growth. The submissions from marketing and credit had been predictable. Marketing felt that restrictive credit policies cut sales growth; credit was worried about higher bad debt and ballooning accounts receivable. It seemed that each department was more worried about his or her own area than in meeting overall corporate goals or the parent company's objective of higher sales growth and, of course, higher profits.

Credit control took place at Phillips by first assigning a credit customer to one of five categories. The assignment was based on the size and financial condition of the company, and new customers were asked to submit financial statements. These along with checks with commercial credit agencies were used to evaluate the risk of selling on credit to the customer. Once a customer was approved for an open account, he was free to order from Phillips with very little restrictions, and as long as his payments were within certain guidelines, no further examination of the customer was made.

The five risk classes are shown in Exhibit 29-1. Class A consisted of the Blue Chip Fortune 500 companies. These companies were considered risk free. Class B companies were almost as strong as Class A. Class C companies were those with high debt in their balance sheet and a credit history of late payments. The company currently sold on credit to A, B, and C companies but not to Class D and Class E companies. Class D companies were those who had a low credit rating and were in some type of financial difficulty. It was expected that, though Class D customers would eventually pay, it would be a long and difficult task to get money from them.

Tom Willis, the marketing manager, had long advocated selling to the Class D customers. He argued that these customers for the most part were able to get credit from Phillips's competitors, and that Phillips's could pick up a large number of customers with a 15% contribution margin by granting credit. Currently, these customers were sold on a cash basis, mostly C.O.D. and because of the bureaucratic problems at the sales end and the need for cash by the customer, sales in fiscal 1981 were expected to be negligible.

Ms. Dixon, the credit manager, was opposed to selling to the new class. She argued that the expected recession in the economy would make her department's job difficult with respect to current customers, and that adding the new class would seriously affect the operations of her department. She estimated that in addition to the higher bad-debt expense, accounts receivable would rise due to

Exhibit 29-1 Analysis of Credit-Risk Classes

Risk Class	Sales if Credit is Granted (in $000)	Current Sales (in $000)	Expected Bad Debt (in Per Cent)	Average Collection Period (in Days)
A	4,000	4,000	0	28
B	9,000	9,000	.5	35
C	6,000	6,000	1.0	41
D	5,000	0	4.0	70
E	3,000	0	6.0	95

the expected average collection period of seventy days on the new accounts, and the credit department would have to spend an additional $27,000 on billing and credit-agency services. Finally, she stated that the controller had estimated that in addtion to the increased receivables, other net working capital would go up about 14 per cent of increased sales. This would cover the higher inventory and other current assets needed to support the higher sales.

Marvis asked Dixon to submit a plan for reducing the average collection period and bad-debt expense in the event the new class of customers were to be sold. Dixon had said that there were two alternatives. The first involved hiring an assistant credit manager, who would have responsibility for the Class D accounts only and would cost the company about $25,000 in wages and benefits. Dixon estimated that the assistant would reduce the average collection period by two days and that bad-debt expense for the class would fall from 4 per cent to 3.6 per cent.

The second plan involved installing a complicated computer-based accounts receivable tracking system. The new system would be leased from a software vendor for $72,000 a year and would require an assistant credit manager. The new system would be set up to control bad-debt expense, and in addition to being used for the Class D customers, it would have benefits for Class B and Class C credit as well. The system was expected to reduce bad-debt expense of Class D to 3.3 per cent of sales, of Class B by .1 per cent, and of Class C by .2 per cent.

As Marvis reviewed this data he knew that he would have to make two decisions. The first would be whether to start selling to Class D customers on credit. If he decided to do so, he would then have to decide whether to leave the Credit Department unchanged or to add the personnel and new systems or the two alternatives described by Ms. Dixon.

SUGGESTED QUESTIONS

1. Compute the incremental profitability of selling to the Class D customers. Assume the required rate of return on receivables and other net working capital is 15 per cent, but that no personnel or system changes are made in the Credit Department.

2. Compute the profitability based on the data in Question 1, but assuming the first alternative is adopted for the Credit Department.

3. Compute the profitability based on the data in Question 1, but assuming that the second alternative is adopted for the Credit Department.

4. Make a recommendation to Phillips as to whether or not the Class D customers should be granted credit and, if so, what should be done with the Credit Department. Use the quantitative analysis and qualitative factors in your recommendation.

Myter Motor Works

Accounts Receivable— Change in Credit Terms

In its 1984 annual reports, Myter Motor Works had to explain how, for the first time since 1937, the company had managed to lose money. The trend in income had been downward for three years and, finally, for fiscal year 1984 the company experienced a loss of $3.2 million on sales of $42 million. The income statement for three years is shown in Exhibit 30-1.

The loss in 1984 did not mean that Myter was in any type of difficulty. The firm had endured in Sandusky, Ohio, ever since the Civil War, and given the permanence of its market share it was likely to last. The company had been started by a nephew of the second wife of Salmon P. Chase, U.S. senator and Ohio Governor, and in order to capitalize on the relationship, the new business was named Chase Machine Works. This name lasted until the late 1860s, by which time Chase had become chief justice of the United States and a fairly unpopular figure. The company was then renamed Sandusky Machine Works. The company acquired its third and present name when the grandson of the founder desired to make it sound more national than regional and christened the then forty-year-old company the Myter Motor Works.

Myter had been started to manufacture ordinance during the Civil War, its founders thinking that their connections to Chase, who served as secretary of the Treasury in the Lincoln cabinet, would win them quite a few government contracts. This did happen, but when the Civil War ended in 1865, the company was forced to move into more traditional lines of manufacture. By 1885, it had a broad line

Exhibit 30-1 Myter Motor Works: Income Statement

	1982	1983	1984
Sales	27,654,000	32,543,000	38,654,000
Cost of Manufacturing	21,574,000	26,345,000	33,678,000
Gross Profit	6,080,000	6,198,000	4,976,000
Sales and Administrative Expenses	4,465,000	4,876,000	5,021,000
Interest Expense	543,000	675,000	1,256,000
Income Before Tax	1,072,000	647,000	(1,301,000)
Taxes	478,000	217,000	(497,000)
Net Income	594,000	430,000	(804,000)

of specialized manufacturing tools, and it prospered until the recession that followed World War I. In 1921 the firm was forced to sell off most of its machine-tool operations, leaving it with only its electric-motor division.

The forced change was fortuitous for Myter, as the increased use of electric motors and related parts in industrial, commercial and residential goods made the company prosperous during the 1920s. The company survived the 1930s sustaining small but manageable losses and the prosperity of the post-World War II economy lifted the company to record sales and record profits. In 1980 the company was one of the leading independent electric-motor manufacturers.

The electric-motor industry in the 1980s was divided into two major groupings. A large part of the market was dominated by the large, diversified industrial manufacturers, such as GE and Westinghouse. However, a majority of the market was represented by a very large number of small, independent firms, such as Myter. While the GEs and the Westinghouses sold to the specialty side of the market, Myter and its competitors produced standardized motors that had applications in home appliances, small industrial machinery, heating and air conditioning, and other commercial uses. While Myter produced motors ranging in size from one-quarter horsepower to twenty-five horsepower, it was its one-half horsepower to five horsepower motor line that accounted for much of its sales and profits.

The mainstay of its line was a trademarked group of motors termed the M-1. This line ranged in size from one-quarter horsepower to two horsepower and accounted for about one-third of Myter's total sales. The motors were sold in a standard "off-the-shelf" configuration or could be manufactured on a customized basis with fittings to meet whatever application was needed. About one-third were sold this way, the rest being sold with standard fittings that were either used as-is or were modified by the purchaser.

The company had been concerned in recent years about the deterioration in its profit margins. Despite the fact that the economic recovery of 1983–1984 produced above average sales growth, the net income figures did not follow the sales trend, and in 1984 the company experienced its first loss since the depression. Concern over financial problems led to the formation of a Strategic Marketing Committee made up of the vice-presidents for marketing, finance, and planning. The committee was charged with the responsibility of developing a strategy which would restore profit margins.

Since it was the most important line of the company, the committee focused on the M-1 motors. A staff report was commissioned on the critical area in the market and expected future trends. At a meeting on October 29, 1984, the committee met to consider the contents of that report. It was hoped that the meeting would begin to lay the foundation for strategies that would restore the company to profitability.

The director of market research, Alice Chatsworth, provided summary of the findings. The critical element in the small electric-motor industry was the competitive position of product. While each manufacturer liked to boast that his product was superior to others, and gave their lines names such as "NeverDie," "LifeLong," the fact of the matter was that the motors of different manufacturers were essentially the same, and for almost all applications the units were interchangeable. The decision by a customer was made on the following basis:

1. Price.
2. Terms.
3. Warranty.
4. Quality of the product.
5. Delivery.
6. Intangibles.

The research director further explained that the order of the listing was somewhat misleading, as quality of the product was probably as big a factor as price for a customer. However, because the technology of electric motors was essentially unchanged since their invention, and since the quality of the major suppliers was indistinguishable, customers took quality of the product for granted and did not rate it very high in their decision to choose a particular supplier. Chatsworth warned that the study should not be used in any way to justify production changes that might reduce the reliability of the product line, since a lower quality of product might cause some customers to stop considering Myter motors altogether.

The area of intangibles in the report included such items as customer relations, something at which Myter excelled. Because of its older facilities, manufacturing costs were higher at Myter than at many of its competitors, who had located to the Sunbelt. As a result, Myter had somewhat higher prices, but through customer relations and superior marketing efforts, along with delivery and guarantees that were as good as any in the industry, it had been able to maintain a slight price differential above market until 1982. The recession in 1981–1982 and the recovery that followed found many customers with a more focused outlook on prices. In order to hold its share and expand unit sales, Myter had been forced to bring its prices more into line with the rest of the industry, and these price reductions on selected lines had contributed to the margin decline.

It had been hoped that as a result of the new pricing strategy, increased unit sales would offset the lower prices, more units sold would increase total profits. This had not worked out because of an unforeseen development, the strength of the U.S. dollar and resultant competition from foreign markets. The strong U.S. dollar in 1983 and 1984 had the effect of lowering the price of imported units, and these imports captured a larger share of the market than had been expected or forecast. Because of the perference for domestic products, better delivery schedules, and other factors, U.S. companies had been able to keep prices above import prices without totally losing the market. The current forecast was that while the strength of the dollar was expected to peak in late 1984 or early 1985, the dollar was not expected to fall and that import prices would probably remain steady.

In view of this analysis, most of which was already known to the committee, Chatsworth was asked to list and evaluate the options that were open to Myter. Chatsworth had expected this question and indicated that there were three possible strategies. The first involved a massive cost-cutting effort, leaving the current market price unchanged, and increasing the margin on each unit sold. Chatsworth indicated that she had reviewed production techniques with the engineering group and found that little was left to be done in the Ohio and Illinois factories, the main production facilities of the company. For the M-1 line, variable cost of production on the marginal units was at about 60 per cent, and the Engineering Group felt this was as low as they could go without relocation. Several Texas and North Carolina sites had been investigated, but relocation to those sites would take two to three years and thus could not help the short-run problem.

The second alternative was to continue with the intitial strategy of price reductions designed to increase market share and generate high total profits on higher volumes. Chatsworth indicated that this strategy was the one with the greatest risk, became there was no guarantee that competitors would not simply match Myter prices, leaving the same market shares, lower prices, and lower margins. The vice-president of marketing also pointed out that unlike consumer products, a lower price of industrial products, such as motors, would not stimulate a higher demand. Demand for industrial products was derived from the demand for the final product. Since the motors were only a small component of total cost for the manufacturers, it would not be expected to stimulate higher demand.

The third alternative proposed by Chatsworth was a change in the terms of sale by Myter. Myter's current billing policy was to create and send an invoice at the same time that the product was shipped. The goal was to have the invoice arrive with the shipment. Current terms were net thirty, the industry standard. Enforcement of this policy was difficult, due to the competitive nature of the business. Many customers took sixty days or longer to pay, and though Myter could express displeasure, its only alternative was to cease selling on open credit, which would simply serve to drive the customer to a competitor.

While Myter tolerated some delays, customers who took longer than ninety days were placed on a list and contacted personally by the corporate controller. Unless there were mitigating circumstances, the customer was told that failure to improve payments would result in being denied credit. The effect in many cases was to lose the customer to a rival supplier, but in this way the average collection period was maintained at about sixty-seven days and bad-debt expense was kept to 1.5 per cent of sales. Both of these measures were below the industry averages of eighty-two days and 3.2 per cent respectively.

The proposal that Chatsworth made was that Myter change its terms from net thirty to net forty. The reasoning was that many companies who had uneven cash flows and difficulties in meeting Myter's current terms would feel more inclined to purchase from Myter. They would know that while the terms would state net forty, in effect they would have about seventy-five to eighty days in which to make payments before Myter became concerned. The advantages of this strategy was that current prices could be maintained, and the expanded sales would be highly profitable due to the 40 per cent gross margin expected on additional sales. Furthermore, Chatsworth felt it was unlikely that the rest of the industry would try to match the more lenient credit terms. Many competitors were smaller and did not have the financial resources to support higher receivables, while others sold to more marginal customers and already had de facto credit terms that were equal to Myter's proposed terms. Summary data on the progam is shown in Exhibit 30-2.

Major opposition to the plan came from Vice-President of Finance George Price. Price raised several points in opposition to the plan.

Exhibit 30-2   Analysis of Change in Credit Terms, M-1 Motor Line

Existing Sales	$12,345,000
Average Collection Period	67 days
Current Terms	Net 30
Proposed Terms	Net 40
Estimated Sales Increase	$2,350,000
Variable Cost on New Sales	60%
Average Collection Period on New Total Sales After Credit Policy Change to Longer Terms	77 Days
Additional Credit and Collections Cost	
Personal Additions	$72,000
Additional Collection Efforts	$35,000
Allocated Fixed Overhead	$14,000
Bad-Debt Expense	
On Existing Sales	1.50%
On Total of New Sales and Existing Sales	2.50%
Other Net Working Capital Investment	$250,000
Required Rate of Return on Investments	18%

1. By changing the credit terms, customers who were used to paying in thirty days or slightly more would then pay later. This would increase the balance on receivables of the existing customer base with no appreciable benefit.

2. While there would be substantial additional profit based on a sales increase of $2.35 million with a 60 per cent variable cost, other costs would also rise. Two additional people would be needed in the credit and collections area at a fully loaded cost of $36,000 each, and additional administrative expenses in collecting the accounts would be $35,000. Also, corporate allocations of fixed corporate overhead to the credit and collections department would increase by $14,000. This allocation was to cover the corporate expense and was based on the number of people in each department.

3. Bad debt expense would rise not just for the new accounts but for some existing accounts as well. With more lenient terms, it would be more difficult for the collections people to recognize customers who were candidates for bad debts, and the newer customers were likely to have a higher likelihood of bad debts than the existing customer base.

4. In addition to the increased investment in receivables, higher inventories would be needed to support the higher sales and other net working capital items would also increase. With a sales increase of $2.35 million, Price put the increased net working capital investment, exclusive of receivables, at $250,000.

Chatsworth replied that these points had been taken into consideration. The bad-debt expense was expected to increase to 2.5 per cent of total sales from 1.5 per cent, and the average collection period on total sales would rise to seventy-seven days from its current level of sixty-seven days. Investment in receivables and other net working capital should earn at least 18 per cent, which was the required rate of return on other investment projects.

The committee felt the strategy merited further consideration, and Chatsworth was instructed to prepare a more detailed analysis of the profit implications of the proposed change in credit terms.

SUGGESTED QUESTIONS

1. What is the current level of accounts receivable on the existing sales level?

2. What would the increase in receivables on the existing sales be if the new policy is adopted?

3. What is the cash investment in receivables generated by the new sales?

4. What is the total incremental cash investment in assets generated by the new sales level?

5. What is the incremental profit on the new sales?

6. What are the incremenatl costs from the new sales?

7. What is the incremental cost of the increased cash investment in assets generated by the new sales?

8. On economic grounds, should the new policy be adopted?

toy city **TOYS**	Toy City Toys

Inventory Models—EOQ

The plans for expansion of Toy City Toys, Inc., into a new line of plastic building-block toys were all set except for one rather important consideration, namely, which of two potential suppliers would supply the high-grade plastic for the blocks. Normally, a supplier would be chosen solely on the basis of price, but uncertainty in the plastics industry and the importance of having a reliable regular supply meant in this case that price would only be part of the decision. Since interruption of a production line was an extremely costly event, delivery considerations were almost of equal importance to cost of product in making the decision about a vendor.

The new line of building blocks for Toy City would employ a high-grade, single-color plastic suitable for processing in the company's patented injection molding process. After delivering specs to several potential suppliers, only two companies made serious bids for the business. As both bids were based on an annual volume close to the estimated annual needs of Toy City Toys, a sole supplier would have to be selected.

Ordinarily, price would be the major criterion, particularly in this situation in which the price of the low-cost supplier, Cobo Plastics, of San Jose, California, was $44 per thousand pounds lower than that of Union Plastics. Cobo's bid of $580 per thousand pounds it was significantly lower than the company's budgeted cost too, and it almost guaranteed profits in excess of the budgeted amount. However, Cobo was a small, specialized company, and its ability to deliver on a regular basis was at best questionable in the mind of the director of purchasing for Toy City Toys. Despite the fact that Cobo would be producing the material in a plant in San Jose, less than forty miles from Toy City's facility in nearby San Francisco, Cobo wanted a three-week lead time between order date and delivery date. This rather long time was necessary because Cobo used its production facilities for several products, and a switchover to the type of product desired by Toy City might take one to two weeks.

The other competitor for the business was Union Plastics, a division of a Fortune 100 company and Triple A rated in all areas, including production and delivery. Even though the Union Plastics plant was located in southern California near Long Beach, Union guaranteed one-week delivery following receipt of an order. Union had the capacity to start production of any product on an almost immediate basis, and Toy City's experience in the past with Union Plastics had been excellent. Ordinarily, Union would have received the order with little or no discussion, except for the fact that their price was not nearly as competitive as Cobo's.

Toy City Toys was started in 1903 by a German woodcarver, Alex Sternum, soon after he emigrated to the United States at the age of twenty-seven. Sternum had arrived in New York with just enough money to take a train across the country to California. In San Francisco he raised some cash by selling wood toys that he carved from scraps of lumber. His financial success came a decade later when he designed a set of wooden buildings, homes, fences, street cars, and people, which he sold under the trademark of Toy City. The line was an immediate success, and Sternum set up manufacturing facilities just outside of San Francisco. He initially called his company the Black Forest Toy Company, but after America's entry into World War I he wanted to eliminate the German reference and took the name of his most popular line.

The company grew in the 1920s by specializing in high-quality, rather expensive wooden toys and expanded upon the Toy City line by adding toy autos, animals, farm buildings, and the like. The marketing strategy was to price a starter set of the Toy City at a low price, then sell additions at a high markup. By the 1930s a second generation of customers was buying the toys, and the company reached sales of $5 million in 1932 at the height of the depression. Production was temporarily diverted during World War II to war materials, but following the war the baby boom supplied the company with its period of highest growth.

Because of its success with wooden toys, the company was slow to adapt to plastic, and from 1955 and 1980 it barely broke even. In 1980 the Sternum family hired a new management team with the directive to move the company forward in a high-growth mode. A public offering of stock raised $7 million in new cash to finance the growth, and a marketing-research group and product-development group were formed to generate a new toy line for the 1980s. The joint effort of these two groups produced the proposed new building-block collection, Toy City Blocks.

Toy City Blocks were to be interlocking plastic blocks with which children could build vehicles, houses, animals, space ships, and other toys. The original concept of Toy City was to be used. A starter set was priced very low, but additional sets would carry a very high price tag. The marketing-research group found that the name Toy City still carried weight in the marketplace, and the purchasers of the old Toy City wooden toys were likely to purchase the new product. Initial sales were estimated at $20 million in the western and southwestern United States with a gross margin of better than 40 per cent.

Design and manufacture of the new blocks soon revealed that a special type of plastic would have to be used in their manufacture. The plastic would have to be sufficiently hard to withstand abuse by three to seven year olds, who were the primary market, yet supple enough to snap into place with little or no difficulty. After specifications for the plastic were developed, manufacturers were invited to bid on becoming sole suppliers to Toy City Toys. Eleven bids were received; all but two were over one dollar per pound and thus eliminated because at that price the entire project would have to be scrapped. Cobo bid $580 per thousand pounds; Union bid $624.

Union had expected to be the low bidder, because its large, automated facilities could be easily utilized in the production of the material. Cobo Plastics was a surprise. After receiving the bid the Purchasing Department of Toy City Toys investigated the company and learned that it had been started in the mid 1960s as a specialty plastics operations. The company carved a niche in the market by not going head to head in competition with the large chemical firms that dominated the industry. It had good, experienced, talented management, a strong balance sheet, and the reputation of delivery of quality material on schedule. The only difficulty in selecting Cobo was its limited production facilities. Because it was small, significant time was needed to switch from one run to another, and it was for this reason that a three-week delivery time was given, as opposed to one week with Union.

The decision in selecting a supplier of the critical raw material for the project was the joint responsibility of Purchasing Manager Burton Reynolds and Plant Manager Charles Seafort. Reynolds had been the major supporter of Cobo Plastics and felt that it was well worth going with the lower price, despite the longer lead time and somewhat higher uncertainty. Seafort on the other hand was concerned primarily with production and indicated that a smooth production cycle was the greater requirement of the project. Seafort felt that the higher price of Union Plastics was justified in view of the greater reliability and shorter lead time.

To settle the dispute, a meeting was held on July 1, 1983. The meeting consisted of Reynolds, Seafort, and Vice-President and Chief Operating Officer Duncan Smith. Smith had asked Seafort to present the critical data for the project, which is shown in Exhibit 31-1.

Any size order could be filled in units of one thousand pounds. The first year's production was estimated to require 6,780,000 pounds based on a five day-week, single-shift production schedule. With holidays and other off days, production was expected to be about 244 days per year. Production for the new building blocks was scheduled to begin on Monday, October 1, 1983.

Based on a recently completed study, and experience in other areas of the company, Seafort estimated that the cost of placing an order was $250 regardless of which supplier was used. This cost covered the time for preparation of the order, follow-up with the supplier, and unloading operations. The nature of the product was such that this cost was constant regardless of how much was ordered.

Also of critical importance in the decision was the amount of safety stock that the company would want to keep on hand. Because the plastic was relatively indestructible, had no value for theft, and did not become technologically obsolete, the company had decreed that its policy would be to keep relatively larger amounts in inventory as a safeguard against interruption of production. Company policy on this issue was to provide for a safety stock of a least 10 per cent of annual production requirement. Seafort estimated that proper safety stock for the plastic if the Union were chosen as supplier would be 750,000 pounds, while if Cobo were chosen, at a minimum 1,000,000 pounds should always be on hand.

It was this higher amount of safety stock that formed the basis for Seafort's economic arguments in favor of Union over Cobo. Seafort pointed out that there was a carrying cost to inventory, and that this cost was considerably greater than the cost of borrowed funds nec-

Exhibit 31-1   Components of the Carrying Cost of Inventory for Medium-Sized Manufacturing Firms (in Per Cent)

Cost of Funds	14
Handling and Storage	4
Insurance and Other Expenses	3
Obsolescence, Theft, Spoilage	4
Total Carrying Cost	25

essary to finance the inventory. Seafort presented a copy of a manufacturing study that showed the costs of inventory.

Seafort argued that this percentage should be assessed against the average inventory balanced and that these cost should be added to the total cost of purchasing the material when determining the economic desirability of one supplier over the other. While he had no figures to support the conclusion, he argued that because of the higher inventory requirements from Cobo, when the dollar carrying cost of this additional inventory was added to the cost of the material, the economic advantage of Cobo would disappear.

Reynolds agreed that the carrying cost of inventory should be considered in examining the overall economic advantage of one supplier over another. However, he disagreed with the 25 per cent figure, stating that since the material was not subject to obsolescence or theft, that component of the carrying cost should be removed. Smith agreed that 21 per cent be used as the correct carrying cost but was not certain which of the two suppliers provided the maximum economic benefit to Toy City.

SUGGESTED QUESTIONS

1. Using the data from the case and Exhibit 31-1, for each supplier compute the EOQ.

2. For each supplier, compute the number of orders per year and explain why they differ.

3. What would be the approximate order date and amounts for the first and second orders placed for supplier Cobo and supplier Union. Assume Toy City Toys plans an equal rate of production year-round.

4. For each supplier, compute the average inventory that Toy City would have in units and in dollars.

5. Using both the carrying cost and the cost of the material, which supplier provides the most economic source for Toy City Toys?

Eiger Mountaineering Equipment Company

EIGER
MOUNTAINEERING EQUIPMENT

Line of Credit Versus Commercial Paper

Eiger Mountaineering Equipment Company was a significantly different operation following its acquisition by the conglomerate General Manufacturing. An immediate change in operations was the necessity to clear all major financing transactions with the parent company's vice-president of finance, Tony Hacker. While Eiger was to be maintained as a separate, stand-alone subsidiary of General, Hacker wanted to be certain that any large financial transaction was consistent with company policy and made sense from an economic point of view.

Eiger's immediate problem in late 1981 was the planning for financing of its seasonal inventory and receivables needs. The treasurer of Eiger, Alan Creston, had estimated that Eiger would need approximately $15 million in seasonal financing in the early part of 1982, a figure somewhat larger than the previous year's but certainly in line with the level of business that Eiger expected to do in 1982. In the previous five years Eiger had engaged in seasonal borrowings of amounts between $9 million and $12 million.

Creston had just finished a meeting with Hacker in which he had outlined the potential financing requirements for Eiger. The proforma financial statements, shown in Exhibits 32-1 and 32-2, showed the traditional increase in cash required in the first and second quarters of the year, with the ability to pay off the seasonal loan coming from excess cash flow in the later part of the year. Creston had sought Hacker's approval to go ahead with negotiations on a line of

Exhibit 32-1 Eiger Mountaineering Equipment: Pro-Forma Income Statement, 1982 (in $000)
Quarter Ending

	March 31	June 30	Sept. 30	Dec. 31	Total
Sales	24,500	27,600	17,300	11,800	81,200
Cost of Goods Sold	13,900	16,500	9,800	6,700	46,900
Gross Profit	10,600	11,100	7,500	5,100	34,300
Administration Expenses	3,100	3,400	3,600	3,700	13,800
Selling Expense	2,400	2,800	1,800	1,200	8,200
Interest	1,700	2,400	2,500	2,200	8,800
Income Before Taxes	3,400	2,500	(400)	(2,000)	3,500
Taxes at 46 Per Cent	1,564	1,150	(184)	(920)	1,610
Net Income	1,836	1,350	(216)	(1,080)	1,890

credit with General's bank but instead came away with a second alternative to the seasonal line of credit, issuing commercial paper.

Until September, 1981, Eiger had been an independent company, manufacturing outdoor camping, recreational, and climbing equipment. The company was headquartered in Denver and traced its roots to 1882, when its founder, German immigrant John Eiger, decided there was more money in making mining equipment than there was in prospecting. Eiger set up shop in the back of a bar in Denver and started making mining supplies to outfit the wave of prospectors looking for gold in the Colorado hills. He found that there was a steady demand for the pans, picks, shovels, and other equipment in the outlying communities and set up a distribution system by horse-drawn wagon to supply stores in the small mining towns that sprang up in the foothills of the Rockies.

By 1910, the prospecting business was completely dead, but Eiger had seen a steady demand in the nonmining frontier household products he produced or distributed. During the next two decades he built his business into the major manufacturer of ropes, tents, packs, special clothing, and other outdoor items that were everyday needs for families who lived far from civilization. The company gradually obtained a reputation for high quality, and the Eiger brand name was readily accepted.

In the early 1950s, the company noticed that its products were being ordered by an increasingly larger number of amateur campers and climbers, people who wanted the professional quality that came from a company like Eiger. In 1955 the company started catalog sales and increased its line to be able to supply complete camping and climbing equipment. In order to move away from the household character of the company and capitalize on the glamor of mountain

Exhibit 32-2 Eiger Mountaineering Equipment Company: Pro-Forma Balance Sheet, 1982 (in $000)

Quarter Ending

	Dec. 31 1981	March 31	June 30	Sept. 30	Dec. 31
Assets					
Cash	1,700	2,400	2,900	2,300	2,100
Accounts Receivable	14,900	19,800	25,500	17,000	13,100
Inventory	17,000	26,000	22.000	19,000	15,900
Other Current Assets	3,000	3,000	3,000	3,000	3,000
Total Current Assets	36,600	51,200	53,400	41,300	34,100
Net Plant	15,600	17,900	18,600	16,200	15,400
Other Assets	3,100	3,936	3,086	4,770	4,490
Total Assets	55,300	73,036	75,086	62,270	53,990
Liabilities and Net Worth					
Accounts Payable	11,600	13,400	12,500	7,800	10,500
Other Payables	5,300	6,200	5,900	4,700	5,100
Accrued Items	2,300	3,400	2,700	2,500	2,300
Short-Term Debt	6,700	18,500	21,700	13,200	4,200
Total Current Liabilities	25,900	41,500	42,800	28,200	22,100
Long-Term Debt	8,600	8,600	8,600	8,600	8,600
Other Liabilities	2,500	2,800	2,200	4,200	3,100
Total Liabilities	37,000	52,900	53,600	41,000	33,800
Common Stock	5,000	5,000	5,000	5,000	5,000
Retained Earnings	13,300	15,136	16,486	16,270	15,190
Total Liabilities and Net Worth	55,300	73,036	75,086	62,270	53,990

climbing, the company became Eiger Mountaineering Equipment. By 1960, it had reached sales of $20 million annually.

The company made its first public offering of stock in 1973 and used the proceeds to finance expansion of its manufacturing plants to further broaden its line. By this time it had set up a network of retail stores in the western states but served all of the United States with its catalog operations. In early 1981, the company was approached by General Manufacturing. After several months of negotiations, the stock of the company was purchased for a total of $54 million. This left the heirs of John Eiger very wealthy and the company a wholly owned subsidiary of General Manufacturing.

General Manufacturing realized that the most valuable asset of Eiger was its reputation as an independent supplier of high-quality goods. As part of the purchase agreement Eiger was allowed to operate independently, with a few exceptions. One of those exceptions was the finance area, in which all major financing decisions had to be discussed with General's financial management staff.

The critical financing problem that faced Eiger in late 1981 was the financing arrangement for its seasonal increase in working capital requirements. Sales of Eiger products were concentrated in the spring and early summer. This meant a buildup of inventory in the early part of the year followed by an increase in receivables in the late spring and summer from sales to independent stores. This cash imbalance corrected itself later in the year, as collections were available for paying down borrowings necessary to support the seasonal increases in assets. The trend in working capital and the estimated requirements are shown in Exhibit 32-2 for the four quarters of the coming year, fiscal 1982.

Seasonal financing was a common occurrence for Eiger, and every year the company had arranged a seasonal line of credit with its commercial bank. This year the short-term funding requirements were estimated at $15 million, but since Creston could not be certain of the total needs, he expected to secure a line of credit of $20 million which would give him enough of a cushion to fund any unexpected shortfalls in cash flow. Negotiations with the bank had indicated that the line would be available at 18 per cent annual rate of interest, with a 1 per cent commitment fee assessed against the unused amount of the line. Before accepting this proposal, Creston set up a meeting with Hacker to apprise him of the situation and to determine if Hacker had any alternatives.

In the meeting with Hacker, Creston learned that it would be possible for Eiger to issue commercial paper to fund its seasonal needs. Normally, a company the size of Eiger would not be able to enter the commercial paper market, which was restricted to large, triple-A companies. However, now that Eiger was a part of General Manufacturing, it could issue commercial paper in the name of, and with the guarantee of, General. Hacker felt that commercial paper rates in 1982 would average 16 per cent, substantially below the bank rates that were being charged Eiger for its line of credit.

Creston would have immediately chosen the commercial paper route except for two other things that he learned from Hacker. One was that the commercial paper would have to be marketed through a dealer, with a charge of one-eighth of one percentage point for each issue. On an annual basis for ninety-day paper, this charge would be incurred four times. The second factor in issuing commercial paper was that Eiger would be required to obtain a back-up line of credit equal to the amount of commercial paper that would be issued. Hacker thought that $15 million would be sufficient, and Creston felt that the line could be obtained for a 1 per cent commitment fee on the unused portion.

Finally, there was one other factor that complicated the decision. General Manufacturing would have a new stock issue in 1982, and some of the proceeds might be invested in Eiger. Hacker was not certain how much would be available, but he told Creston that it might be that Eiger would need only $5 million or $10 million in outside financing, as opposed to the projected $15 million. Creston knew he would have to take this factor into account in deciding whether to go with the commercial paper or line of credit.

SUGGESTED QUESTIONS

1. For the line of credit, compute the annual interest cost of borrowing $5,000,000. $10,000,000. $15,000,000.

2. For the line of credit, compute the commitment fee expense for borrowing $5,000,000. $10,000,000. $15,000,000.

3. What is the annual percentage cost of using the line of credit for $5,000,000? $10,000,000? $15,000,000?

4. For the commercial paper, what is the annual interest expense of issuing $5,000,000? $10,000,000? $15,000,000?

5. For the commercial paper, what is the total cost and effective percentage rate, including the dealer charge and commitment fee (assume paper is issued four times a year), for $5,000,000? $10,000,000? $15,000,000?

6. Based on your analysis, which alternative is the less expensive for each level of borrowing?

part V

Special Topics in Financial Management

Clearview Food Products

Lease Versus Purchase

Joan Higgins, president of Clearview Food Products, liked to describe her company to bankers, sales representatives, and other professional personnel with whom she came into contact as "hippies gone wild." It was a fun description, but it was not true in the sense that the owner-operators of Clearview were hippies or had ever been. The only wildness she had ever seen was a party early in the year to celebrate the company's passing the $3 million in annual sales, and as it was a nonalcoholic party, the wildness was very limited.

Still, the company could trace its roots to the hippie movement and the cultural revolution that went with it during the early 1970s. In 1973 a group of fourteen college students from Colgate University in upstate New York decided that graduation from college left them prepared for a life that they did not want to follow. The academic side of college had trained them for a place in regular society, the social side of college had exposed them to a drug and alcohol related life which they rejected as strongly as a job offer from Wall Street. With no place to go and a common interest in natural foods and healthy living, they founded a food cooperative in a small village outside of Hamilton, New York.

The initial assets of the company were an old truck and an older warehouse. The activities of Clearview consisted of purchasing locally grown organic foods and selling them to local residents. After several months of this, barely making enough to keep the members of the group from leaving for the better paying jobs of the city, two important things happened. The first was that a food-purchasing cooperative in Syracuse asked the company to make regular deliveries. Its orders were enough to double the basic volume of the company. The second thing that put the company on the road to greater earnings was that a California manufacturer of natural foods contacted the group about acting as a distributor for all of New York State, including New York City.

It was the second event that propelled the company into a transformation from a small distributor into a multimillion-dollar food company. It turned out, that Clearview's location in mid-state New York was almost ideal. From that location it could serve Buffalo, Rochester, Syracuse, Albany, Binghamton and, of course, New York City. With the cash flow generated by selling on a cash basis to food cooperatives and others, and the increasing number of food lines that Clearview took on as distributor, the company soon found that it was too large to function as an informal partnership. In 1977, the group incorporated as Clearview Food Products and became a full-line distributor of natural and organic foods, selling to grocery stores, restaurants, and local food cooperatives.

The company's operations in New York City were particularly successful, because its location gave it significant cost advantages. Clearview was able to distribute to New York City at a lower cost than companies that actually resided in the metropolitan area. While its competitors were paying high New York City rates and rents, Clearview found that loaded trucks could leave its plant at 4 A.M and service all major customers at the same time as city-based companies. Clearview's reputation for quality and service established it in the important New York City market.

Although a business in name, and a corporation in the legal sense, Clearview was really a cooperative effort by its employees. Every employee was required to own at least one hundred shares of stock in the company. When an employee joined the company and served a probation period, he or she was given the opportunity to purchase the stock. The company financed the purchase by withholding a monthly payment from the paycheck. Upon leaving the company, the employee was required to sell the stock back to the corporation. All transactions were done at net book value per share, so that the existing shareholders were neither harmed nor made better off by the new shareholders. The only way that employees could make a profit from their holdings was by increasing the equity of the company by increasing profits.

In the beginning, all management decisions were made by a vote of all the shareholders, one share, one vote. However, as the company grew larger and more complex, decisions were delegated to various committees. The president was responsible for reviewing all major decisions, drawing up a position paper, and presenting the decision to the appropriate committee. These decisions involved policy and, once policy was set, the groups within the company had the authority to take whatever actions were necessary to implement the policy. For example, once it had been decided to expand into nearby Pennsylvania, the purchasing and marketing personnel implemented the program without further approval by the governing committees.

The members-owners of Clearview recognized that their way of managing the business would not work for everyone. Their success was based on the close spirit of cooperation and purposes exhibited by the group. The only exception to the above method was for a major change in the strategic nature of operations. In late 1982 it was proposed that the business expand into food processing. For all of its existence the company had existed only as a distributor. However, the credibility generated by the excellent service and products given its customers convinced many of the company that they could process and market foods under their own name.

The proposal generated significant controversy, for it would mean a major change in operations, philosophy, and finances. As a distributor, selling on a cash basis but purchasing on a credit basis, the company had little cash-flow problems. However, by diversifying into production and processing this would change. Significant capital would be required to support production equipment, inventory and, for the first time, credit sales.

After reviewing the possible problems with the new program, it was decided to implement the new strategy on a trial basis. A pilot program would be set up, and if the project was successful those in charge would be given authority to expand. The processing activity would use a small sector of the current warehouse, and since the warehouse had once been a small factory, all necessary utilities were in place. The warehouse would serve as a repository for the inventory, and the existing distribution system would handle the Clearview products as easily as the other lines.

The critical factor in the new project would be the processing equipment. After surveying manufacturers, the project group settled on an equipment series manufactured by Processing Equipment Corporation. The equipment for the pilot project had a list price of $75,000, and as Clearview did not have anywhere near that level of cash reserves, it was decided to finance the entire purchase. Clearview had no bias in favor of or against debt, to them it was just another way of doing business.

One alternative for the financing was a bank loan, secured by the equipment. A local bank with whom the company had been working since its inception had agreed to finance the entire amount, at an annual rate of 15 per cent. In order to help with the cash flow of the company, the bank agreed to receive payments on an annual basis. The loan would be a five-year term loan, with five equal payments made at the end of each of the next five years. Some members of the company had suggested other banks, but given the fixed-interest rate and the ability to make payments at the end of the year, instead of monthly, the project committee agreed that if bank financing were used, they would go with this scheme.

The second alternative was to lease the equipment. Processing Equipment Corporation had its own captive finance company, PEC Financing, Inc., whose function was to provide lease financing to customers of the parent corporation. PEC Financing Corporation indicated that it would provide a five-year lease for a rate of $12,000 per year, and that it would match the terms set by the bank, that is, the payments would be made in a lump sun at the end of each of the following five years. The equipment had a ten year life, but Clearview estimated that five years would be as long as they would use it. At the end of five years the experiment in food processing would either be such a success that newer and more modern equipment would be used, or else the project would be abandoned.

The project committee had been charged with evaluating the two proposals summarized in Exhibit 33-1 and determining which was the most economical. The committee quickly divided into two camps, those who wanted to finance with the bank loan and those who wanted to finance by leasing. The strongest arguments appeared to be in favor of the bank loan. Those advocating that position argued that by purchasing the equipment outright they would be entitled to a number of economic benefits denied by leasing. These benefits included a 10 per cent investment tax credit that would be realized at the end of the first year, tax benefits from the interest component of the payment and from depreciation, and real-

Exhibit 33-1   Data of Processor Lease (in Per Cent)

Vendor	Processing Equipment Corporation
Lessor	PEC Financing, Inc.
Purchase Cost	$75,000
Physical Life	10 years
ACRS Life	5 years
ITC	0.1
ACRS Basis	$71,250
Interest Rate	0.14
Loan Term	5 years
Lease Payments	$12,000
Lease Term	5 years
Salvage at end of 5th Year	$22,000
Tax Rate	0.4

ization of the salvage value at the end of the fifth year, which was estimated to be $22,000.

If they leased, the ITC and the salvage value would belong to the lessor. They also pointed out that at a lease rate of $12,000 per year they were effectively paying $120,000 for equipment that sold for $75,000, since to enjoy the use of the equipment for its full physical life would require another five-year, $12,000 per year lease. Those in favor of leasing argued that since the lease payment was tax deductible, the total cost was far less, and that leasing the equipment would leave bank debt available for other projects where leasing was not available, or for emergency cash needs.

SUGGESTED QUESTIONS

1. Compute the loan payment for the purchase of equipment and construct an amortization table to determine the interest expense each year.

2. Using this information, depreciation and other factors in the case:

    a. Compute the net cash flows per year for the loan option.

    b. Compute the present value of these flows discounted at the after-tax cost of debt.

3. Compute the present value of the after-tax lease payments at the after tax cost of debt.

4. What is the net advantage of leasing? Based on this and the other factors, what would you recommend?

Quark Tool Company

Hedging Foreign-Currency Risk

Quark Tool Company was an Iowa based company that never made a single sale outside of the United States. Then the company found itself with potentially the largest single order in the history of the company, but with a catch. An independent agent in Europe reported he was ready to close a deal on the sale of a Model 670 Computer Controlled Automatic Lathe, one of the newest and most sophisticated pieces of equipment in the company's product line. The penetration of the European market by an American company in this field was almost unprecedented, and the sale could open a whole new territory for Quark, if indeed the company could manage the financial problems associated with the sale, and the catch that was mentioned above.

Quark was a typical example of a part of the industrial base of the United States in the mid-1970s. The company had been founded in the 1880s in Cedar Rapids, Iowa, as a manufacturer of industrial tools and lathes. As the economy and the country grew, so did Quark, and by the mid 1950s the company had sales of $40 million, a profit margin approaching 10 per cent, and a very strong market presence in the specialty tool-and-die industry. However, increasing import competition in the 1960s left the company near bankruptcy, and it was only after the purchase of the company by its employees in 1971 that the company was able to maintain itself as a going concern. The last three years had been profitable (see Exhibit 34-1), but this had come only on the strength of major cost-cutting measures and had followed a decade of losses.

Exhibit 34-1   Quark Tool Company: Statement of Revenues and Expenses (in $000)

	197x	197y	197z
Revenues	125,788	154,333	174,333
Cost of Goods Sold	66,543	78,960	97,655
Gross Profits	59,245	75,373	76,678
Operating Expenses	24,335	31,238	36,755
Income Before Interest and Taxes	34,910	44,135	39,923
Interest	11,267	13,544	17,890
Income Before Taxes	23,643	30,591	22,033
Taxes	11,254	14,379	10,320
Net Income	12,389	16,212	11.713

In the mid-1970s, the company had changed its strategic goals, realizing that only through specialization and product differentiation could it survive the onslaught from foreign competition. Until that period the company had manufactured a broad line of specialty tool-and-die equipment, industrial machinery, and various wood and metalworking lathes. However, after the near demise of the company from better and less expensive foreign models the new employee-owners changed tactics. They kept the most popular and most profitable line of their existing products but spent all of their development and marketing resources on design and production of specialty tools with highly sophisticated electronic controls.

This new line had been a moderate success, it carried a much higher price than the typical product, and a single piece of equipment was often priced at $300,000 or more, as opposed to the $75,000 to $125,000 cost of its older product line. Sales had been brisk, but the long lead times for design and production often meant a six-to-nine month delivery schedules, and the finances of the company had been strained by the need to support the investment in inventory during the production of the equipment. However, the company found itself with a modest backlog and growing acceptance of its products by the large industrial manufacturers, and having survived the recession of 1974–1975, Quark had a high degree of confidence in being able to build on the favorable trend of the next three years.

Despite its success, the company was reluctant when approached by an independent manufacturer's representative, Myron Macenko, who wanted the right to market the company's new line in Europe. Arthur Wendle, president and CEO of the company, still harbored memories of how foreign competition had nearly ended the life of Quark, even through the success of the new line had been in part because of the technical superiority of the product to European competition. However, agreeing to allow the independent representative to market the company's product in Europe did not cost anything.

Macenko simply served as a sales agent for the company and was only compensated on the basis of a sale of the product. Wendle signed a five-year exclusive agreement with Macenko for marketing rights in France, Germany, Italy, Belgium, and Greece.

Wendle throught very little of the matter until nine months after he had signed with Macenko, when he received word that the agent had arranged the sale of a large version of the company's Model 670 Automatic Lathe to a firm in Germany. The terms of the deal called for delivery to a freight terminal in Des Moines one year from the date of the contract, and the price was DM 1.25 million, which at the current exchange rate of 40 cents per Deutschmark meant a $500,000 deal. This was substantially above the current quotes the company had been making to its customers, and even after a hefty commission to Macenko, the deal was an excellent one for Quark. Wendle sent the contracts to his legal staff and soon turned to other matters.

The legal staff returned the contracts, approved, but with a memorandum setting forth a problem that Wendle had not realized at the time of making a verbal agreement for the sale with Macenko. The price of the contract called for payment of DM 1.25 million in one year when the equipment was constructed and delivered. The legal memorandum pointed out that while the current exchange rate was 40 cents, the actual amount realized by Quark would depend upon the exchange rate one year from now. The value of the mark had fluctuated substantially in the last eighteen months (see Exhibit 34-2), and a fall in the value of the mark would leave the company with less than its expected price. The way the contract was written, Quark would have to assume all of the exchange-rate risk, for Macenko had stated the purchaser was unwilling to commit to a price in U.S. dollars.

After receiving this communication, Wendle called a meeting of the executive group of Quark to discuss the problems. Milton Poley, vice-president of finance and corporate treasurer, presented three reports from respected economic forecasting services concerning the movement of the mark. The rate of the mark against the dollar as forecasted for one year for the three services in shown in Exhibit 34-3. Poley summarized the forecasts. When Wendle remarked that the forecasts did not help, nobody in the room disagreed with him.

Poley went on to list several options that Quark would have with respect to the exchange-rate risk if they accepted the contract. One alternative would be to accept the risk. He pointed out that in the event that the mark rose against the dollar, the company would make even more money than it had expected from the deal. If it fell, then the losses in the exchange rate would just have to be taken against the potential profit in the deal. Poley said that he could not

Exhibit 34-2 Dollar Value of the Deutschmark, Prior 18 Months

January	0.3550
February	0.3595
March	0.3789
April	0.4123
May	0.4367
June	0.4214
July	0.4568
August	0.4976
September	0.4456
October	0.4267
November	0.4187
December	0.3965
January	0.3761
February	0.3479
March	0.3690
April	0.3863
May	0.3965
June	0.4002

Exhibit 34-3 Forecasts of the Deutschmark One Year from Today

Econosultants Services	0.4480
Corrado International	0.3589
Data Services Centers	0.3950

guarantee anything, but that he expected the forecasts shown in Exhibit 34-3 represented the maximum fluctuations of the mark in the coming twelve months. Wendle however pointed out that in the preceding eighteen months the mark had been outside both the upper and lower boundaries of the forecast.

The second alternative, explained Poley, was to hedge the transaction in the foreign-currency futures market. The mark was selling at .3850 dollars for delivery in one year, and contracts were available in DM 125,000 denominations. Poley said that the company could short ten contracts to cover the deal. He explained that if the mark rose against the dollar, the hedge would lose money, but this loss would be offset to some degree by the increase in dollars received from the DM 1.25 million sale of the equipment. If the mark fell, the gain on the hedge would offset to some degree the loss incurred by having to exchange the DM 1.25 million at a lower rate than .40 dollars. (See data in Exhibit 34.4).

A final method for hedging the transaction would be to create a

Part V: Special Topics in Financial Management

Exhibit 34-4   Relevant Financial Data

Current Exchange Rate, Deutschmark	$0.4000
One-Year Forward Rate	$0.3850
One-Year Borrowing Rate for Deutschmarks	12.00%
One-Year T Bill Rate	10.95%
Future Contract Denomination	DM 125,000

liability in marks equal to the receivable. This could be done by borrowing DM 1.25 million, converting to U.S. dollars, and investing the proceeds for one year in one year T bills. Poley explained that at the end of the year, when the T bills matured, the funds would be converted into marks and used to pay the interest and principle on the loan. Had the mark declined in that year, the loss would be offset to some degree by the profit on the borrowings, because less dollars would be needed to pay back the mark loan. Had the mark risen, the gain on the contract would be offset by the loss on the loan deal, that is, the company would have to pay back more in marks than could be purchased with the proceeds from the liquidation of the one-year T bills.

Wendle agreed that the company should explore some type of hedge, but wasn't sure whether or not the two situations explained by Poley would have the same effect if the mark were to rise as when it falls. He asked Poley to prepare an analysis of the two types of hedges to determine how much the company would gain or lose if each forecast of the rate in one year came true.

SUGGESTED QUESTIONS

1. Show how the computation is made to get the value of the contract to $500,000.

2. What would the value of the deal be if the exchange rate in one year were as the Econosultants forecast? The Carrado forecast? The Data Services forecast? The one-year forward rate?

3. Assume Quark hedges by selling ten contracts, show what the gain or loss on the hedge is and the total value of the deal from the sale and the hedge, assuming

  a. The Econosultants forecast is correct.
  b. The Corrado forecast is correct.
  c. The Data Services forecast is correct.
  d. The one-year forward rate is correct.

4. Assume Quark hedges by borrowing DM 1.25 million, converts the loan to dollars, and invests it in one-year T bills. What is the

total value of the deal (the gain or loss on the hedge plus the dollar value of the sale), assuming
   a. The Econosultants forecast is correct.
   b. The Corrado forecast is correct.
   c. The Data Services forecast is correct.
   d. The one year forward rate is correct.
5. Evaluate your results and make a recommendation for Quark.

Lestrade Laboratories

Tax Computations

As a small, regional commercial laboratory, Lestrade Laboratories, Inc., had led a rather peaceful life. The company had been organized in the early 1900s by John Lestrade, a former Scotland Yard inspector who had left his native Britain for the more sociable climate of Detroit, Michigan. Under the meticulous care and management of a former police official, the company had grown and prospered through the years. The daughters of the founder had remained with the company, so that in late 1983 the company was still being run by a direct descendant of John Lestrade.

Lestrade Laboratories did most of its work on a contract basis with state and local governments and with various private corporations that needed one-time analyses. The company had been relatively small until the mid-1970s, when environmental legislation had substantially increased the demand for chemical analysis of industrial wastes. Lestrade was a $2 million company when it got its first big contract from the Wayne County Environmental Protection Agency to test industrial waste for toxicity. Lestrade was successful in that contract and soon established a reputation as a reliable and independent lab. Government agencies were quick to use the company, as were private industries that wished an unbiased and acceptable source of industrial waste analysis.

The growth of the company in the mid-1970s had led the then president, Irene Adler, to bring in qualified financial managers to keep the company profitable in its new business areas. The vice-president of finance, John Watson, had gradually brought on a professional staff of young M.B.A.s to supplement his own work, and by late 1983 the financial staff consisted of Watson, a controller, and Tobias Gregson, who was director of accounting and taxes. Gregson had recently left a national C.P.A. firm to join Lestrade and had been given responsibility for the accounting system and for tax reporting and compliance.

The problems facing Gregson involved tax analysis of the 1983 income for the company. As he reviewed expected 1983 results, Gregson noted the following areas as ones that demanded his attention.

1. *Reporting on a Normalized or Flow Through Basis.* Lestrade Labs was no different than other companies that Gregson had seen in his work as a C.P.A. in its treatment of depreciation. The company's depreciation expense stemmed almost entirely from its purchase of laboratory equipment. The company had the option of using accelerated depreciation methods and did so whenever it was financially desirable. Since the company was generally profitable, use of accelerated depreciation was a regular practice.

The question facing Gregson was whether or not to report on the income statement using actual taxes paid or tax liability under straight-line depreciation. The concept was the question of flow-through versus normalization, and the issue arose because taxes were lower under accelerated depreciation than they were under straight line. This was due to the fact that the company had made extensive purchases of equipment in the last several years to support its growth. Later in the life of the equipment the straight-line depreciation used for book purposes would be higher than the accelerated depreciation used for tax purposes, but the equipment was still sufficiently young so that accelerated depreciation provided for higher depreciation expense than straight line.

Under the normalization method of accounting, the income statement was presented as though straight-line depreciation had been used in computing taxes. Taxes were computed using straight-line depreciation, although for tax purposes accelerated depreciation was used, which resulted in lower actual tax payments. The difference between the tax liability as stated on the income statement and the actual taxes paid was credited to a deferred tax account.

The rationale for this method was that normalization gave a more accurate picture of the company's financial position. Since accelerated depreciation did not change the total amount of taxes paid but their timing, the argument was that a more level flow of tax payments than low-tax payments early in the life of an equipment purchase and high tax payments late in its life was the appropriate accounting. In normalization, the deferred tax account would increase during the early years of the equipment and then decline to zero as the depreciable life was reached.

The main argument for flow-through was that it presented a report which showed the tax expense as the actual tax payment. Under flow-through, straight-line depreciation is used for the income statement, but the tax liability is the actual taxes paid, using the accelerated depreciation to compute the tax payment in a separate schedule. Where flow-through is used, taxes are low during the early years of the life of equipment and higher during later years. A secondary benefit of flow-through is that during periods of high capital investment, the income statement shows higher net income under flow-through than through normalization because of the lower tax payments.

In analyzing the issue, Gregson learned that the expected income before taxes and depreciation for the year 1983 would be $978,546 and that straight-line depreciation expense would be $367,543. Accelerated depreciation was expected to be $486,234.

The tax schedule that Gregson would be using is as follows:

Exhibit 35-1   Corporate Income Tax Rates, 1983

Amount	Tax
0–$25,000	15%
$25,001–$50,000	$3,750 + 18% of Amount over $25,000
$50,001–$75,000	$8,250 + 30% of Amount over $50,000
$75,001–$100,000	$15,750 + 40% of Amount over $75,000
Over $100,000	$25,750 + 46% of Amount over $100,000
Capital Gains	28%

2. *Computation of the Investment Tax Credit.* Gregson had been informed that purchase of equipment eligible for the investment tax credit had been made during the year. He had asked the controller for a report according to depreciable life and had received the following information.

Equipment with 3-Year ACRS Life	$54,600
Equipment with 5-Year ACRS Life	17,500

3. *Tax on Sale of Equipment.* Gregson had been told that during the year a piece of test equipment had been sold to the state of Michigan. The equipment had originally cost $375,000 five years ago when it was purchased. It was sold for $420,000 and had been carried on the books of the company at its original cost, less depreciation. The net book value on a tax basis was $197,000.

SUGGESTED QUESTIONS

1. Compute the income statement under the normalization method and under the flow-through methods.

2. What difference, if any, is made in net cash flow to the company from choice of one method over the other?

3. Compute the total amount of investment tax credit.

4. Compute the total tax liability to the company from the sale of the equipment. Assume this tax liability is in addition to the taxes from ordinary income.

Southeastern Tennessee Electric Company

Depreciation Methods

The Southeastern Tennessee Electric Company was unusual in many ways, one being that it was the only private stockholder company in the middle of the TVA system in western North Carolina and eastern Tennessee, and another being that despite its name it was headquartered in North Carolina and not Tennessee. Southeastern, as it was known among its employees and customers alike, was located in Andrews, North Carolina, near the Tennessee border. It provided electric power to a small region of western North Carolina and eastern Tennessee.

Southeastern generated electric power from the seven hydroelectric dams it had built along the rivers of its region and from two coal-fired generating plants near Knoxville. The company had been founded in the 1920s to bring electricity to the small towns of the region and to serve the suburbs of Knoxville. The company had survived the depression but had not grown, as TVA gradually took over much of the rural service area and the larger private companies expanded to meet the needs of Knoxville and Asheville. In late 1982 the company had revenues of $152 million and a customer base of 135,000.

The company had been able to prosper for two reasons. One was that a large portion of its power came from hydroelectric sources and was not affected by the rapid rise in the cost of oil and coal that occurred in the mid 1970s and early 1980s. The second was that Southeastern was a regulated monopoly and was given exclusive rights to provide electricity to its service area. No other company could come in and offer customers electricity.

As a regulated utility, Southeastern's rates were set by utility commissions in the states in which it operated. The essence of the regulation was that the company would be allowed to earn a fair and reasonable rate of return. This rate of return was defined as the rate the company would have been able to earn in a perfectly competitive economy, in other words, the cost of capital under competitive conditions. The rates the company was allowed to charge were in theory designed to cover all operating costs and to provide a net income that would yield the shareholders a reasonable return on their investment.

A critical aspect of all public utility was the degree of capital intensity. While normal manufacturing firms had a fixed asset turnover of 3 to 4 times, it was not unusual for a public utility to have a fixed asset turnover of .25 to .50. This meant that while each dollar of fixed assets generated $3.00 to $4.00 in sales for the manufacturing company, each dollar of fixed assets generated only 25 to 50 cents of revenue for a utility. Management of fixed assets was one of the most crucial areas of control for any public utility, and Southeastern was no exception.

Recovery of fixed-asset investments for Southeastern and public utilities was done through depreciation. As a part of the rate-making process, Southeastern was allowed to treat depreciation as an operating expense. This meant that although depreciation was a noncash expense, the company was allowed to recover the expense from the ratepayers through its rates. In this way the company recovered the cost of the equipment over its useful life. For rate-making purposes, the company was allowed to use straight-line depreciation based on the useful life of the asset.

For tax purposes, however, the utility was allowed to compute accelerated depreciation and to base its actual tax payment on accelerated depreciation. The company adopted the normalization method of accounting in working with accelerated depreciation, meaning that for rate-making purposes it computed taxes as though it paid straight-line depreciation. The taxes as computed under straight-line depreciation were considered expenses as far as the ratepayers were concerned, and rates were set to allow the company to recover the taxes as computed under straight-line depreciation. The difference between taxes paid under accelerated depreciation and taxes computed under straight-line depreciation were accrued as deferred taxes.

In 1981 and 1982 there were significant changes to the tax laws, including the computation of depreciation. Prior to 1981 the two major methods of accelerated depreciation were sum of the year's digits and double declining balance. In 1981 and 1982 regulations were enacted to change the rules for property placed in service after those dates. The new laws set up the Accelerated Cost Recovery System (ACRS), which significantly shortened the time over which depreciation took place. Part of the rationale of the new law was that with high rates of inflation, historical cost depreciation harmed businesses, as they were unable to replace the depreciated equipment at its historical cost. By shortening the depreciation period, Congress hoped to stimulate business investment by providing cash flows on a more timely basis.

The fixed-asset accounting for Southeastern was a small department, headed by a director of fixed assets and a small staff. The group was led by Jamie Winters and had responsibility for accounting of all fixed assets in the operations. It was also the responsibility of the group to compute depreciation on a straight-line basis for regulatory purposes and to compute accelerated depreciation for the tax department to use in computing the tax payments.

In early 1983 Winters called his staff together to consider a request that had come down from the company's president. The CEO had requested the Fixed-Asset Accounting Group to prepare an analysis of the impact on the new ACRS system and to focus specifically on the value of using ACRS over the previously employed methods of SYD and DDB. To illustrate and better understand the impact of the new rules, the president had asked the group to demonstrate the impact of the new rules on the proposed purchase of a $500,000 auxiliary generating unit. That unit was placed in service on January 1, 1983, and served as a back-up in one of the coal-fired units in the event of failure of a main generator. Although not usually in service, it was allowed to be described as useful plant and equipment by both regulatory and tax regulations.

In researching the project, Winters found that the equipment under consideration would have a ten-year life for straight-line depreciation for regulatory and reporting purposes, and that it qualified for a five-year life for ACRS purposes. The appropriate ACRS rates are shown in Exhibit 36-1.

The equipment would also qualify for the 10 per cent investment tax credit and it was assumed that this would be taken. Under ACRS, in order to prevent a double tax break, the depreciable basis of the equipment was reduced by 50 per cent of the ITC. There had been no real logic behind this, the 50 per cent had resulted from a compromise between those who wanted to eliminate all of the ITC from the depreciable basis and those who had not wanted to eliminate any of it. The other relevant information in the project was that the equipment was expected to have a zero salvage value. ACRS was

Exhibit 36-1   ACRS Depreciation Rates

Year	3 Year	5 Year	10 Year
1	25%	15%	8%
2	38%	22%	14%
3	37%	21%	12%
4		21%	10%
5		21%	10%
6			10%
7			9%
8			9%
9			9%
10			9%

unaffected by salvage since the depreciation rates were applied against the full basis of the equipment, with any salvage or sale treated as ordinary income when it occurred if it was above book value, but straight-line and SYD methods both reduced the basis by the salvage value.

In examining the rates in Exhibit 36-1, Winters was considering how to show the president that ACRS did provide a benefit over other methods of depreciation, even though the ACRS method looked on the surface as more of a straight-line method over a shorter life.

SUGGESTED QUESTIONS

1. For straight-line depreciation compute the depreciation expense for years 1–10.
  a. Compute the cash flow value of depreciation assuming a tax rate of 46 per cent.
  b. Compute the present value of the cash flows assuming a discount rate of 15 per cent.

2. For SYD depreciation, compute the depreciation expense for years 1–10.
  a. Compute the cash flow value of depreciation assuming a tax rate of 46 per cent.
  b. Compute the present value of the cash flows assuming a discount rate of 15 per cent.

3. For DDB depreciation, compute the depreciation expense for years 1–10.
  a. Compute the cash flow value of depreciation assuming a tax rate of 46 per cent.
  b. Compute the present value of the cash flows assuming a discount rate of 15 per cent.

   4. For ACRS depreciation, compute the depreciation expense for years 1–10.

   a. Compute the cash flows from depreciation assuming a tax rate of 46 per cent.

   b. Compute the present value of the cash flows assuming a discount rate of 15 per cent.

   5. Compare your results. How would your results change if the salvage value of the equipment were very high, say $200,000?

⅄STANDARD⅄ Publishing Company   Standard Publishing Company

Merger—Pooling Versus Purchase

In the highly publicized world of mergers and acquisitions, and headline makers like Bendix, Allied Chemicals, Conoco, and the like, the acquisition of Graphic Designs by Standard Publishing was worth only a small line of type or at most a paragraph in the business-news weeklies. The merger was completely friendly, there were no disagreements about the price on either side, no outside forces, and no acrimony. In short, the proposed merger was a traditional, well-thought-out business transaction that, when it is over, should be beneficial to both parties. The only issue that remained was for Standard to decide if it was going to do a "stock deal" or a "cash deal." It was solely their decision because Graphic Designs was indifferent as long as the price was the same.

In the spring of 1985 Standard was a 122-year-old New York City–based publisher of business and professional books, journals, and magazines. The company published a long list of business and computer-related titles, seventeen business and computer magazines, and three professional journals for the business-computer industry. The company was best described in the words of one security analyst as "old-line solid." The impression was that the company was good, but not spectacular, its business steady and not subject to wide swings and fluctuations in either sales or earnings. The company was often written up, sometimes in its own publications, as a model of a well-run business. The company's stock traded on the New York Stock Exchange and in late spring, 1985, was selling at a very respectable twelve times estimated fiscal 1985 earnings.

Part V: Special Topics in Financial Management

Standard's forecasted income statement for the coming fiscal year and balance sheet for the fiscal year which ended on June, 30, 1985 are shown in Exhibits 37-1 and 37-2. The company expected to have just over a half billion in assets and sales of almost $1.5 billion. The company's debt position was relatively high, but its solid history and its lack of sensitivity to the business cycle gave it the ability to issue an additional $100 million to $150 million in new debt to finance growth. This debt capacity came in part from the very high margins the company enjoyed, a result of entering business areas where it dominated the competition, and in part from a strong control function, which kept both direct costs and overhead far below industry averages. Despite a high debt ratio, the company's interest coverage was so large that the major rating agencies gave the company double-A ratings.

Growth for Standard had come primarily through development of new publications. In the last decade the company had made a few modest acquisitions, all for cash and most at slightly above their book value. Unamortized goodwill would be about $17.5 million in 1985 and it was being written off at a rate of $1.2 million a year. Standard adopted the regular practice of writing off goodwill over a forty year period. The company's policy with respect to acquisitions

Exhibit 37-1   Standard Publishing Company: Balance Sheet

June 30, 1985 (in $000)

	Standard Publishing	Graphic Designs
Cash and Marketable Securities	22,780	4,560
Accounts Receivable	145,890	22,566
Inventory	117,863	8,765
Other Current Assets	6,543	621
Total Current Assets	293,076	36,512
Land	13,455	3,550
Plant and Equipment, at Cost	398,560	12,540
Less Accumulated Depreciation	187,650	4,560
Net Plant and Equipment	210,910	7,980
Goodwill	17,500	0
Total Assets	534,941	48,042
Accounts Payable	44,312	8,765
Accrued Wages and Taxes	56,780	4,321
Short-Term Debt	15,689	4,532
Total Current Liabilities	116,781	17,618
Long-Term Debt	178,950	4,320
Total Liabilities	295,731	21,938
Total Equity	239,210	26,104
Total Liabilities and Equity	534,941	48,042

Exhibit 37-2   Standard Publishing Company: Pro-Forma Income Statement

Year Ending June 30, 1986 (in $000)

	Standard Publishers	Graphic Designs
Net Sales	1,467,895	124,566
Cost of Goods Sold	678,902	68,998
Gross Margin	788,993	55,568
Operating Expenses	417,888	23,498
Operating Income	371,105	32,070
Other Expense Interest	23,788	1,239
Goodwill Amortization	1,200	0
Income Before Taxes	346,117	30,831
Taxes	166,543	13,444
Net Income	179,574	17,387

was to follow the fortunes of small companies in related fields. As these companies grew and prospered, they would be approached by Standard to see if they were interested in a possible merger. If there was an indication of interest, negotiations would be started, and in 62 per cent of the cases these negotiations had led to a successful merger. Once acquired, the companies would be operated as independent divisions, unless there was so much overlap with existing Standard business that a consolidation was cost effective.

The current attention of the acquisitions department of Standard had been focused on an upstate New York company called Graphic Designs. The company had been started seven years ago by three computer engineers who had been working for the nation's largest computer company. They had all done extensive research into computer-aided design and computer-generated graphics, and when their employer expressed little interest in commercial development, they purchased the rights to the technology and set up their own company. Each of the founders contributed $250,000 in capital, and the remainder of the funds came from a venture-capital company. In 1981 the company had been so successful that it was able to repurchase the stock from the venture-capital firm (at a handsome profit to the venture capitalists). In 1985 the company was in the hands of the three founders. Each owned one-third of the one million shares outstanding.

Graphic's business was organized along two major divisions. The CAD part consisted of the purchase of off-the-shelf computer equipment and then modifying it with special memory boards and other peripherals to produce what turned out to be some of the finest equipment available for computer-assisted design work. The equipment was near the top of the range in terms of price, but the quality was so superior that the company enjoyed large sales and possessed a 1.75 year backlog. The second division consisted of computer generated graphics design. This division produced hardware and software that produced high resolution computer-created graphics. The revenues of this division came partly from the sales of equipment to large users, and partly from the sale of in-house graphics services to smaller customers, who could not afford to purchase equipment for themselves.

Standard had been attracted to Graphic Designs for several reasons. One was that Graphic's operations would fit well with the diversification program that Standard had implemented four years earlier. That program had charted a course for Standard in which it would move into new but related businesses. At that time, Standard saw computer services as an outgrowth of the publishing business and Graphic Designs' current businesses certainly fit that need for Standard. A second reason for the interest in Graphic Designs was diversification. Many hi-tech companies relied on a single product and a single technology, and hence were highly vulnerable to any change in the market. Graphic Designs had the lock on the technology but was not dependent on a single aspect of that technology.

A third reason involved the technical superiority of the Graphic Designs products and its engineering staff. The company had attracted some of the finest engineers in the field and its forty-six patents gave it a two-to-three-year lead over its rivals. The company had been putting a greater distance between itself and its competition. If a shakeout in the computer industry were to occur, Graphic Designs would be expected to be one of the survivors. Finally, Standard was impressed by the management team of Graphic Designs. Assuming an acquisition was made, Standard intended to operate the company as a stand-alone division, with as much autonomy as possible. Its feeling was that with Standard's ability to raise capital and Graphic's technical and managerial skills, Graphic Designs would grow and prosper even more than it had in the past.

When Stanley Fair, vice-president of mergers and acquisitions for Standard, first approached Jake Williams, president of Graphic Designs, about a possible merger, Williams was very cool to the idea. However, when Fair mentioned that Standard might be willing to pay as much as $50 million for the company, Williams's attitude changed considerably. After Fair explained Standard's plan to continue Graphics as a stand-alone division, with current management and a heavy capital infusion, Williams eagerly entered into the negotiations. The two men met regularly during April and May, 1985, and Williams made detailed financial statements available to Fair. In mid-May, 1985, Williams stated that he and his partners would sell for $100 million, about eight times projected 1984 earnings and less than six times 1985 projected earnings. Based in part on the

Exhibit 37-3   Information on Common Stock
June 30, 1985

	Standard Publishers	Graphic Designs
Number of Shares	22,000	1,000
P/E Ratio	12	na
EPS, 1985	$6.20	$11.45

financial data shown in Exhibits 37-1 and 37-2 Fair agreed in principle to the deal.

Fair took the proposal to the Executive Committee at Standard for final approval. That committee was composed of Fair, H. James Gentry, the chief financial officer, Benjamin Pierce, the president and chief operating officer, and Lionel Hawes, the chairman of the board. While the company needed board approval for the acquisition, approval by the Executive Committee was tantamount to approval by the board, which almost never objected to any major strategic move by the company. After a formal presentation of the projected financials, the qualitative description of the company, and the justification of the acquisition price, Fair obtained the agreement of the Executive Committee for the merger.

The only question that remained was how was Standard to pay for Graphic Designs. The proposed merger would be the largest ever attempted by the company, and previous mergers had been made by purchasing out of excess cash. However, with the projected year-end balance sheet shown in Exhibit 37-1, it was clear that Standard did not have the cash to make this purchase. Gentry indicated that there were two ways open. If Standard wished to purchase the company for cash, it could sell $100 million in 15 per cent subordinated debentures in a private placement and use the funds for the purchase. Alternatively, it could issue stock worth $100 million at current prices and exchange this stock for the common stock of Graphic Designs. A summary is shown in Exhibits 37-3 and 37-4.

Gentry went on to explain that under the stock plan, the merger would be considered a pooling of interest. However, with the debt plan, the merger would be treated as a purchase. Gentry told the

Exhibit 37-4   Plans for Standard Acquisition of Graphic's

Plan A   Standard sale of $100 million (net) in subordinated debentures, proceeds used to purchase all of Graphic's on a purchase accounting basis.

Plan B   Standard would issue sufficient stock to purchase all outstanding shares of Graphic's at a deal value at $100 million based on current price of the Standard stock. Merger would be a pooling of interest.

committee that there were benefits and drawbacks to each plan. Under the pooling concept, no goodwill would be created to be written off against earnings, but the additional shares that would be issued might reduce the EPS of the company and have a depressing effect on the price of the stock. Gentry pointed out that the stock plan would give large chunks of stock to the current owners of Graphic Designs, but that this would not affect the control of Standard.

Under the purchase arrangement, goodwill would be created to the extent the price was above the fair-market value of the assets of Graphic Designs. Gentry said that his preliminary evaluation of Graphic Designs indicated that the inventory could be written up by $10 million and the fixed assets by $20 million by debiting the accumulated depreciation account. This write-up would increase depreciation expense by $2.5 million in the first year of the merger and increase cost of goods sold by $6 million in the first year. The goodwill that was created would be written off over forty years. Finally, Gentry pointed out that under the purchase plan, the company would incur additional interest expense that would not be present under the pooling plan.

Fair responded that he had discussed the two different approaches with Williams, and that Williams had indicated that the shareholders were willing to accept either of the two plans. Thus it was up to Standard to determine which of the two methods of acquisition it wished to pursue.

SUGGESTED QUESTIONS

1. Construct the balance sheet for the combined companies for June 30, 1985, assuming the merger takes place under a pooling of interest.

2. Construct the balance sheet for Standard after the debt is issued but before the merger takes place.

    a. Construct Standard's balance sheet after the merger takes place by purchase accounting with the proceeds from the debt.

3. Construct the pro-forma income statement and compute EPS for Standard for fiscal 1986 under pooling. Under purchase. Assume a tax rate of 47.75 per cent on *taxable* income.

4. Based on your results, make a recommendation for the way the merger should be done and support it. Be sure to take into account cash and noncash charges in the income statement.

5. List and explain at least three reasons why the type of merger should make a difference to Williams and his partners.

The American Electric Company

Merger Terms

The American Electric Company of Farrington, Connecticut, was one of the most prestigious of all U.S. corporations. In addition to its size, strength, products, and other operating characteristics, it was also known for its ability in the strategic-planning area. In a very real sense, the company operated as a graduate school of strategic planning, as middle- and top-level executives often moved from American Electric to take control of other Fortune 500 companies. It was thus with a certain amount of embarrassment and concern that the company found itself in mid-1985 with the rather lowly price-earnings ratio of seven on its common stock.

The company traced its roots back to Thomas Edison. In 1895, the Utica Electric Company purchased certain patents involving electric motors from the inventor, changed its name to The American Electric Company, and began marketing a more powerful and more efficient line of electric motors. By the 1920s, the company had plants in two dozen states, and it easily survived the 1930s to become one of the major defense contractors during World War II. At the end of the war, the company developed a strategic plan that eliminated its dependence on any one sector of its business. In the postwar period, American Electric devoted its capital resources to providing consumer goods through its small- and major-appliance division, and industrial products through electric motors and parts.

In the 1980s, American Electric was a $5 billion company, with sales coming from three major groups. The defense group manufactured jet engines, jet-aircraft equipment and related parts. The consumer group was involved with major appliances, and the industrial group, with electric motors as its mainstay and a rapid growth component consisting of electronic-control equipment. Despite this diversification, which rendered the company almost immune to the business cycle and gave its shareholders constant if not spectacular growth in earnings and dividends, the company's P/E multiple continued a slide that had begun in the late 1970s. For some reason, it seemed the company was out of favor with investors, although on purely financial grounds it was as strong and prosperous as it had ever been.

In January, 1985, the annual Strategy Conference was devoted to an examination of the company's poor standing in the stock market. At the center of the meeting was a report by the investment-banking firm of Klaus Henry, Inc., which had just completed a thorough review of the company. It included a presentation by top company financial officers on the future sales and earnings outlook. The report concluded that

While the American Electric Company is as well run as ever, with significant prospects for the future, the bulk of its business remains in old-line industrial goods. Growth prospects for the company will be less than others in the position unless the company changes its basic strategy and begins to pursue a more growth oriented strategy.

The report finished with a discussion of the basic businesses of the company and concluded that if American Electric were to once again become a Wall Street favorite, it would have to begin a program of aggressive acquisitions.

At the conclusion of the meeting, the Mergers and Acquisitions Group was charged with locating suitable acquisition candidates. While the group was free to pursue any acquisition it felt was in the best interest of the company, it was requested to concentrate on companies with at least $300 million in sales, in businesses that were complementary to the existing operations of American. Given the company's relatively conservative debt policy, it was strongly recommended that negotiations with potential candidates be done on the basis of a stock deal with a pooling accounting treatment. American had done both cash and stock mergers in the past, and the overwhelming bias in the company was for the merger by exchange of stock, as this method increased the equity of the company without stock-issuing costs and prevented the balance sheet from being loaded with goodwill.

In the spring of 1985 the group vice-president of mergers and acquisitions made an informal proposal to the president of American Electric that the company explore the possibility of merging with the G.S. Foster Company. Kenneth Coffey, who had headed the acqui-

Exhibit 38-1   The American Electric Company: Income Statement

Year Ending September 30, 1985 (in $000)

	American Electric	G.S. Foster
Sales	5,098,765	765,432
Cost of Sales	2,987,564	416,544
Gross Profits	2,111,201	348,888
Operating and Administrative Expenses	876,544	212,329
Operating Income	1,234,657	136,559
Other Income	256,788	54,321
Interest Expense	445,670	23,455
Income Before Taxes	1,045,775	167,425
Taxes		
Federal	412,344	109,876
State and Local	23,670	13,455
Net Income	609,761	44,094
Number of Shares (Year End)	85,200	36,700
Earnings Per Share	$7.16	$1.20

Note: The financial statements have been reconstructed to a comparable basis

sition activity at American Electric told the company's president, Alfred Possman, that the Foster Company appeared to be an almost ideal merger candidate, given the merger profile presented at the strategy meeting. He wanted approval to open up negotiations with his counterpart at Foster with the objective of reaching an agreement in principle that could be taken to the respective boards for approval. Possman gave the approval, and working through the company's investment-banking firm, Coffey held a series of meetings through the spring with officials at Foster.

As a part of the process, Foster provided Coffey with a set of historical financial statements, and a forecast of the company's year-end financial statements. A condensed version of those statements, adjusted for differences in accounting, is presented in Exhibits 38-1 and 38-2, along with the comparable statements of The American Electric Company. Relevant information on the stock of the two companies is presented in Exhibit 38-3. Coffey had studied the prior performance of Foster and had every reason to believe that the information in the projections was valid; he felt confident in making a valuation based on that information.

In late July, Coffey, along with the group vice-president for finance, Perry Dennison, met with Possman to review progress in the merger talks and to determine if the company should make a defin-

Exhibit 38-2 Condensed Balance Sheet for American Electric and G.S. Foster
Year Ending September 30, 1985 (in $000)

	American Electric	G.S. Foster
Total Assets	$4,456,788	$389,776
Total Debt	$2,297,665	$252,344
Total Equity	$2,159,123	$237,432
Total Debt and Equity	$4,456,788	$489,776

Note: The financial statements have been reconstructed to a comparable basis

itive proposal. Coffey reported that the Foster company was sixty-seven years old and had been profitable for the past twenty-two years. Foster's main line of business was equipment-control and metering devices, and its level of technology in the field was considered state of the art. Foster did not have the largest share of the market, but both its digital and analog metering devices were unparalleled in terms of accuracy and precision, and Foster devices were used in every critical project in defense and aerospace applications. The company's stock was widely held, with no single stockholder owning more than 3 percent of the outstanding shares.

Coffey stated that his negotiations with Foster had been friendly, and the question of whether or not to merge really depended upon whether Foster would consider an offer "if the price were right." The purpose of the meeting with Dennison and Possman was to determine what terms Coffey could offer Foster. It was generally agreed that, for a merger the size of Foster, an exchange of common stock would have to be the vehicle of acquisition, but there was very little agreement within the group about the terms of the offer. Basically, a fraction of one share of American would be offered for each share of Foster, but what exactly that fraction would be was the subject of heated discussion.

Dennison's main concern was with the problem of dilution. If American Electric offered to buy Foster at an exchange that resulted

Exhibit 38-3 Relevant Stock Information

	American Electric	G.S. Foster
Price/Earnings Ratio	7	10
Dividends	$2.50	$0.40
Number of Shares	85,200,000	36,700,000
EPS	$7.16	$1.20
Market Price	$50,12	$12.00
Net Income	$609,761,000	$44,094,000

in paying more for EPS for Foster than American was currently earning, the EPS of American would drop and the merger would in effect dilute the earnings per share of American. Assuming the P/E ratio did not change, this would then reduce the share price of American, which as Dennison pointed out was the opposite effect of what the merger program was intended to have. Thus, argued Dennison, the company should not be willing to exchange at a higher ratio than the ratio of EPS of Foster to EPS of American.

Possman pointed out that while Dennison's arguments were cogent, they would result in offering less for Foster stock than the market value. If American were able to offer only the ratio of EPS's, it would be able only to purchase companies whose P/E ratios were lower than its own, since it could not strike a deal that offered lower than current market price. Possman also argued that it was possible that the merger would be seen by Wall Street as a positive step by American and that, as a result, the P/E ratio of American would move to the P/E ratio currently enjoyed by Foster. He suggested that at a minimum the company would have to offer the equivalent value for Foster in American shares, that is, to exchange shares based on the ratio of Foster's price to American's price. This should, he thought, result in at least the current market price for Foster holders and, if the P/E ratio of American rose, then the Foster shareholders would get a price above the current market value.

Coffey then told the meeting that no merger could take place unless the value offered was at least equal to the present value of the shares being purchased; in almost all cases the offer had to be at a substantial premium above the current market. He stated that under Possman's plan, because of dilution, an offering based on the strict ratio of the share prices would result in Foster receiving less than market value unless the P/E ratio of American rose. He argued for an offer of 30 per cent above market value of Foster, stating this was the minimum Foster's officers would be willing to accept. He agreed that this offer would result in dilution, but his discussion with the investment-banking firm serving as adviser to American on the deal assured him that the P/E ratio of American would rise in response to the merger, thus wiping out the effects of dilution.

SUGGESTED QUESTIONS

1. a. What is the current market value of C.S. Foster?
   b. What is the current book value of C.S. Foster?
2. a. Assume that a merger is offered using the exchange ratio of EPS. How many shares of American would be offered for one share of Foster?

    b. What would be the value per share in terms of the current price of American?

    c. What is the net income, EPS, and stock price for American after the merger assuming the P/E remains the same? Assume Foster's income counted for the entire fiscal 1985 year.

    d. What is the value of Foster if, after the merger the P/E ratio stays at seven? Goes to Foster's value of ten?

    e. What is the new price of the stock of American after the merger if the P/E ratio of American goes to ten?

  3. Answer Questions 1A to E above, assuming an exchange based on the ratio of the share prices.

  4. Answer Questions 1A to E above assuming an exchange based on offering Foster 30 per cent above its market price in shares of American.

  5. Evaluate your results. What do they tell you, and what should American do?

Whitaker Manufacturing Company

Convertible Bonds

Jonas Whitaker, chairman of the Board of Directors of Whitaker Manufacturing Company, was faced with what he felt was a typical CEO type problem. He wanted to do something, knew that the thing that he wanted to do was the right thing for the company, but that he would not be allowed to do what he wanted to do because of shareholders, bankers, and other interference. Whitaker wanted the company that bore his name to raise $5 million in new capital to support expected growth over the next five years. Whitaker specifically wanted to issue long-term debt to achieve this purpose, but the current and projected financial statements simply would not allow the company to increase the leverage on its balance sheet by any more than its current levels.

The company's financial statements for 1984 and the forecast for 1989 are shown in Exhibits 39-1 and 39-2. Of critical concern to Whitaker was the state of the balance sheet. Total debt was over 60 per cent of total assets at the end of 1984. The company expected to grow in the coming five years and would be financing a large part of this growth with new debt, both from short-term credit lines and a new long-term debt issue. The result was that, given the company's generous dividend policy, the debt ratio would rise to 70 per cent by the end of 1989, and this would be before the financing of a $5 million requirement. The debt position by the end of 1989 would be extremely high for the company and very high by industry standards. It was possible, but unlikely, that the company could add additional long-term debt to its balance sheet to meet the $5 million

Exhibit 39-1 Whitaker Manufacturing Company: Statement of Income (Consolidated)

	1984	1989 Pro-Forma Before Financing
Revenues	$45,670,000	$88,700,000
Cost of Goods Sold	$27,650,000	$55,800,000
Gross Profit	$18,020,000	$32,900,000
Operating Expenses	$5,679,000	$9,800,000
Interest	$2,350,000	$5,800,000
Income Before Taxes	$9,991,000	$17,300,000
Taxes	$4,050,000	$8,750,000
Net Income	$5,941,000	$8,550,000
Number of Shares	1,500,000	1,500,000
EPS	$3.96	$5.70
P/E Ratio	6	8
Share Price	$23.76	$45.60

need. Only under special circumstances or a special issue could the company expect to increase the amount of debt on its balance sheet. Some type of equity issue was mandated.

Whitaker Manufacturing supplied residential and commercial furniture to retail outlets in the southeastern United States. The company was started in 1867 by two veterans of the Civil War. Their first operations were beside a lumber mill near High Point, North Carolina, and their raw materials were furnished from scraps from that mill. As the economy of the South recovered, the company prospered, and in the mid-1950s it went public, but with the Whitaker family retaining a large block of stock. The next twenty-five years

Exhibit 39-2 Whitaker Manufacturing Company: Balance Sheet

Year Ending Dec. 31 (in $000)

	1984	1989 Pro-Forma Before Financing
Current Assets	18,950	34,500
Fixed Assets	11,432	22,400
Total Assets	30,382	56,900
Current Liabilities	11,234	19,850
Long-Term Debt	10,000	16,000
Preferred Stock	0	0
Common Stock 1,000,000 shares authorized and outstanding	1,500	1,500
Retained Earnings	7,648	14,550
Total Liabilities and Equity	30,382	51,900
Additional Financing Required	0	5,000

represented the most prosperous time for the company. Sales went from a little over $10 million in 1960 to a level of $45 million in 1984. Profits had risen commensurately, and the stock which was originally sold for four dollars a share was selling for over twenty-three dollars a share at the end of 1984.

Whitaker's growth had been primarily financed by internally generated funds and debt. In recent years, the dividend payment had grown substantially, partly to propel the price of the stock upward and partly to provide for income to members of the Whitaker family, which held large blocks of stock. The company had lines of credit with two major North Carolina banks, and its policy was to draw upon these until they reached the maximum, then refund the short-term debt with a long-term debt issue. The long-term debt was usually twenty- to thirty-year debentures, privately placed. Because of the company's profit record, the debt had been relatively easy to place even with the rising debt ratio. In Whitaker's forecast for 1989, long-term debt would increase to $16 million from its current level of $10 million, and current liabilities were expected to increase by over $8 million, although some of this would be noninterest-bearing accruals and payables.

Even with the growth in debt the company expected to find itself short $5 million, and company plans were to raise this sum early in 1985. Jonas Whitaker wanted to raise this money with a $5 million subordinated debt issue. He felt that even with an interest cost of 15 per cent, this would be the cheapest method for raising funds, since interest cost would be tax deductible. In discussions with several investment bankers, Whitaker was told that the 15 per cent was a reasonable number, but they all doubted that the issue could be sold, since it would raise the debt ratio of the company to unacceptable levels. Two of the firms said that they would take the issue, but only on a "best-efforts" basis, and there was no guarantee that the issue could be placed. Any unsold bonds would be returned to Whitaker, and thus the company risked paying the costs of a new debt issue and having little of it actually placed.

The company's attitude about selling stock was that it would avoid such a path if at all possible. The initial public offering had been made to bring in new equity capital and to provide a market for those members of the Whitaker family who wished to sell small portions of their holdings. However, tight control of the company was one of the strategic goals of the owners, and since the initial issue, there had been no sale of common stock. It was this policy which had led the company to its high debt ratio and its problem of financing without access to the debt markets. Unless an alternative could be generated, Whitaker would most likely have to go the common-stock route if it wished to continue its expansion and growth.

After reaching no definitive path with its investment-banking house, Whitaker set up a meeting with Berry and Logan, a local Charlotte investment bank specializing in small companies. Sarah Berry, senior partner in charge of the Charlotte office, had several suggestions for Whitaker. The first was to issue preferred stock. After reviewing the proposal in-house, Whitaker rejected this option on the grounds that it was too expensive. A new preferred-stock issue would cost the company 11.5 per cent after issuing costs, and since the dividends were an after-tax expense, there would be no sheltering of this cost. The idea was completely killed when Berry reported that in her view of the market, such an issue could only be sold on a best-efforts approach.

The second alternative that Berry introduced received a better reception. Her proposal was for a $5 million subordinated, convertible issue of debt. This security would be issued at a conversion price above the current market price of the stock. Assuming that internal projections of growth and profitability were met, the price of Whitaker's stock would rise above the conversion price of the bond. Once that had happened, the company could force conversion by calling the bond, thus converting the debt into equity and relieving pressure on the company's balance sheet. The proposal caught on with Whitaker immediately after Berry concluded that the cost of the issue would probably be in the area of 10.5 per cent, and that as long as the issue was in debt form, the interest would be a tax-deductible expense, lowering the cost even more.

Whitaker asked Berry to explore the market for such an issue, and two weeks later Berry came back with a report that, in her opinion, such an issue was possible, although again it would have to be done on a best-efforts basis. Her recommendation was for a twenty-year, $5 million subordinated, convertible bond. The subordination feature of the bond would allow the company to proceed with its proposed new debt issues without endangering the security of either existing debt or new debt. The issue would carry a cost of 10.5 per cent to Whitaker. Berry said that the prospective purchasers would want call protection, and that the bond should carry a five-year call protection, that is, it would be callable only after five years. Although Whitaker would not be required to call the bond, Berry recommended that the company announce that its intentions were to do so as soon as possible. In this way analysts and investors would regard the issue as future equity, and would discount its importance in calculating the debt ratios of the company.

Given current market conditions, Berry recommended that the bonds be convertible at a price of twenty-seven dollars per share. Given the company's internal projections, as shown in Exhibit 39-1, this would provide for a forced conversion of the issue as soon as it was callable. Even if the future projections were not met, the stock

Exhibit 39-3   Alternatives for $5,000,000 in New Capital

Straight Debt (20 Year)	15.00%
Straight Preferred	100,000 shares at 11.5%
Convertible, Subordinated Debt	10.50% 20-year debentures convertible at $27.00 per share
Common Stock	227,273 shares @ $22.00 per share

should be high enough in five years to allow the company to force conversion. Berry also indicated that her company was prepared to underwrite an issue of common stock at a net price to the company of twenty-two dollars per share. She noted, however, that this would require issuing 227,273 shares to raise the $5 million. She pointed out that after forced conversion at twenty-seven dollars a share, the company would have less shares outstanding for the same amount of capital were it to issue the convertible bond. Details are shown in Exhibit 39-3.

SUGGESTED QUESTIONS

1. **a.** How many shares would each $1000 bond be equal to?
   b. What would the bond's conversion value be at date of issue?
   c. What is the conversion premium for the bond as stock.
2. If the 10.5 per cent bond did not have the conversion privilege, that is, sold as straight debt, what would its value be?
3. If, after the bonds were issued, the stock fell to five dollars per share, what would be the likely price of the bond? Why?
4. If interest rates rose, but the stock price remained constant, what would likely happen to the price of the bond? Why?
5. Reconstruct the 1989 pro-forma income statement for Whitaker for the following cases:
   a. The company has issued straight 15 per cent debt.
   b. The company has issued the convertible debt, and not forced conversion.
   c. The company has issued convertible debt, and forced conversion at the beginning of 1989.
   d. The company sold stock for twenty-two dollars per share in 1984 instead of issuing the convertible bond.
   e. The company financed the deficit with short-term debt until the beginning of 1989, then sold stock at the share price shown in Exhibit 39-1 for 1989.
6. Summarize and interpret the results in Question 5.

CASE 40

The Case of the Beleaguered, Burgled Balance Sheets

Balance Sheet Characteristics

It was one of those typical San Francisco days, by three o'clock the fog and the clouds had made it seem like dusk, and with streetlights lit and the honking of rush-hour traffic, it seemed like a good time to close up early. I was about to tell Nessie to forward my calls to Joe's back booth when I heard the door to the outer office open and saw Nessie admit the kind of client you don't mind staying late for. She was tall, troubled, and not wearing the kind of rags you pick off the rack at K Mart.

I opened a fresh pack of smokes as Nessie called on the intercom, *"A new client, Sam. Do want to see her today or should I ask her to make an appointment?"*

I told Nessie to tell her to wait for five minutes, then bring her in. I wanted to beat her to the punch, so when she came in I told her what I thought had brought her to a medium-class private eye with a reputation for keeping the police out of affairs the police usually belonged to.

"Look, honey, you're two years out of Stanford, working a master's degree in comparative lit., part-time, while you sling hash at an all-night diner in North Beach. Your boyfriend promised to marry you after you got him through a Ph.D. in Chaucer, and now he and his diploma are gone.

"You want me to find him and put some heat on him for treating you this way."

She looked at me with real squinty eyes and muttered, "Close, Sam," and I immediately liked the way she took up my first name.

"I got a B.A. in accounting from Cal., and I'm working on an M.B.A. at night from State. I'm a financial analyst at Bank of United States, and I told my boyfriend to scram when he couldn't come up with his share of the rent. I'm talking to you because somebody is out to get me at the bank and I need help."

So, it was the old get-the-new-girl-on-the-block routine. I'd seen it last year in a case in Silicon Valley, and now it looked like the scam had moved to the city.

"So it's personal protection you want. Well, it can be expensive, but I guarantee you nobody will come close to you that you don't want to get close to you."

"Right on target again, Sam." She snarled at me with a slight sarcastic twinge. *"It's not me they want, it's my promotion, and unless I put some files back together someone other than me is going to be head of the bank's new planning group."*

I told Nessie to put some coffee on and be prepared to stay late, but Nessie told me to shove it and walked out. It had been that way ever since Gloria Steinem had been in here asking me for help in the kidnapping of her eyeglasses. I put the coffee on myself and settled back to listen to an old story with a new twist.

It took a while to get the whole picture, what with the sobbing and light crying, but I finally pulled myself together enough to understand. It turned out that Heather Lockliss had spent two years as an analyst with the bank, being given more and more authority until she was next in line for a coveted spot as head of the systemwide Financial Planning Group. She and two other young turks were angling for the ticket to the executive washroom.

Late last night Lockliss had been given a file on five companies that had applied to the bank for a line of credit. Her job was to review the statements and make a report to the Friday-morning Loan Committee. All the top officials of the Bank would be there, including Mr. Big (James Big, president and CEO), and a good presentation would put her first in line for the promo.

Heather had put the material in her desk at 5:30 last night, but when she got there this morning the desk had been rifled. All the material was still there, but the papers were all mixed up and the tops containing the names of the companies had been chopped off. All she had was a mixed-up bunch of financial statements and a one-way ticket to a teller's booth. Whoever was out to get her hadn't played favorites. A second copy left with the other analyst had the same treatment. There was no way to tell which statements belonged to which companies.

I asked her to give me what she had, which wasn't much. The five companies were (1) The American Greedy Telephone Company, big talkers who ran local telephone companies all around the country,

(2) Hi-Charge National Bank, a local concern whose forte was change for a five spot, (3) South Buffalo Meatpackers, their motto was "Sell it or Smell it," (4) Fly-By-Night Airlines, they'd take you where you wanted to go provided you didn't ask too many questions, and (5) Ptomaines Drug Stores, a national chain with a questionable reputation. They put the cigarettes right next to the cough medicine.

The best piece of evidence was a schedule Heather had worked up just before she left. It showed the balance sheets of the five companies as a per cent of total assets. It wasn't much to go on, but I marked it Exhibit 40-1 and told her for a dinner date and a C-note a day I'd help her out. She took me up on both offers, let me in the office with her employee pass, and I started to do some snooping on my own. Dinner fell apart when she told me she didn't go to restaurants that gave out game cards.

The next afternoon I called Heather over to my office. I told her I had something for her and not to worry, the presentation would take place Friday as planned.

"Have you got the material, do you know who did it?" she asked in that whiny little voice that irritated everyone so badly.

"Yeah, I know who did it. Last Monday, after you left, you let yourself in through the employees after-hours door. You took the folders from both your office and your co-worker's, did the surgery on the papers, and put them back. You kept a copy some place so you could pull it out at the last minute at the meeting tomorrow and make the grade.

Exhibit 40-1   Balance Sheet

December 31, 1984 (as a Per Cent of Total Assets)
COMPANY

	A	B	C	D	E
Cash	29.3	1.5	12.1	9.7	5.8
Accounts Receivable	0.1	4.2	12.2	50.4	7.3
Inventory	0.1	0.8	11.9	3.9	52.9
Net Plant	0.7	87.8	53.6	31.6	30.3
All Other Assets	69.8	5.7	10.2	4.4	3.7
Total	100.0	100.0	100.0	100.0	100.0
Payables	5.7	7.4	12.8	15.7	20.3
Other Current Liabilities	88.6	2.3	4.6	3.3	11.0
Long-Term Debt	1.6	39.9	56.7	40.1	22.8
Other Liabilities	0.5	7.5	5.8	11.4	4.1
Preferred Stock	0.0	4.1	0.2	1.2	0.0
Equity	3.6	38.8	19.9	28.3	41.8
Total	100.0	100.0	100.0	100.0	100.0

It's too bad, baby, but somebody's going to take the fall for this one, and it's going to be you."

She looked at me with those squinty little eyes and said in that calm, collected voice I had heard from a thousand other dames in the same position, "Nice try, Sam. Monday night I was in Vegas on a junket. Here's the airline ticket, rental car receipt, and a notice from the casino that unless I settle my tab they're going to break a couple of knee caps."

Well, you don't always strike pay dirt, but I told her to go back to work and at five o'clock I would have the five companies sorted out for her. As she left I took out Exhibit 40-1 and asked myself how in the world I was possibly going to do that.

SUGGESTED QUESTIONS

1. Help Sam out. Figure out which companies are A, B, C, D, and E.

2. Who really did the caper?

PART VI

Microcomputers and Spreadsheet Programs

CHAPTER 1

An Introduction to Personal Computers

THE PERSONAL COMPUTER

A personal computer is just that, a computer designed for use by a single individual. In this way, it is different from the minicomputer or a mainframe. Until the advent of personal computers, computers were large, multi-user machines, which performed a variety of tasks for a large number of individuals within an organization. The personal computer changed all that, allowing individuals to have their own machines. While personal computers can be linked in so-called networks, the most predominant use of a personal computer is still one person, one machine.

In terms of operations, a personal computer is no different than any other computer. Many people think of computers as smart; in fact, they are only logical. The best way to think of any computer is as a very loyal, very fast servant, capable of doing things that any human being could do if given enough time. If you enjoy giving orders, knowing that no matter what you command, the thing will do, you will get great satisfaction from a personal computer. Even if you do not have this desire for command, you can still take some satisfaction from the fact that a computer will make every effort to do whatever you tell it.

A computer has mathematical integrity, but it will execute any command given to it, regardless of its truth. By mathematical integrity, we mean that the computer will add two plus two and get four, all the time. You cannot, within most systems, override this internal mathematical integrity. The computer will perform mathematical functions correctly to as many decimal points as you would ever need, each computation taking only a fraction of a second. Indeed,

223

the major, but not only, advantage of a computer is its ability to perform complex or simple mathematical tasks in a very short time and to do them with such reliability that the answer is correct without any additional confirmation.

You should not, however, confuse mathematical prowess with intelligence. While a computer may produce the correct mathematical answer, there is no assurance that the numbers entered into the computer were the correct numbers or that the particular activity that was performed was indeed the correct activity for the information required. Assume, for example that you are constructing a computer program that will produce an income statement. You may, either through ignorance of accounting or through a simple mistake in entering the instructions to the computer, tell a computer to find the net income by taking the income before tax and adding the tax expense to it. Since the computer has no accounting background and has never sat for a C.P.A. or even filled out its own tax return, it has no idea that the correct procedure is to subtract the tax expense, so it will cheerfully give you the wrong answer, carried to as many decimal points as you desire.

The above example does not mean the computer was not acting logically. Logic to a computer means doing things in a rational, consistent manner. For example, if you tell the computer to find the value of X in the following expression,

$$X = A + ((B-C)^*D)^5 \qquad (1)$$

it will take the value of B, subtract C from it, multiply the answer by D, raise that result to the fifth power and then add the value of A to it. If instead, equation (1) is written as follows,

$$X = A + B-C^*D^5 \qquad (2)$$

which is the same expression, without the parentheses, then the computer will take the value of D, raise it to the fifth power, multiply that result by C, subtract that value from B and add the value of A to get the value of X. The numerical result will be significantly different from the result in (1), even if A, B, C, and D are the same numbers in (1) as they are in (2).

The point is that the computer is a very literal animal. Unless what you request violates mathematical conventions, such as asking it to divide by zero, and unless you fail to provide it with the proper information in the proper format, the computer will do exactly as it is told. This is both its strength and its weakness. As a machine which will do exactly as it is told, it is 100 per cent reliable. You can generally count on any operation being performed as requested, without having to go back and recheck the answers. However, though it will do exactly as it is told, it has no way of telling you whether what you have asked it to do, while internally consistent, violates some proper method of doing things. The computer merely computes, it does not pass judgment on the sanity of what it does.

THE MAKEUP OF A PERSONAL COMPUTER SYSTEM

The popularity of the personal computer has spawned an entirely new industry, the manufacture of equipment that is added to a system. This extra equipment can make a personal computer do things faster, in more colors, and in all sorts of different ways. In effect, a personal-computer system is very much like a car, you can get the basic model which will provide you with transportation, or you can add an almost unlimited number of options which allow you to make the trip easier and more comfortable, without changing the nature of the car. In terms of getting you from A to B, though, the basic automobile does just as well as the one loaded with options.

There are a seemingly infinite number of options for a personal computer. We want to focus on those most critical to operations:

1. The Monitor.
2. The Keyboard.
3. The Central Processing Unit and Internal Memory.
4. The External Storage System.
5. The Printer.

A typical setup for a personal computer work station is shown in Figure 1-1.

Figure 1-1   A Typical Setup

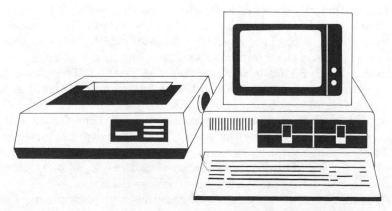

The Monitor

The activity that is done on a personal computer is viewed on a televisionlike screen called a monitor, or cathode ray tube display. In some cases the monitor is actually a home TV set, although this is generally not desirable since the resolution of the screen is usually not sufficiently detailed for most computer work. The best monitor is one that is specifically designed for use with a computer.

Monitors come in either color or monochrome versions, and the monochrome may or may not have graphics display capabilities. Color monitors add nothing to the ability of the computer to do its basic functions; their chief benefit is in the display of graphics. The ability to display in color comes at the cost of higher resolution, though, and unless color graphics are required, a monochrome monitor is equal to or superior to a color monitor. The color monitor may be either a composite video signal or RGB. There are technical differences between the two, but essentially the RGB monitor gives greater resolution and is the one recommended for any color work.

The monochrome monitors are typically green or amber on a black screen, although white on black is also available. The monochrome monitors are also less expensive. The drawback to a monochrome monitor is that it cannot be used for graphics display without special modifications to the computer, and when it is used for graphics the display will be inferior to the color RGB monitor. However, since the majority of applications in the business community for a personal computer are text and number related, the lack of graphics capability of a monochrome monitor is usually not an issue. In some systems the monitor is built in. The Compaq portable computer has a nine-inch monochrome green screen with graphics capability. The monitor may have its own switch, or it may automatically turn on when the computer is switched on.

When the computer is in operation, the letters and numbers that are entered into it are simultaneously shown on the monitor. In effect, the monitor serves as a piece of paper, showing what the operator has written. A key to understanding the monitor is the cursor. The cursor is a blinking space or indicator which shows exactly where you are on the monitor. As you type in letters and words, the cursor will automatically move to the next position. The cursor is also moved by using the keyboard, and for most programs this is done by special keys called arrow keys, or by a combination of shift keys and letter keys. There are typically four of them, for the four directions, and depressing the proper one will move the cursor in that direction. Cursor movement is dependent upon the program and system you are using, however, so always check before starting a program to determine exactly how to move the cursor.

It is important to use the cursor movement keys in moving the cursor, and not the space bar or the backspace key. The space bar is actually a character key to the computer, an invisible space. In other words, there is a character there, but you cannot see it. The cursor keys are best for moving the cursor. That is what they are designed for and they can help you to avoid embarrassing and difficult-to-correct errors.

The Keyboard

The typical computer keyboard is derived from the electric typewriter. While every make and model has a different keyboard, they have enough similarities so that once you are familiar with one, it is very easy to switch to a different machine. The keyboard for the typical personal computer is shown in Figure 1-2.

The first thing one notices about the keyboard for a personal computer is that it has a larger number of keys than the typical electric typewriter. These keys can be divided into the following categories.

1. *The Letters and Numbers.* These keys correspond to the keys on a typewriter. In most cases they are laid out in the same format as a typewriter, and they are used in the same way as a typewriter. The keys are lowercase, and the uppercase letters, or capitals, can be accessed by depressing a shift key while striking the letter key. Capitals can be engaged continuously by pressing a "capitals lock" key, but be careful. On some machines this key may only provide for capital letters. To use the symbols, punctuations marks, and other items that lie above a key, such as the @ symbol which is above the number 2, the capital lock key may not work. On the IBM PC, for example, this can only be used by depressing the shift key at the same time as striking the number 2 key.

A word of caution is necessary in discussing the keyboard. On a regular typewriter, some number keys and letter keys are interchangeable. You might, for example use the lowercase L in place of the number 1, since both look almost the same on the paper. You cannot do this in using a personal computer. The computer treats all letters as letters only. You must be specific in designating letters

Figure 1-2   The Typical Keyboard

F1	F6	Esc	1	2	3	4	5	6	7	8	9	0	−	=	←		Lock 1		Lock 2
F2	F7	Tab	Q	W	E	R	T	Y	U	I	O	P	[	]		Ent	Pg	↑ Up	−
F3	F8	Shift	A	S	D	F	G	H	J	K	L	:	;	"		←	Hme	→	+
F4	F9	Ctrl	\	Z	X	C	V	B	N	M	<	>	/	Shift	●	End	↓ Dwn	
F5	F10	Alt										Caps Lock		Insert		Delete	

and numbers. Similarly, the lowercase X cannot be used as a multiplying symbol, as the computer reads this as a letter. In most systems the askerisk, *, is used as the multiplication symbol. You should always check whatever program you are working with to determine exactly what arithmetic function corresponds to what symbol on the keyboard. Most programs will operate as follows:

+	Addition
−	Subtraction
*	Multiplication
/	Division
∧	Power

2. *The Shift Keys.* A personal computer has a shift key for capitals sometimes designated with an arrow, and this key works the same way as a shift key on a typewriter. However, a computer may have the keys perform other functions too. In order to use the keys for the other function, a control key or an alternate key is sometimes on the keyboard. These keys operate as second and third "shift" keys and allow the keyboard to perform a large number of functions. For example, with some computers and some word-processing programs, holding down the control key and a specific letter key at the same time might cause the cursor to move, cause an indentation at the beginning of a paragraph, or cause a paragraph to reform itself from single spaced lines to double spaced lines.

3. *Special Function Keys.* A third grouping of keys is special-function keys. These keys are what strongly differentiate a computer keyboard from a typewriter keyboard. Some of these keys have a specific task, and some are programmed by the particular software (computer program) that you happen to be using. Among the most useful of these keys is the escape key, often with ESC on it. This key will erase your last entry or will enable you to get out of difficulty if you have done something wrong and have to start all over again. Other special-function keys are the "print screen" key, which causes the printer to print a copy of the entire screen, a delete key, which will delete the letter at the cursor, and movement keys that will move the cursor a page at a time.

On the IBM and some related computers, some special-function keys are found on a numeric key pad. The numeric key pad is usually in addition to the numbers on the top row of the computer, but performs the same function. The arrangement of numbers in a numeric key-pad sequence makes it easier to enter large batches of numbers. On the IBM, the cursor movement keys are also on the numeric key pad and those cursor keys will be used unless the key above the cursor pad, called NUM LOCK is pressed once. In that case the numbers will be entered when the numeric pad is used. To get back to the cursor movement keys, press NUM LOCK again. The NUM LOCK key is what is termed a toggle switch. Pressing it once engages the function, pressing it again turns if off.

One group of special-function keys is generic, in that they will perform any special function that is programmed for them. On the IBM there are ten of these keys to the left of the main keyboard section. They are simply labeled F1, F2, F3, and so forth to F10. Not every program uses them and you have to know how a specific program uses the special-function keys in order to take advantage of them. On the Lotus 1-2-3 spreadsheet program, for example, depressing the F1 key puts the help screens on the monitor, allowing you to temporarily interrupt your work and learn more about whatever it is you want to do with the program. When you are through using the help function, depress the ESC key to return you to the worksheet. Almost all programs will use the function keys and the shift-type keys to allow you to do certain operations.

4. *The Enter or Return Key.* One key is critical to the operation of the keyboard and the personal computer. It is known as the enter key, and sometimes called the return key, because it is similar in position if not in function to the return key of an electric typewriter. The key is usually located just to the right of the main part of the keyboard, and will have the word "Enter" or "Return" or a bent arrow on it. This is the key that actually enters the data you have typed, or the instructions you have given, into the memory of the computer. Until this key is depressed, everything you have done may show up on the screen of the monitor, but it is not inside the computer.

In effect, what the enter key does is tell the computer that you are ready for it to accept some data. For example, you may be working with a program that prompts or questions you to "Enter the Sales for the Past Quarter." If you type $1,234,333 and do nothing else, you can expect the numbers to sit there, just staring at you on the screen. The computer does not know you are finished, and being a patient beast (you can go off for hours and it just sits there waiting for you to continue), it waits for you to tell it you are finished writing the number. This is done by pressing the enter key. In a few cases, a computer can accept input without the enter key; for example, when it is looking for a yes or no answer it can go ahead as soon as you have typed "yes" or "no." In most cases, though, you must press the enter key in order to get the information into the memory of the computer.

The Central Processing Unit

The central processing unit (CPU as it is known in computerese) is the heart of the machine. It contains all of the circuits and chips that make the machine go. A personal computer is built around a single chip, whose design and dimensions define what the computer can do and how fast it can do it. The key chip, known as a microprocessor, is the key element in computing, and the main reason why an IBM PC is different from an Apple IIe and why a DEC Rainbow is different from an Apple Macintosh.

The chips are frequently categorized around how many bits of information they handle in each transaction. The Apple II is built around an 8-bit chip, meaning it handles 8 bits of information in each processing action. The IBM PC and the majority of personal computers used in the business world are 16-bit machines, built around a chip known as the 8088 made by the Intel Corporation. The Apple Macintosh is built on a Motorola microprocessor that handles 32 bits of information at a time. In general, the more powerful the chip, the better and faster the machine, but this does not mean that the 32-bit machine is a more desirable computer than a 16-bit machine, or that the 16-bit machine is more functional than the 8-bit machine. The utility of the machine is determined by its ability to meet the needs of the user, and that can only be judged by comparing an actual computer with the specific requirements of the operator.

The popularity of the 16-bit machine is not based on its technical superiority but on the wide array of applications software written for that type of machine. One of the major misconceptions about the personal computer is that one must be a programmer in order to get full use and value from it. The opposite of that situation is closer to the truth, in that the majority of users have little or no programming knowledge. They use the machines with preprogrammed software, and among the most popular are the electronic spreadsheets which are covered in the second section of this chapter and the remaining chapters. The utility of a computer is not in its power or speed but in the job it can do for the user.

The CPU is probably the most critical part of the personal computer, but it is also the part for which the least amount of knowledge is required by the user. The reason for this is that the CPU operates without any necessary activity by the user. In effect, the relationship between the CPU and the user should be that between an individual and the telephone. The modern telephone is a complex system of electronics, a very sophisticated piece of machinery that can perform all sorts of communications tasks. However, use of the telephone requires no knowledge of its technical operations, only the knowledge of how to make it do what you want it to do. The personal computer's CPU is the same way, it can be fully utilized without understanding the technology. And that is exactly how most users function.

Storage Devices

A computer is said to have a memory. The difference between a computer and a regular typewriter is that once you have typed the character, the typewriter has done its job. It no longer remembers what you typed, and is ready to accept the next character.

A computer has an internal memory as part of the CPU, it remembers what has been entered in it. Unfortunately, with the exception of "bubble" memories, which are not usually available on personal computers, once the computer is turned off it has instant amnesia. Thus, in order for a computer to be effective there must be some way of storing the information so that a program or data does not have to be entered all over again.

Typically, computers use one of three types of storage devices. Small home computers use a cartridge that is plugged into the computer. The cartridge is made up of a read only memory chip (ROM) which contains the information hard wired in the chip. When the cartridge is inserted into the machine the computer reads the instructions from the chip. This type of memory device is not suited to a personal computer, though, because new information cannot be written onto the chip. The computer can take information already on the chip, but it cannot update or alter the chip. This makes the cartridge suitable for computer games and similar activities but impractical for business operations, for which user-provided data must be stored.

A second type of storage device is magnetic tape. Some early personal computers and some home computers use recording tape and a tape recorder as their storage medium. This is an improvement over the cartridge because new data and programs can be written onto tape and the programs and data on tape can be modified. However, for personal computers, tape storage is relatively slow; that is, it takes a long time for the computer to find the information on the tape, and read it from the tape or to write information onto the tape. Coleco's Adam home computer utilizes a high-speed tape drive, but so far tape has not been the major storage medium for personal computers.

The third and most popular type of off-line storage for personal computers is an electronic disk. The disks comes in various sizes, with the 5¼-inch floppy disk being the standard although some machines use an 8-inch disk and the Apple Macintosh uses a 3½-inch disk. The disks have a magnetically sensitive surface which allows the computer to write data onto the disk and read data from the disk. The advantages of the disk system are its speed, its relative low cost, and its relative high capability in storing large amounts of information. In some cases the disk can store more information than can be held in the computer's memory.

The computer reads the disks by means of a disk drive. This device turns the disk so that its "heads" can pick off the relevant information. A disk drive may be built into the CPU or it may be a separate unit. On most newer machines, one or two drives are built into the unit. Two is the more desirable configuration. The reason for this is that with two drives, a program disk can be in one drive and a data disk can be in the other. The computer can read instructions from the program disk and read and write data to the data disk without having to stop while the user changes disks, as is the case with the single-disk system. Depending upon the type of machine and the type of drives, a disk might be single-sided or double-sided. The advantage of double-sided drives is that a larger amount of data can be stored on one disk. Single-sided disks should not be used on double-sided drives.

The standard disk is a 5¼-inch floppy disk. It is designed to be inserted and removed from the drive as necessary. A second type of disk that is common in personal computers is the "hard" disk. This is a higher capacity storage disk that is built into its drive, that is, it cannot be removed as the floppy disk is. The drive itself may be built into the computer or it may exist as a separate item linked by cable to the machine. The advantage of a hard disk is that with its high-storage capacity, a large number of programs that are frequently used can be stored on the disk. The programs can be used by calling them into the computer's memory from the disk, and one does not have to insert a floppy disk or, more importantly, worry about damage to a floppy disk. The hard disk is particularly useful if you are switching between programs, that is, using a spreadsheet program to develop a table to be inserted into a word-processing table. Also, because of its high-storage capacity, a hard disk is useful for storing large amounts of data that would be used in a data base.

The disk drives must be designated if you are using more than one, because the computer must know which drive to go to to obtain information and which drive to write information to. External drives should be labeled, A and B, and A is the default drive or the first drive the computer would look to for information. If the drives are built in, the left-hand drive is usually Drive A and the right-hand one Drive B. If half-height drives are used, they may be stacked one on top of the other, in which case the top drive is typically Drive A and the bottom drive is Drive B. You should also consult an operations manual before working on a machine for the first time, to determine which is Drive A and which is Drive B, otherwise you may never get going. The hard disk is typically labeled Drive C, but again you should always check the operations manual for the exact designation.

Printers

The information put into the memory of the computer can be displayed on the screen of the monitor, and the output of the computer program can also be displayed, but the monitor is not a suitable device for conveying information to a third party. In order to make a permanent record of your input or output you need a printing device. The printer is used to make a listing of your coding in your program so that it can be examined, modified, debugged, or given to another person, and the printer is used to produce a hard copy of your output so your results can be shared with other persons.

There is a large number of different types of printers available for personal computers, but the two most common types are dot-matrix and daisy-wheel printers. The dot-matrix printer works with a printing head that is composed of wires that form each letter by having the ends of some of the wires press ink against the paper. This method produces the typical "unfilled" letters that we associate with computer generated printing.

The advantage of the dot-matrix printer is that it is fast and inexpensive. Some dot-matrix machines are advertised to print as fast as 160 CPS (characters per second), although in typical uses speeds at 40 CPS to 80 CPS are more likely. The disadvantage is the quality of the print. While advances have been made with dot-matrix printers so that some expensive ones print almost letter quality, most are not suitable for letter writing or for a presentation. However, for a draft or work where high quality of printing is not needed, a dot-matrix printer is by far the best machine. Also, for graphics output, such as a bar graph or a line graph, the graphics printer is the one to use. Daisy-wheel, letter-quality printers either cannot do graphics at all or are very slow at the task.

The second major type of printer is the letter-quality, daisy-wheel printer. It derives its name from the printing process. The letters are at the end of spokes, in a small plastic wheel. The printer positions the proper spoke on the paper, and strikes it with a hammer through a ribbon. Since the wheel must turn to the correct letter, and the whole print mechanism moves to the proper space on the paper, a daisy-wheel printer is usually slower than the dot-matrix printer. However, the print is letter quality (the standard by which letter quality is usually judged is the printing from an IBM Selectric typewriter), and the more expensive daisy-wheel printers can print at speeds of 40 CPS and higher.

The printers themselves, particularly the dot-matrix printers, are very versatile and are capable of doing a large number of "tricks." The dot-matrix printer, for example, can approach near-letter-quality type by making multiple passes over line, moving slightly off the letter at each pass so that the dots begin to fill in the spaces and the character fills up. The printer is controlled with printer-control codes or with commands in the particular software you are working with. Lotus 1-2-3, for example, has a section where you can specify the printer codes before printing a spreadsheet. To fully control the printer, consult the printer manual or the documentation of the software you are using.

One final word of caution. Most printers have a small memory and store the printer-control codes. This means that as you change from one software package to another, or from one print task to another, the printer might operate using the previous set of control codes. The safest thing to do is to shut off the printer for a few seconds, which will cause its memory to lose whatever information was transmitted to it. Turning the printer back on puts the printer on the default settings, and then you can go forward with your work. This is particularly important if someone else has been using the machine and you start up without going from a cold start.

THE DOS SYSTEMS

Every computer has to have a basic housekeeping set of programs and instructions which tell the computer how to operate. For most personal computers this set of programs is known as the disk operating system (DOS). Although a number of DOS's exist, the two industry standards are the MS-DOS, the microsoft disk operating system, which is used on most 16-bit computers, such as the IBM and its compatibles, and the CP/M system. The system will come on a disk for disk-operated machinery and the disk will contain a number of very useful and very necessary programs.

One of the most important functions of the DOS is to enable preprogrammed software to run on the machine. Almost all preprogrammed software must have certain DOS programs in it to run, but since the DOS package belongs to someone other than the program company, the software is shipped without these programs. This means that before any system can be run for the first time, the appropriate DOS programs must be loaded onto that disk. This is done in a procedure called an install process, and it is explained in the documentation with all software. Fortunately, once the install process is done, it never has to be done again, so unless you are using software for the first time you need not worry about this. However, if you are using a new piece of software, be certain to consult the documentation for the proper installation procedure, otherwise it just will not run.

A major function of DOS for the user is that it provides an operator with a variety of useful programs that make operating a personal computer much easier. The DOS programs include demonstration programs, which teach the basics of operating the computer, and utility programs, which allow a user to do a large number of housekeeping chores. The most commonly used DOS programs are probably the copy programs. These programs allow you to copy a single program (sometimes called a file) or an entire disk to a new disk. This is very important, because you must keep back-up copies of your work in case of accidental damage or erasure of the primary disk. You should be warned, however, that it is illegal to make back-up copies of copyrighted software unless you purchased the software yourself and use the copy only for yourself. Many software programs are "copy-protected," which will defeat the copy program in the DOS.

Other useful DOS programs allow you to obtain a directory of your disk, that is, a listing of all the programs or files on the disk, programs that allow you to erase, and programs that check the disk to see how much space has been used and how much is left. This last is very important, since a full disk will not take additional information, and in some cases the program will "crash." A crash does not mean anything physically has happened to the equipment, but it does mean that the computer will have to be restarted and that anything you have done that has not yet been saved to a disk is lost. A crash almost always means having to redo something.

DISK HANDLING AND CARE

The two things that are handled the most by the user of a personal computer are the keyboard and the disks. No special instructions are needed for the keyboard, just type the characters that you want to type. But disks need special handling and care, and the failure of a disk can mean the loss of several weeks worth of work. The following comments apply directly to the use of a 5¼-inch floppy disk, but the practices are good for using with any system and any disk type.

A floppy disk is a fragile thing. It should be handled as little as possible. The disk is enclosed in a cardboard jacket. It should be picked up by holding the cardboard cover. Avoid touching the exposed part of the disk. Disks should be stored upright in their paper jackets in a plastic case. Laying them flat will not damage them, but the flat disk almost always gets something placed on it. Disks do not like heat or dust, and an inexpensive plastic case is the best place for them when they are not in the computer.

Insert disks in the computer after removing the jacket. The manufacturer's label should be up, and the notch on the left. The disk should slide easily into the disk drive, and the door of the disk drive should then close easily. The disk drives themselves require little care or concern, but there are two rules to obey. The first is to never remove a disk when the drive is operating. A small red light will be on when the drive is rotating. As long as the light is on, leave the drive alone. If the system gets hung up and the drive continues to run long after it should have stopped, shut off the computer and restart. The second rule is to leave the doors of the drive open after removing the disk, closing them causes the heads that read the disk to touch. With disk drives, the rule of "shut the door after you leave" is not valid.

Every disk should be labeled, and most disks are sold with a peel-off adhesive label that is stuck to it. Ideally, this label should be written upon before it is affixed to the disk, but sometimes this is not possible. If you have to write on a disk label after it is on the disk use a felt-tipped pen and press softly. Most labels have several lines, so be sure to leave room for updating or adding new information. A new label can be pasted over an old one, but this cannot be done too many times.

SAVING AND FORMATTING

The reason you want to be careful with the disks is that a lot of blood, sweat, and tears, not to mention time, has often gone into the program or file that is on the disk. A disk can be replaced cheaply, but the data on it may take days to replace. Usually the way to get data on a disk is to type it in through the keyboard. A very good policy when working in any system is to stop every so often and save your work on the disk, even if it is incomplete. A program or file is saved to a disk by giving the file a proper name and using the save function of whatever system or program you are in.

Saving as you go along is useful because it protects you against all sorts of mistakes. A power failure will erase all of the computer's internal memory, so in the event of a power failure all you have is what has been saved on the disk. It's a lot easier to start again from where you last saved on the disk, and that can be done by calling the file back into the computer's memory. Admittedly, power failures are pretty rare, but crashing the computer and hanging it up is not so rare. By frequently saving a program, if you have to restart the computer, most of your program or data is on the disk. It is also important to know that when you save a file whose name is already on the disk, the old file is erased and replaced by the new version.

This is good if you are saving your file as you go along and the old version is no longer needed, but be careful you do not accidentally replace a file you wanted to save.

Before a blank disk can be used, it must be formatted. Formatting consists of the computer reading the disk and placing certain "marks" on it so that as data is written to the disk, the computer knows where to find them. It is important that you have formatted blank disks before you start, because your work cannot be saved to an unformatted disk, and you cannot stop in the middle of what you are doing to format the disk. A good practice is to format disks right after you purchase them, so that they are ready to use. Formatting a disk erases all files already on the disk. Once a disk is formatted, it can be used repeatedly or until it is filled up with data you do not wish to change or lose.

Formatting can usually be done in one of two ways. The DOS disk for your computer will have the format utility on it. For MS-DOS for the IBM you format a disk by having the DOS disk in Drive A, the blank disk in Drive B, and typing the underlined portion below

A⟩ <u>Format</u> B<u>:</u>

the A⟩ is the DOS prompt, telling you the computer is ready to accept instructions. After typing this, the screen will give you the directions for formatting as many disks as you have or need.

A second method for formatting involves a particular applications program. Many applications programs, such as Lotus 1-2-3, have their own utilities programs on the disk with the spreadsheet program. These utilities programs will copy a file, copy a disk, and also format a disk. If a DOS disk is not available, or you just want to use the applications program, follow the instructions in the manual. In either case, you always want to make certain that you have a supply of formatted disks when you start your work.

GETTING UP AND GOING

Most users of personal computers will be using preprogrammed software, that is, a program or system that someone else has developed. Few people do their own programming. In order to use a system, after it is installed, one simply inserts the disk in Drive A, inserts a formatted disk, either blank or with data, in Drive B, and turns on the machine. For most programs, the program disk will contain what is known as an autoexecute batch file. After the machine has performed a few diagnostic tests to determine if it is working and set up correctly (for example, that the disk-drive doors are closed), the computer will read the batch file and load the appropriate program from the disk. At that point all you have to do is follow the instructions in the documentation or as they come on the screen.

In some cases, after inserting the disk and turning on the machine, you will get the DOS prompt. For the IBM PC and others using the MS-DOS system it will look like this

A⟩

This is the machine's way of saying it is ready for you to do something. To run the particular piece of software, you may then type the program name and press the enter key. For example, to run Lotus 1-2-3, you would have

A⟩ Lotus ⟨Enter⟩

Throughout this writing the ⟨Enter⟩ will be used to signify pressing the enter or return key. After doing this, the program will run as it is supposed to. Consult the manual for the name of the program in order to make it run from a DOS prompt.

EXPERIMENTATION

Can a user harm a computer? Yes, striking the computer, drives, or keyboard with force will invariably damage the machine and make it ineffective. Can you damage or harm the machine without physical violence, that is, will mistaken key entries damage the computer? The answer is no. If the computer does not like what you are doing, it either will not accept the commands or it will hang up and crash. The computer will become so confused it simply refuses to do anything else. The remedy, then, is to start over, by either depressing certain keys that will reboot the disk or by turning the machine off, waiting several seconds, and turning it back on.

Thus, the user is free to experiment without fear of wrecking the machine. The very worst that can happen is to have to start over by rebooting the disk and recalling the program and the data. Much of learning how to use a computer involves experimentation with the keyboard, the "what happens if I do this" activity. Far from being apprehensive, a user should be encouraged to experiment. Like riding a bicycle, computers are best examined in a hands-on environment. If you want to know what something does, try it.

This does not mean that experimentation is totally safe. If you hang up the computer and have to reboot and start from scratch, you will lose all that has been put into the computer's memory but not stored on disk. Therefore, if you are about to try something you haven't done before, save your partially completed work to a disk before you venture into unknown territory. If fact, you should save the partially completed work to a disk on a regular basis. If you mistrike a key and have to start again, you can recall the data and start from your last save.

CHAPTER 2

An Introduction to the Electronic Spreadsheet

THE ELECTRONIC SPREADSHEET—WHAT IS IT?

Probably more than any other development, the creation of electronic spreadsheet programs for personal computers stimulated the growth and development of the machines. These programs are used more than all other types of programs combined. For many users, if the personal computer could do nothing else but electronic spreadsheets it would justify its purchase price.

The electronic spreadsheet is a preprogrammed package that enables a user to manipulate, store, and print out complex financial analyses without knowing any computer programming. In a real sense, all of the work has been done for you by a third party; the user merely inputs his data the way he wants them, defines relationships among the different elements of the data, and leaves it to the computer to determine the end result. For the most part, the work follows simple English and algebraic logic, meaning that even an individual who has never been on a computer before can be creating work in less than an hour of study or preparation time.

Each spreadsheet program is unique unto itself, and while no one has counted, there are probably well over fifty different packages to choose from. This does not mean that learning one package does not help you in learning another, for the programs have far more in common than they have differences. This chapter is about the common features of electronic spreadsheets, and the items discussed here should apply to most programs. The following three chapters then

240

discuss three of the more commonly used systems in detail. If you understand the basics, you should be able to use any system after a short study of the program's manual or documentation.

The electronic worksheet creates a work area in the computer and displays a part of this work to the user. The work area is defined by a series of columns and rows. The columns are labeled by letters of the alphabet, A, B, C, and so on (or by numbers) and the rows by numbers, starting with 1 and going as high as the number of rows possible. This layout may be very large, several hundred columns by several thousand rows. The monitor will show only a portion at a time, the exact amount depending upon how wide the individual columns are. A typical display of the work space, termed a *spreadsheet,* is shown in Figure 2-1. Essentially, what happens is this. Each intersection of a column (letter) and a row (number) forms a cell. Into this cell a user can enter numbers, words (termed labels or text), or a formula. The term *spreadsheet* is derived from the accountants ruled paper, which consists of columns and rows into which data or labels are written. The program thus creates a report that consists of the entries in the individual cells.

To illustrate how this works, consider the representation of the partial income statement in Figure 2-2. In this spreadsheet, we have used the computer's cursor arrow keys to move the cursor to the following cells and make the entries shown in Table 2-1. The words and numbers are input without commas or dollar signs. The program will then have them appear in a traditional format, to make them easier to read. The results, printed out in Figure 2-2, show exactly the information put in. Notice the numbers printed in cells D14 and D16. In D14 we told the computer to subtract 90,000 from 150,000, which it did. Then it printed only the result of that operation. Sim-

Figure 2-1   A Typical Spreadsheet Configuration

Columns

	A	B	C	D	E	F	G	H	I...
Rows									
1									
2									
3									
4									
5									
6									
7									
.									
.									
.									

Part VI: Microcomputers and Spreadsheet Programs

Table 2-1   Data for Figure 2-2

Cell	Entry
C2	Partial
C4	Income Statement
C6	XYZ Company
A10	Sales
D10	150000
A12	Cost of Goods Sold
D12	90000
A14	Gross Profit
D14	150000 − 90000
A16	Gross Profit Percent
D16	60000/150000

Figure 2-2   Data from Table 2-1

```
        A       B       C       D       E       F       G       H
1
2                    Partial
3
4                    Income Statement
5
6                    XYZ Company
7
8
9
10  Sales                    150000
11
12  Cost of Goods Sold        90000
13
14  Gross Profit              60000
15
16  Gross Profit Percent     40.00%
17
18
19
20
```

ilarly, in D16 we told the computer to take 60,000, which is the result of the computation in D14, and divide it by 150,000. The printout then showed the result of that operation, .4 or 40 per cent.

Now suppose we made a mistake. It turns out the cost of goods sold was not really $90,000 but $95,000. In that case, we can go back and change the value of cells D12, D14, and D16. The new entries would be as shown in Table 2-2, resulting in the spreadsheet in Figure 2-3.

Table 2-2   Data for Figure 2-3

Cell	Entry
D12	95000
D14	150000 − 95000
D16	55000/150000

Figure 2-3   The Altered Spreadsheet

```
       A       B       C       D       E      F        G       H
 1
 2                   Partial
 3
 4                   Income Statement
 5
 6                   XYZ Company
 7
 8
 9
10  Sales                      150000
11
12  Cost of Goods Sold          95000
13
14  Gross Profit                55000
15
16  Gross Profit Percent       36.67%
17
```

Obviously, there is some benefit to this procedure, but it is difficult and time consuming to go back and change all of the cell values. There is an easier way of doing things. Let's go back to our original set of computations and the data in Table 2-1. With respect to the calculations, there is something we can do in terms of what goes in cells D14 and D16. Instead of entering the actual numbers, let's make the following entries:

Table 2-3   Logic Entered in Spreadsheet

Cell	Entry
D14	+d10 − d12
D16	+d14/d10

What we have done is tell the program to place in D14 whatever value is in D10, less the value in cell D12. Similarly, we have told the computer to place in D16 whatever value is in cell D14, divided by the value in cell D10. After we do this, the spreadsheet will still look like Figure 2-2, and it may appear that we have not made any improvements. But the benefits from entering the values in cells D14 and D16 in formula rather than in actual numerical value can be seen when we change a value in D10 or in D12. Suppose we go back to the spreadsheet and change those values as follows:

Table 2-4   New Sales and Cost Data

Cell	Entry
D10	160000
D12	120000

If we make these changes, and no others, our spreadsheet will now look like Figure 2-4. Cells D14 and D16 will automatically recalculate their values to reflect the new values in cells D10 and D12. This then is the great value of the spreadsheet programs. If all of our spreadsheets are set up so that all the calculations are done in terms of cell references rather than numbers, then changing any one of our data numbers will change all the numbers all the way through the program that depend on that one number.

Figure 2-4   Spreadsheet with New Data

	A	B	C	D	E	F	G	H
1								
2								
3								
4			Partial					
5								
6			Income Statement					
7								
8			XYZ Company					
9								
10	Sales			160000				
11								
12	Cost of Goods Sold			120000				
13								
14	Gross Profit			40000				
15								
16	Gross Profit Percent			25.00%				
17								

This concept creates a very powerful financial-planning tool. If in developing an analytical spreadsheet, no matter how complicated, where all computations depending on sales are referenced by the cell in which the sales number resides, then any change in the sales number will automatically be reflected in all the computations that use the sales number. The spreadsheet might be a hundred columns by a thousand rows, but in a matter of minutes a change in sales can create a new spreadsheet that contains all of that information.

GETTING AROUND THE SPREADSHEET

Essentially, when you have called up the spreadsheet from your program you are faced with a matrix of cells. The spreadsheet is much larger than can be shown on the computer screen at any one time, and you can only be in one cell at a time. When you first call up the spreadsheet, the cursor will begin in a specific position on the spreadsheet, typically the "home" position or cell in the upper left-hand corner, cell A1. The particular spreadsheet program will indicate to you exactly where in the spreadsheet you are, usually by highlighting the particular cell and by stating the current cell either above or below the spreadsheet. In Figure 2-5, we see the way the

Figure 2-5   The Lotus 1-2-3 Spreadsheet Screen

```
A1:
                                                            READY
          A      B      C      D      E      F      G      H
 1
 2
 3
 4
 5
 6
 7
 8
 9
10
11
12
13
14
15
16
17
18
19
20
```

spreadsheet looks for a Lotus 1-2-3 program. The current position of the cursor is given by the notation A1 (in the upper left-hand corner).

The same part of a spreadsheet is shown in Figure 2-6 for a spreadsheet from the Supercalc 3 program. Here the current position of the cursor is given in the lower left-hand side of the screen. Again the cursor is in cell A1, awaiting instructions.

Most movement in the spreadsheet is done by means of the cursor-movement keys. On most systems these will be the four arrow keys or a combination of the control key and a letter key. Each time the cursor key is hit, the cursor moves to the next cell in the appropriate direction. As you move from cell to cell, the address will update in the appropriate location on the screen, so you always know where you are.

Moving the cursor key can take long if there is far to go. Consequently, many systems have "express" methods for moving quickly

Figure 2-6   The Supercalc 3 Screen

```
|      A  | |  B  | |  C  | |  D  | |  E  | |  F  | |  G  | |  H  |
   1
   2
   3
   4
   5
   6
   7
   8
   9
  10
  11
  12
  13
  14
  15
  16
  17
  18
  19
  20
> A1
Width:   9   Memory:382 Last Col/Row:A1     ? for HELP
   1 >
F1 = HELP; F2 = Erase Line/Return to Spreadsheet; F9 = Plot; F10 =
View
```

in the worksheet. These express methods are typically the following (although, always check to make sure of the method that works with your spreadsheet program):

1. *The GOTO Command.* Most programs have a set key or key sequence that enables you to direct the cursor to a specific cell address. Invoking this command and the cell address, and then pressing the enter key will send the cursor to that address.

2. *Page Up and Page Down Keys.* On the IBM PC and similar machines, there are special keys that move the screen an entire page at a time. These keys, typically, work only with the up and down movements, not left and right, so movement up and down can be quicker than left and right. This should be kept in mind when deciding in what order you will be entering data, labels, or formulas.

3. *Scroll-Lock Keys.* The scroll-lock key locks the cursor on a specific place on the screen. When you have done this, pressing the arrow keys moves the spreadsheet behind the cursor rather than moving the cursor. This can be helpful in reducing time if you want to keep the cursor in the middle of the screen to see other cells while you are typing in the cell in which the cursor resides.

MAKING ENTRIES IN THE SPREADSHEET

The purpose of the spreadsheet programs is fivefold, the first is to allow you to develop sophisticated and detailed financial models and calculations; the second is to allow you to do so in a quick and efficient manner; the third is to allow you to save the spreadsheet so it can be used later; the fourth is to permit you to print out the spreadsheet; and the fifth to allow you to make changes in certain significant variables and to have the computer, rather than the user, recompute the model with new data. In this section, let us consider how to go about the process of inputting information into the cells.

Before making any entries into a computer spreadsheet, determine in your own mind what you are doing and what you want the final product to look like. Remember, the output will be in exactly the same form as the input, so it helps to know what you are doing before you start. Don't worry, though, if you decide to change after you begin; the spreadsheet programs have ultimate flexibility. You can, with most programs, even decide to insert a row or column in the middle of the spreadsheet if you find you left some element out and did not leave space for it. After you get experienced with spreadsheet programs, it is fairly easy to compose a spreadsheet while sitting at the terminal. For a first experience, though, it is better to make notes about how you want the spreadsheet to look.

After you have an idea of how the spreadsheet will look, call up the program, get into the spreadsheet mode, and begin. Start by entering something in a cell. This is done by typing whatever you want to type and then hitting the enter or return key. On the screen you will see what you are typing next to the cell indicator, and after hitting the enter or return key it will be placed in the cell. What you have typed may or may not actually show up in the cell, but it will always show up next to the cell indicator.

Effectively, there are three types of entries that can be made into a cell. One type is a label or alphacharacters. For example the first line of an income statement is often labeled *Sales*. If you are making an income statement, you can type the word *Sales*, hit the enter key, and the word will appear in the spreadsheet on the screen. Any character key can be used to make a label, even numbers, but you have to be careful to tell the system that you want a number to be a label rather than a piece of data (more on this later). With a label, whatever you type will appear in the cell.

The second type of information you can put in a cell is data. Data are numbers and are entered without any other characters, that is, no commas, dollar signs, or parentheses for negative numbers. If you want these items, the program can be instructed later on how to display the numbers, but they are always entered in plain number form. The decimal point is entered by using the period key and negative numbers are entered by typing a − before the number. No spaces should be used in entering numbers.

The third type of entry is a formula. The formula can either be user-created, such as the formula +b7−b8, which is entered in cell B9 and tells the computer to enter into B9 the value in B7, less the value in B8. In some cases, the formulas are predefined by the spreadsheet program, that is, in developing the program the creators have designated certain codes to do a specific mathematical calculation. For example, in Lotus the @ sign in front of a set of characters indicates a Lotus preprogrammed formula, and the @ sign must be followed by a certain character string. In Lotus, @AVG (b7.b14) says enter in the current cell the average of the values in the cells from B7 through B14.

Earlier we said that the cell may or may not show what was entered in it. In the case of a formula, the cell will not display the formula on the screen, but the result of the formula. If, however, you look at the cell indicator outside the spreadsheet, it will show what is in the cell. Thus, as you work with the spreadsheet you will be constantly looking at both the spreadsheet itself and the cell indicator for the particular cell that you are in. You will notice as you make cell entries in formula that the computation suddenly appears in the cell.

In making entries into cells there are two questions that invariably come to the mind of the user. These are (1) what do I do if I make a mistake, and (2) what happens if the column is not wide enough to accept my entry. The answer to the first question is relatively easy. One way of correcting an error is to simply go to that cell and write the correct entry, hitting the enter key after writing the new entry and watching the program. Essentially, what will happen is that the program will replace the old entry with the new entry, and it is as though the old entry never existed. Of course, to make the new entry permanent, the spreadsheet must be saved at some time prior to turning off the machine.

Notice that in using this method for correcting an entry, the entire entry must be retyped. This method of correcting an error is easy if the entry is short. However, if the entry is long, particularly if it is a long, complicated formula then retyping it can be a burdensome task. In this situation there is a second method for correcting an error, the edit function. To use the edit function, go to the cell you wish to change and engage the edit function for the particular program you are using. This will be explained by the program. For Lotus 1-2-3, for example, it is engaged by pressing the F2 key on the IBM PC. In the edit mode, the cursor is on the entry after the cell indicator. Using the backspace, delete, and arrow keys, the cursor can be positioned to the correct place on the item and the correction or change made. As always, when you are finished, press the enter key to put the new entry into the cell.

The problem of a column not wide enough to take all of the entry has equally easy solutions. First of all, the program stores all of the entry if there is not enough space on the screen to display it, as long as the entry does not exceed the program's limit, which is usually well over one hundred characters. This means that for a long formula, for example, it is not necessary that the column be sufficiently wide to display the formula. All that it is going to be displayed is the answer, and if the column is wide enough to display the answer, then the system will work without any changes.

In many cases, though, you will have labels or numbers that are wider than the column. In this situation, several alternatives are available. First, columns are set to what is called a default width when you start the program, say nine characters. Some programs will borrow from the column next to it if there is nothing in that column. Thus, anything over nine characters will spill over into the next column. Using two columns in this way, in effect, gives you the equivalent of one eighteen-character-wide column.

If, however, you wish to widen the column, which you may have to do to accommodate large numbers, then the programs will allow you to do so. All programs have variable width columns, and by consulting the documentation, you can determine exactly how this is done. The older programs tend to have only one width of columns for the entire spreadsheet—that is, when you widen one you widen them all. The new programs, such as Lotus 1-2-3 and Supercalc 3 have variable width columns. This means you can make each column a different width and is particularly helpful since your label columns are likely to be much wider than your number columns.

GLOBAL AND RANGE

One of the most important concepts in spreadsheet programs is that of global and range. The term *global* refers to the entire spreadsheet, and a global change or a global command affects the entire spreadsheet. For example, in the discussion about changing column widths, it would have been correct to talk about a global column width. Invoking the global column-width command changes the column width of every column. It is well to remember that when you do something globally, you have done it all over the spreadsheet.

The term *range* refers to a portion of the spreadsheet. A range is a subsection of columns and rows within the spreadsheet. It is defined in terms of its upper-left-hand corner cell and its lower-right-hand corner cell. For example, the range A1:C6 would be the section of the spreadsheet with cell A1 in the upper left corner, cell C1 in the upper right, A6 in the lower left and C6 in the lower right. Since the subsection of the worksheet is a rectangle or a square, by defining any two diagonally opposite corners you have defined the dimensions of the rectangle. There is no limit on the size of a range—it can be as big as the worksheet or as small as a single cell; it can be a column or a row.

The range concept is important because it is the way in which you give the program many of its commands. The most common use of the range concept is in printing. It is highly unlikely that you would want to print out an entire spreadsheet. In most cases, you will want to print only a portion. You transmit this information to the program by telling it to print a certain range. This is extremely useful because it means that your spreadsheet can be a very large financial model from which you can print a variety of reports. In advanced uses, you can assign names to the ranges and use the names in commands so that you do not have to remember the coordinates of a particular range.

FILE MANAGEMENT

In computer talk, the word *file* is more likely to be a noun than a verb. A file is another name for a program. In working with spreadsheet programs, a file is the spreadsheet you are currently working with. There are a number of things that can be done with files, but the two things almost all spreadsheet users will do is to save files and to load files. As discussed in Chapter 1, the spreadsheet that is created is stored only in the RAM of the computer, when the computer is turned off, whatever was in its memory is gone forever. Since it is almost certain that you will want to come back to any work which you have done, you must make a permanent copy of the work.

In working with spreadsheets, the process of making a permanent copy is known as saving the worksheet to a file on a disk. The exact process is done by the specific commands in the program you are working with, but saving a worksheet file can be done with all programs. In doing this the worksheet is given a name, which should be a combination of letters and numbers, with no spaces or special characters involved. You will remember what the worksheet is about if you give it a name related to its content. Once a file is saved, it can be recalled (loaded or retrieved) by using commands in the particular program you are using.

Several things should be remembered when using files. First, you should save the spreadsheet every so often to insure that if something happens to the machine—such as a power failure or software crash—a day's work is not lost. For most programs you can stop, save the file, and then continue with your work. A second point is that when you use the name of an existing file, the existing file is replaced by the new file. This is good if you are updating a spreadsheet, but be careful and do not give a new spreadsheet the same name as one you want to keep. Finally, save copies of the file on two separate disks. This second save is a back-up; it protects you against disk damage or loss.

FORMAT

We have already used the term *format* in discussion of the preparation of a disk for storage of a spreadsheet. However, in working with spreadsheet programs the term format has a second meaning.

As has been indicated earlier, all data are entered as they exist, without commas, dollar signs, or parentheses for negative numbers. In most cases, however, a user will want data displayed in a more conventional manner to make the data easier to read and to give it a more professional look.

This process is done through commands in the spreadsheet program. With most programs, formatting can be done on either a global or range basis, that is, you can format the entire spreadsheet or only a specific portion of it. If most of the spreadsheet is to have one format, the easiest thing is to format on a global basis and then go back and format the different areas on a range basis. Range formatting will always override global formatting. Again, each program will be different in how a user does formatting, but all should allow standard formats, such as parentheses for negative numbers, dollar signs, commas, and per cent signs. The formatting process will also allow the user to control the number of decimal places displayed.

COPYING AND REPLICATING

A spreadsheet is easy and quick to construct because the program allows the user to copy labels, data, and logic all through the spreadsheet. In many cases of a multirowed or multicolumned spreadsheet, the specific logic or labels need be written just once, because they can be copied into subsequent cells that use the same logic or labels. As an example, consider the following portion of an income statement and assume it is being constructed on a spreadsheet:

Figure 2-7   Partial Income Statement on a Spreadsheet Program

	A	B	C	D
		XYZ Company		
	Partial Income Statement, Year Ending Dec. 31,			
		1982	1983	1984
11	Income Before Tax			
12	Tax			
13	Net Income			

Now assuming you were constructing a spreadsheet to do this, you would enter the labels "Income Before Tax," "Tax," and "Net Income" in cells A11, A12, and A13 as shown. In the B column you would enter the following:

B11	230000
B12	.46*B11
B13	+B11 −B12

This would indicate that you have previously determined that income before tax was \$230,000, and that number is entered in cell B11. You want the program to calculate cell B12 on the basis that the tax liability is 46 per cent of the income before tax, and so you make that entry in cell B12. Finally, since net income is income before tax, less tax, you indicate that the value of cell B13 is the value of cell B11 minus the value of B13. When you have done this, your spreadsheet will look like the following (remember, the worksheet displays the results of cell calculations, not the cell entries):

Figure 2-8   Partial Income Statement with Data

A	B	C	D
	XYZ Company		
Partial Income Statement, Year Ending Dec. 31,			
	1982	1983	1984
11 Income Before Tax	230000		
12 Tax	105800		
13 Net Income	124200		

Now we want to do the same thing for columns C and D, but instead of rewriting the formulas for cells C12 and C13 and D12 and D13, we will copy the logic in cells B12 and B13 to that section of the spreadsheet. This is done by methods specific to each program, which can be learned by consulting the subsequent chapters of this book or by consulting the program manual. When we do, the entries in the range C12:D13 will be as follows:

Cell	Entry (Copies from Column B)
C12	.46*C11
C13	+C11 − C12
D12	.46*D11
D13	+D11 − D12

The interesting thing to notice is that when the copy operation is performed, it is done on a relative basis. Thus, the copying preserved the relationship between cells B11 and B12 in computing B13 and in copying the logic to the C column. When you copied to column C it did not place in C13 + B11 − B12 but +C11 − C12. The program knew that you wanted the same relationship in column C as in column B, not the exact same cell entries. This understanding is very important in being able to use a copy or replicate a command in a spreadsheet program. Essentially, what happens is that the copy-replicate activity copies relationships between cells to new cells in the spreadsheet, and it is this function that allows a user to construct a spreadsheet of many columns or rows where the logic is identical.

Perhaps you do not want to copy relationships but rather a specific formula to a series of cells. For example, in the above situation instead of computing the tax amount as

$$.46^*B11, .46^*C11, \text{etc.}$$

you may want to compute it as

$$+A2^*B11, +A2^*C11, \text{etc.}$$

where cell A2 is the place where you have stored the tax rate. In this case, once you have entered the formula in cell B12, if you copy to C12 and so on, it will not be done correctly; that is, cell C12 will have in it

$$+B2^*C11$$

because the program is using its relational logic to copy. In this case you must tell the program you want to anchor the copying with cell A2. This can be easily done but is specific to the program you are working with. For example, in Lotus 1-2-3 you do this by entering in cell B12

$$+\$A\$2^*B11$$

When you do this, the program will compute cell B12 in the same way as before, but when you copy from cell B12, the A2 value will not change. Putting in the $ overrides the relational copying and makes the copying absolute. Other programs allow you to do this in a similar fashion.

HINTS AND IDEAS

In working with a spreadsheet program, there are a number of ways to do things. Probably the easiest way to learn the alternatives is to sit down at the computer, call up the program from the disk, and begin. However, this is frequently inefficient, and efficiency is what using a computer is all about. After all, the reason you go to so much time and trouble to learn a system is to save yourself time and trouble in the future.

With a spreadsheet program, you should first have an idea about how you want the spreadsheet to look. You might first set up and print a series of tables with the labels only so that you will have a picture of what the finished product will look like. You might then pencil in the numbers or data that will go in the different cells, and pencil in the formulas that you will use for the cells which do calculations. If you then call the particular spreadsheet from a saved file on a disk (you did remember to save the spreadsheet before you quit?) you can start to enter the data and formulas.

In constructing the spreadsheet put as much as possible in logic form rather than in actual numbers, because the more logic you have, the easier it is to make a change in any significant variable. A good idea is to devote part of the spreadsheet to certain key elements, such as tax rates, interest rates, growth rates, discount rates, and so on. Then, within the program, you can refer to that cell rather than keying in the actual rate. If you have to make a change, you go to the one cell that contains the rate or key information, and that change will be reflected through the entire spreadsheet.

It is usually a good idea to save formatting of the spreadsheet for the end of a session, after everything else is complete. But, such things as widening a column should be done as needed. You will want to see if the columns are wide enough for the program to display your entries. If you make the columns too wide, you can always narrow them down again in the finishing-up process.

Finally, you should not be afraid to experiment and test certain things. As previously indicated, you cannot really harm the computer from the keyboard and in most cases pressing the escape key will undo whatever damage you have done to your spreadsheet. However, remember that you can hang up the computer and have to reboot, in which case the work you have done since your last save will be lost. If you are going to experiment, save your file first. If you are the nervous type, make a back-up. Then you can go ahead without any worries, because you can always return to where you were by starting over.

CHAPTER 3

Using Lotus 1-2-3

This chapter will take you through the steps necessary to use Lotus 1-2-3 in solving the case problems in this text and in solving many types of financial problems. Before beginning, a couple of things need to be said. First of all, the Lotus 1-2-3 program is a very sophisticated spreadsheet program, capable of doing many more things than those discussed in this chapter. Also, experienced users will find that they can do things faster and easier than the methods discussed here permit. This chapter is not meant to produce an expert Lotus user, or even an efficient one. Its goal is to produce a user who can develop, save, and print spreadsheets, to provide a user with the basic skills that will enable him or her to further develop prowess in the program. When you can master the techniques of this chapter, you should have no difficulty in mastering the advanced skills by reviewing the user's manual, using the help function, or just plain experimenting.

A second point is that this discussion of Lotus is tailored to the IBM PC and its compatibles. In most cases, each point is applicable to a user no matter what type of machine is employed; but if the program does not act as it should and you are using a non-IBM machine, it may be that machine differences are causing the difficulty. You should have no hesitancy in examining the manual if you have trouble at a particular point.

Finally, the assumption is made that the user has a program which has been properly installed for the computer, monitor, and printer that is being used. As discussed in Chapter 1, an installation process is necessary to configure a program to your specific system and to use certain programs that belong to the makers of the computer or the operating system. This installation process is done just once, so if the program has been used before it should be ready to go. If it has not, the operating manual will take you step by step through the installation process.

GETTING STARTED

In order to begin using Lotus 1-2-3, you need the Lotus program disk and a blank, formatted disk, which will be used to store the spreadsheet. If you have not formatted the blank disk, do so before you start, as you cannot do it after you have begun. You should insert the program disk in Drive A and the blank disk in Drive B and then turn on the machine. In most situations, your system will be self-booting, that is, the computer will go through its self-checking routine, possibly ask you to enter the date and time, and then go directly into Lotus 1-2-3. If it does not, it will display the DOS prompt, which in the IBM and related systems looks as follows:

A⟩

with a blinking cursor after it. This means the computer is waiting for you to tell it what to do. In this case, type

Lotus ⟨enter⟩

where ⟨enter⟩ means to press the return or enter key, and the Lotus 1-2-3 program will be loaded into the RAM or memory of the machine.

After Lotus 1-2-3 is loaded, you will be faced with the main menu. This first menu is shown in Figure 3-1. Lotus 1-2-3 is a menu-driven

Figure 3-1   The Lotus 1-2-3 Access Screen

```
Lotus Acess System V. 1A (C) 1983 Lotus Development Corp.          MENU
- - - - - - - - - - - - - - - - - - - - - - - - - - - - - - - - - - - - - - - -
1-2-3 File-Manager Disk-Manager PrintGraph Translate Exit
Enter 1-2-3 -Lotus Spreadsheet/Graphics/Database program
============================================================================
```

Tue 01-Jan-80
0:00:29am

program, which means that when a user has to make a choice of several things to do, the options are displayed for selection. In 1-2-3, the cursor serves as a pointer and the enter key as the selector. Pressing the enter key means taking the choice that the cursor key is on, which is highlighted. The cursor key is moved by the cursor movement keys, that is, the arrow keys. In 1-2-3, you will want to choose the first selection, designated 1-2-3 which is where the cursor is currently residing, so your instructions are simply to press the return or enter key to continue into the program.

At this point the disk drive will light up and make a quiet noise as the computer reads the 1-2-3 program from the disk into memory. When it stops, you will be faced with either a Lotus 1-2-3 logo (for release 1.0) or some text with the instructions to "strike any key to continue." Regardless of what you see, the next step is to strike any key, at which time the screen will display the upper left corner of the spreadsheet, as shown in Figure 3-2. The cursor should be resting in cell A1 and the cell indicator above and to the left of the spreadsheet will so indicate. You are now ready to begin to begin.

Before beginning, the user should know two things. Lotus 1-2-3 has an on-line, built-in help function, which is like a small manual. A user can get into the help menu at any time by pressing the F1 key. The help screens tell about certain aspects of the program. To

Figure 3-2   The Initial Lotus 1-2-3 Screen

```
A1:                                                           READY
                A     B     C     D     E     F     G     H
1
2
3
4
5
6
7
8
9
10
11
12
13
14
15
16
17
18
19
20
```

use the help screens, you move the cursor with the arrow keys to the help index, and press return or enter. Then you move the cursor to the item you wish to know more about, and press enter. The screen will display information about the subject. You can return to the point you were at in the spreadsheet at any time by pressing the ESC key.

A second point is that the menus in 1-2-3 that allow you to do such things as save or print a file are accessed by pressing the / key before doing anything else in a cell. The / key serves several purposes. In 1-2-3, / serves to call up the menus if it is the first key pressed when the cursor is at a cell, and it serves as the divide function in an arithmetic formula. One can leave the menus by pressing the ESC key as many times as necessary or by selecting a quit option in the menus. We will explore the menus in later sections of the chapter as we discuss topics that require their use.

MAKING ENTRIES IN THE CELLS

If you have followed the procedures so far you will be ready to start making entries in the cells. The entries will be either numbers, labels, or formulas. For numbers, the procedure is simple: Move the cursor to the cell in which you wish to make the entry, type the number, and press the enter key. The number will appear in the cell and you can go forward to your next step. Two points should be made here. The first is that the numbers are entered without dollar signs, commas, or any other character except the decimal point. These items are provided for in a formatting process. The second point is that the arrow key, rather than the enter key, can be pressed after typing the number. This enters the number in the cell and moves the cursor one cell in the direction of the arrow key. This speeds up the process if you are entering numbers that are consecutive.

The second type of entry you might want to make is text, which is termed a label in 1-2-3. A label is usually a word or set of words, although occasionally a user wishes to define a set of numbers as a label. To type a label, simply move the cursor to the correct cell and begin typing the words. Again, pressing the enter key or one of the cursor movement keys will cause the entry to appear in the cell. Capitals and lower cases are done using the traditional shift keys or the "caps lock" key. If the "caps lock" is engaged you will be so notified by the message "caps" in the lower right portion of the screen.

Sometimes you may confuse the program if it thinks you are typing a number when you want a label. Suppose, for example, you want to put a label at the top of a column of numbers, and the label will signify values for the first quarter of 1984. You desire to enter the label "1984-1." If you type this in, however, the display in the cell will read "1983." What has happened is that the program thinks you want the value of 1,984 less 1, which is 1,983. You have to signify to the program that the item you are typing is a label and not a value.

This differentiation is done in 1-2-3 by means of a label prefix. Lotus 1-2-3 distinguishes labels from numerical value by inserting a character before the label. You will notice, for example, that when you start to type a label that starts with a letter, a box in the upper right corner says "label" and that the label you are typing begins with an ' after the cell indicator in the upper left corner (see Figure 3-3). This ' is a label prefix and tells 1-2-3 that the entry is a label. It is automatically inserted when the program knows you are typing a label, as when you begin with a letter. Thus, if you want to type a number as a label, you must begin by typing the character ' and then the number. Lotus 1-2-3 will treat the entry as a label and will not display the ' in the cell or in the printing of the spreadsheet.

Actually, the ' character in 1-2-3 does more than indicate a label. It tells the program to position the label flush against the left margin of the cell. It may be that you want to label centered or flush against the right margin. In these cases you will use a different label prefix, the carat ^ for centering and the quotation marks " for right margin flush as the label prefix. Again, typing either of these or the ' will indicate to Lotus that what follows is a label and the label prefix will not show up in either the cell or in the printout. Remember, too, that you can always tell what 1-2-3 is thinking about your entry by consulting the indicator in the upper right corner.

Many of the entries you will want to make in 1-2-3 will be formulas. Often, these formulas will be of the nature of taking an entry in one cell and adding to or substracting from it the value in another cell. For example, you may want to compute net income by taking

Figure 3-3   Lotus 1-2-3 Screen Showing 1984 Typed as a Label in Cell A1

```
A1: '1984                                              LABEL
           A       B       C       D       E       F       G       H
1        1984
2
3
4
5
6
7
8
```

the value in the cell that holds income before tax and subtracting the tax amount from it. To enter formulas in 1-2-3 you simply type them in, making sure that any parentheses in the formulas conform to standard algebraic logic (the program will compute the inner parentheses first). However, if your formula begins with a cell reference there is a problem. If you want to say

$$B7-B8$$

Lotus 1-2-3 will read this as a label and print in the cell B7-B8, because any time an entry starts with a letter Lotus assumes it is a label. To tell 1-2-3 it is a formula, the + sign must be placed before it, that is, the formula must be written

$$+B7-B8$$

at which time 1-2-3 will recognize it as a formula and compute the answer. Incidentally, the cell addresses may be written in either uppercase or lowercase letters.

Finally, the Lotus 1-2-3 program has a number of preprogrammed formulas, called @ formulas, that enable you to do many mathematical tasks with a minimum of key strokes. For example, assume you want to compute the average for the values in cells B7 to B11 and put that average in cell B13. You could do this by typing the following entry for cell B13

$$(+B7+B8+B9+B10+B11)/5$$

making sure you have the parenthesis. Otherwise, only cell B11 would be divided by 5. But you could use the @ formula for averaging. An @ formula consists of the following:

the @ character followed by a code to signify which @ formula is used followed by other information and a range in parentheses.

For example, the @ formula for computing an average is

$$@avg(beginning\ cell.ending\ cell)$$

For the above computation, the formula would read:

$$@avg(b7.b11)$$

In using @ formulas, the beginning and ending cells must be separated by at least one period (it can be more) and that there are no breaks or empty cells in the range. Empty cells are typically read as zero by the program, and if these are present it will give you the wrong answer. The @ formulas are described in the manual and are also shown in the help screens. In 1-2-3, @ formulas exist for most common mathematical, statistical, and financial applications. Remember, they do not have to be used, but they save time and effort.

One final point about cell entries is that the entry may be too long for the cell width. In this case, 1-2-3 will display a label by borrowing from the adjacent cell if it is empty; otherwise it cuts the label off at the end of the cell. It still remembers the entire label, so that later when the column is widened the entire label will be printed out. If the cell is not wide enough for the number, the display will be **********. You must then widen the column to see the answer. As far as formulas are concerned, since they are not displayed in the cell the column width does not matter, as long as you do not exceed 1-2-3's maximum value for a cell, which is 240 characters.

THE EDIT FUNCTION

After having made entries into cells, the next logical question is how to correct or change an entry. The simplest way is to write the new entry over the old one, that is, move the cursor to the cell, type the new entry, and press the return key. This will cause the new entry to replace the old one in the cell and you can continue with the work.

In the event that the entry in the cell is very long and complicated, and the change in it is very small, you may want to use the edit function to change the entry. Depressing the F2 on an IBM PC, or a similarly designated key on another machine, puts the program in the edit mode. When this happens, the entry in the cell appears after the cell address indicator, and the program is ready for any changes. In the edit mode, the keys function somewhat differently. The cursor arrow keys move the cursor within the entry after the cell address line. The backspace key deletes the character to the left of the cursor, and the delete key, which normally does not do anything in 1-2-3, will delete the character above the cursor. In the edit mode, the program is in an insert mode, which means that typing any character inserts that character at the point of the cursor.

To exit from the edit mode press the enter key after you have made your changes. The change will be put in the cell, and you can continue building the spreadsheet. One other point should be made: if you make an unacceptable entry in a cell, an open parentheses, for example, the program will automatically put you in the edit mode. It will not allow you to make the entry and move on until you have corrected the problem, which you can do by using the edit activities described above and then pressing the enter key.

THE MENU SYSTEM AND COPYING CELL ENTRIES

Making cell entries into a new spreadsheet will probably cause a user to access the 1-2-3 menu system in order to copy labels, data, or most likely, formula logic from one set of cells into another. The 1-2-3 menu system is the method by which you can do all of the functions described in Chapter 2—copying, saving, printing, and so on. To first access the 1-2-3 menu, position the cursor at any cell and before any typing is done, depress the / key. This will call up the menu shown in Figure 3-4.

In the Lotus menu system, the arrow keys move the cursor to the item you wish to select, and then you can depress the enter key. In the Lotus menus, the choices are shown on the first line. As you move the cursor along this line and highlight the choice, a description of what each choice does is shown on the second line. In many cases, selection of a menu will cause a submenu to appear. For example, by choosing the worksheet menu, you open up a large number of choices for doing things to the spreadsheet. Figure 3-5 shows the menu that appears when the worksheet item on the first menu is selected. Some of these items will be discussed in later sections of this chapter, but you can learn almost everything about the menus by just going through them with the cursor movement and the enter key. Remember, you can always exit from a menu by pressing the

Figure 3-4 The Lotus 1-2-3 Menu Screen

```
A1: '1984                                                   MENU
Worksheet Range Copy Move File Print Graph Data Quit
Global, Insert, Delete, Column-Width, Erase, Titles, Window,
Status
               A        B        C        D        E        F        G        H
1              1984
2
3
4
5
6
7
8
9
```

Figure 3-5 Worksheet Menu

```
A1: '1984                                                    MENU
Global Insert Delete Column-Width Erase Titles Window Status
Set worksheet settings
                 A       B       C       D       E       F       G       H
1                1984
2
3
4
5
6
7
8
9
```

ESC key, and when you exit from the last menu you will be ready
to resume work on the spreadsheet.

The copy function speeds up construction of a spreadsheet. You
can copy labels, but you are more likely to copy logic. Since most
spreadsheets show one-quarter or more of one year, the logic for one
time period can serve for as many time periods as you wish. It needs
simply to be copied into other columns or rows. Remember, though,
that the process copies logic in a relative manner, keeping the relationship between the cells the same, unless this feature is overridden
by a process discussed later in this section.

In order to use the copy function, you have to go through the following steps:

1. Depress the / key. This will cause the menu in Figure 3-6 to
display.

2. Move the cursor to the copy function and press enter key. This
will cause the display shown in Figure 3-7.

3. In the copying function, you are asked the range to copy from
and the range to copy to. You will first enter the range to copy from,

Figure 3-6 The Main Menu

```
A1: '1984                                                    MENU
Worksheet Range Copy Move File Print Graph Data Quit
Copy a cell or range of cells
                 A       B       C       D       E       F       G       H
1                1984
2
3
4
5
```

Figure 3-7   The Copy from Section

```
A1: '1984                                                    POINT
Enter range to copy FROM: A1..A1
             A       B       C       D       E       F       G       H
1          1984
2
3
4
5
6
7
8
9
```

which will be designated by the cell addresses in the upper left cor-
ner and the lower right corner, separated by one or more periods.
For example, if you want to copy from the range designated by cells
A7..B10 you would then type in those cells and press the enter key.
When you begin, the program will already have a cell address telling
it where to copy from: notice which is the current cell of the cursor.
You can disregard this for the time being, because whatever you type
will replace what the program has listed.

4. After entering the cells from which you want the copying to
begin, you are ready to tell the program to where you want the copying to go. Again, you enter the upper left and lower right cells of the
range, separated by periods. For example, you may want to copy to
the range C7..D10, which you would type after the *copy to:* prompt
appears. By pressing the enter key, you complete the copying operation and return to the spreadsheet for additional entries.

Remember, the copying in 1-2-3 is done on a relative basis. If cell
B6 has the logic, $+B4+B5$, then copying to cell C6 will cause the
entry in cell C6 to be $+C4+C5$. If you do not want this to happen,
you must designate the cell entry with the $. Copying by entering $+$
$\$B\$4+B5$ will not change the values of cell B6. When you copy in
this way to cell C6, the entry in cell C6 will become $+\$B\$4+B5$.
Placing the dollar sign before either the column letter or row number
or both will freeze either the column letter or row number or both
when copying.

FIXING UP THE SPREADSHEET

After you have constructed your spreadsheet, a number of options
are available to "clean up" the spreadsheet and make it more pre-

sentable. Three of the more commonly used procedures are changing the column width, inserting label prefixes, and formatting the display of numbers. Other options are available, and a user is encouraged to explore these through either the manual or through experimentation with the menus and the help function. Remember, in the following discussions when you are told to select an option in the menu, you have to move the cursor to the item with the arrow keys and then press the enter key.

Column Width

The column width may be changed either globally, that is, for the entire spreadsheet, or for a single column. To change a single column's width, start by having the cursor on a cell in the column whose width you wish to change. The steps are then as follows:

   1. Press the / key to get to the first menu.
   2. In the first menu select worksheet option.
   3. In the menu that comes up, select column-width option.
   4. In the column-width menu select the set function (selecting the reset will return the column width to the global column width).
   5. Enter the width in characters you wish the column to be.
   6. Press enter key. The column width will change, and you will be put back into the spreadsheet mode, ready to make entries.

A global change will affect the column width of every column, except that individual column-width settings will override the global column-width setting. The steps for doing this are as follows:

   1. Press the / key to call up the first menu.
   2. In that menu, select worksheet option.
   3. In the worksheet menu, select global option.
   4. In the global menu, select column-width option.
   5. Enter the column width you desire and press the enter key. The column widths of all the columns will change, and the program will return you to the spreadsheet.

Label Prefix

As discussed earlier, 1-2-3 identifies an entry as a label by means of a prefix. The default option is the prefix ', which tells 1-2-3 to start the label at the left-hand margin of the cell. You can center the label or align it at the right-hand margin by typing a ^ or a " prior to entering the label. However, in many cases this may slow you down, so you might want to type the labels and then go back and center them or right-justify them.

   This is done in 1-2-3 by means of the range menu. To center or right-justify a group of labels in a single batch, do the following:

1. Type the / key to get to the first menu.
2. In the first menu, select range option.
3. In the range menu, select label pre-fix option.
4. In the label pre-fix menu, select left, center, or right.
5. After this selection, the program will ask you for the range of the insertion of the label pre-fix. You will enter the upper left corner cell and the lower right corner cell, separated by one or more periods.
6. After pressing the enter key the program will make the change and return you to the spreadsheet.

Formatting

As indicated earlier, you enter numbers into 1-2-3 without any commas, dollar signs, or other formats, except demical points. Lotus 1-2-3 gives you the option of formatting the numbers through the range menu. To format a range of entries, you do the following.

1. Press the / key to get the first menu.
2. In the first menu, select range option.
3. In the range menu, select format option.
4. In the format menu you will have a number of choices, with each choice explained as the cursor moves to that choice. Your most common selections will be

Fixed sets the number of decimal places displayed.

Currency sets a dollar sign in front of the number, inserts commas, allows you to choose how many decimal places are displayed, and puts parentheses around negative numbers.

, inserts commas, allows you to choose how many decimal places are displayed, and puts parentheses around negative numbers.

Per cent puts a per cent sign after the number, and allows you to choose how many decimal points you want to display.

5. In the format menu, select the option you want. Answer the questions about how many decimal places you wish displayed, press the enter key, and then answer the question about the range, indicating the upper left corner cell and the lower right corner cell, separating them by one or more periods. Press the enter key to make the format changes and return you to the spreadsheet.

SAVING AND RETRIEVING A FILE

Making a spreadsheet is a lot of work and you probably will not create a final version in a single sitting. However, when you turn off the computer, the spreadsheet that resided in the computer's memory will be gone. Consequently, to work efficiently, you must be able to store the spreadsheet and then retrieve it from a disk.

In 1-2-3, saving and retrieving spreadsheets is done by means of the file menu. In order to save a spreadsheet, you do the following:

1. Press the / key to call the first menu.
2. In the first menu, select the file menu.
3. In the file menu select the save function.
4. The program will then ask you to name the file you wish to save. If you have already saved the file, its current name will appear. You can type the name and press the enter key, or if the name is already displayed, press the enter key. If a file with this name already exists, such as an earlier version of the spreadsheet, the program will ask you if you want to replace the existing file. If you do not, you have to start over and give your current file a different name. If you do, select the replace option, and the computer program will save the file and then return you to the spreadsheet. If you choose to replace the old file with the new, the old version will be gone.

You should make a habit of saving the spreadsheet in stages as you work on it. When you finish, you should make a back-up copy on a second disk. By periodically replacing the spreadsheet with its most current version, you are protected from losing it all in the event of an interruption of the program; and by making a back-up disk, you have protection against loss of your primary disk. A minute or less in saving and backing up can save hours in redoing your work.

The process for retrieving a stored file is to do the following:

1. Press the / key to show the first menu.
2. In the first menu, select the file menu.
3. In the file menu, select the retrieve option.
4. At this point the program will display all of the files currently in Drive B. You should move the cursor to the file you wish to recall and press the enter key. The program will then retrieve the file and it will be available for further processing. Remember, a selection is made in a menu by moving the cursor to that selection and pressing the enter key. Take the cursor to the end of the current list, if there are many files on a disk, and it will call up the next list.

PRINTING THE SPREADSHEET

There are many options available in 1-2-3 for printing the spreadsheet. You can print the spreadsheet, or only a portion of it, as it is displayed on the screen. Be sure that your computer is properly connected to a printer and that your version of Lotus has been properly configured for that printer. The following steps show only the basic printing of a spreadsheet, and you should consult the manual or the help screens to learn about the menu items not mentioned.

In order to print out a portion of a spreadsheet in 1-2-3, do the following:

1. Press the / key to get the first menu.
2. In the first menu, select the print option.
3. In the following menu, select the printer option.
4. In the following menu, select the range option. Then enter the range of the spreadsheet you wish to print (the upper left corner cell, one or more periods, the lower right corner cell, and press the enter key):
5. At this point you should turn on your printer and see that the perforation on the paper is at the top to start a new page. Then select the align option. Nothing will happen, but the program will know that the paper is at the top of the page in the printer.
6. Select the go option. The range you have selected will now print out.
7. When the printing is finished, you may either print another part of the spreadsheet by going back to Step 4 or quit the print function by selecting the quit option. This will return you to your spreadsheet for additional work.

A COMPREHENSIVE EXAMPLE

In order to demonstrate the ability of Lotus 1-2-3 to produce a spreadsheet, we will use it to solve the following problem:

Forecasting Net Income for the Smith Company
It is January, 1986, and the Smith Company has just completed a review of its 1985 results. The income statement for 1985 is shown in Table 3-1. The company would like to produce a report that compares actual 1985 income with a forecast of income for the years 1986 through 1988. In doing so, it will make the following assumptions:

1. Cost of sales will be 65 per cent of sales in each year.
2. Overhead will be 22 per cent of sales in each year.
3. Sales will grow at an annual rate of 14 per cent over the forecast period.
4. Interest expense will grow at a rate of 8 per cent over the forecast period.
5. The tax rate will be 45 per cent.

Table 3-1

Smith Company: Income Statement, Year Ending Dec. 31, 1985

	Actual
Net Sales	$100,000
Cost of Sales	65,000
Gross Margin	35,000
Overhead	22,000
Income Before Interest and Taxes	13,000
Interest	5,000
Income Before Tax	8,000
Tax	3,600
Net Income	4,400

Based on this information and on the information in Table 3-1, use Lotus 1-2-3 to produce a report showing the current income statement and a forecast for the years 1986, 1987, 1988.

To build the spreadsheet, do the following:

1. Globally set the column width to 11 spaces.
2. Set the width of column A to 20 spaces.
3. Enter the heading

    Smith Company
    Income Statement,
    Year Ending Dec. 31,

in cells B1, B2, and B3.

4. We want to enter the critical variables in a separate data section. The reason for this is we want to build the spreadsheet by making reference to these critical variables in case we have to change one. If we do, and the variables are typed only once, the one change will reflect throughout the spreadsheet. Thus we will make the following entries.

Cell	Entry	Cell	Entry
A5	Data:		
A7	Cost of Sales %	C7	.65
A8	Overhead %	C8	.22
A9	Growth in Sales	C9	.14
A10	Growth in Interest Exp.	C10	.08
A11	Tax Rate	C11	.45

5. We are now ready to set up the income statement. We will use the labels in Table 3-1, and four columns—1985 Actual, 1986, 1987, and 1988. We will first enter the year headings by putting 1985, 1986,

1987, and 1988 in cells B14 and E14, consecutively. Then we put the carat symbol, ˆ, in front of the year. It does two things. First it tells the program that the entry is a label and not a number and, second, it centers the label in the column. In cell B15 we type ˄ *Actual* which centers that label just below the year 1985. We will now type the income statement accounts as they are presented in Table 3-1. Net sales goes in cell A17, cost of sales in cell A18, and so on through net income in cell A26. Finally, we type the numbers for 1985 in cells B17 to B26 from the data in Table 3-1. Our spreadsheet now looks like Figure 3-8.

Figure 3-8 Partially Completed Spreadsheet

	A	B	C	D	E
1		Smith Company			
2		Income Statement			
3		Year Ending Dec. 31,			
4					
5	Data:				
6					
7	Cost of Sales %		0.65		
8	Overhead %		0.22		
9	Growth in Sales		0.14		
10	Growth in Interest Exp.		0.08		
11	Tax Rate		0.45		
12					
13					
14		1985	1986	1987	1988
15		Actual			
16					
17	Net Sales	100000			
18	Cost of Sales	65000			
19	Gross Margin	35000			
20	Overhead	22000			
21	Income Before Interest &				
22	Taxes	13000			
23	Interest	5000			
24	Income Before Tax	8000			
25	Tax	3600			
26	Net Income	4400			

6. The next step is the hardest. Until now all we have really been doing is entering labels and values to introduce the variables into the example and to re-create Table 3-1. We will now do the creation of the forecast, and every cell from now on will be a formula. From this point forward the computer will do all of the work.

Our creation of the rest of the spreadsheet will be in two steps. In the first step we will create the entries for column C, and in the second step we will copy that logic into columns D and E. The entries in cells C17 through C26 and their explanation are as follows:

Cell	Entry

C17   +B17*(1+c9)

This takes one plus the sales growth rate (in cell C9) and multiplies it by the 1985 sales in cell B17. Notice that the $ is included to freeze the growth rate so that its cell will not change when we copy the logic for years 1987 and 1988

C18   +$C$7*C17

This takes the value in cell C7 and multiplies it by the value in cell C17. This will cause cost of sales to be 65 per cent of whatever sales is.

C19   +C17-C18

This computes gross margin by subtracting the cost of sales from sales.

C20   +$C$8*C17

This computes overhead by multiplying the overhead per cent times the sales for the year.

C21   empty
C22   +C19-C20

This computes income before interest and taxes by subtracting overhead from gross margin.

C23   +B23*(1+$C$10)

This computes the interest expense by increasing the previous year's interest expense at the designated growth rate.

C24   +C22−C23

This computes income before tax by subtracting interest from income before interest and taxes.

C25   +$C$11*C24

This computes tax by multiplying the tax rate times income before tax.

C26   +C24−C25

This computes net income by subtracting the tax from the income before tax.

At this point we are finished with 1986, and in fact have done most of the work. Our spreadsheet now has the entries in the cells as shown in Figure 3-9, although on the screen, the 1986 column will not show the formulas, but the values they have taken on.

We are now ready to do the second step, which is filling out the spreadsheet by copying the logic into columns D and E as follows:

Press the / key to call up the first menu. In that menu select the copy option. The program will ask the question *Copy From:* and you will insert C17..C26 and press the enter key. The program will then ask *Copy To:* and you will type D17..E26 (which is the range for the

Figure 3-9   Spreadsheet after the Logic for 1986 is Entered

	A	B	C	D	E
1		Smith Company			
2		Income Statement			
3		Year Ending Dec. 31,			
4					
5	Data:				
6					
7	Cost of Sales %		0.65		
8	Overhead %		0.22		
9	Growth in Sales		0.14		
10	Growth in Interest Exp.		0.08		
11	Tax Rate		0.45		
12					
13					
14		1985	1986	1987	1988
15		Actual			
16					
17	Net Sales	100000	+B17*(1+C		
18	Cost of Sales	65000	+C17*$C$7		
19	Gross Margin	35000	+C17−C18		
20	Overhead	22000	+C17*($C$8)		
21	Income Before Interest &				
22	Taxes	13000	+C19−C20		
23	Interest	5000	+B23*(1+C		
24	Income Before Tax	8000	+C22−C23		
25	Tax	3600	+C24*$C$11		
26	Net Income	4400	+C24−C25		

Note: The screen will display numbers, not the formulas as shown here.

Figure 3-10   The Final Version

	A	B	C	D	E
1		Smith Company			
2		Income Statement			
3		Year Ending Dec. 31,			
4					
5	Data:				
6					
7	Cost of Sales %		65.00%		
8	Overhead %		22.00%		
9	Growth in Sales		14.00%		
10	Growth in Interest Exp.		8.00%		
11	Tax Rate		45.00%		
12					
13					
14		1985	1986	1987	1988
15		Actual			
16					
17	Net Sales	$100,000	$114,000	$129,960	$148,154
18	Cost of Sales	65,000	74,100	84,474	96,300
19	Gross Margin	35,000	39,900	45,486	51,854
20	Overhead	22,000	25,080	28,591	32,594
21	Income Before				
22	Interest and Taxes	13,000	14,820	16,895	19,260
23	Interest	5,000	5,400	5,832	6,299
24	Income Before Tax	8,000	9,420	11,063	12,962
25	Tax	3,600	4,239	4,978	5,833
26	Net Income	4,400	5,181	6,085	7,129

D and E columns. After you press the enter key, the program will copy the logic. You have now created the spreadsheet.

7. The remaining step is to clean up the worksheet with the range format commands. We want the numbers in the data section to be in per cent, to have two decimal places, and the numbers in the income statement to have commas with no decimal places, and the first row to have dollar signs.

This is done by accessing the first menu with the / key, then selecting the range option, and within the range option selecting the format option. To create the per cent signs with two decimal points, select the per cent option, answer the decimal question with *2*, press the enter key, and then designate the range of C7..C11, followed by the enter key. To create the dollar signs and commas, with no decimal points for the next sales row, again access the range format selection, and this time choose the currency option. Indicate *0* after the decimal question and then B17..E17 for the range to format. Finally again select the range format menu, select the , option, answer the decimal question with *0* and indicate the range to format as B18..E26.

Your Spreadsheet is now finished and looks like Figure 3-10.

Congratulations, you have now created your first spreadsheet with Lotus 1-2-3, and are on your way.

SUGGESTED QUESTIONS

1. Construct the spreadsheet in the example and print it out.

2. After you have constructed the spreadsheet, determine what it would look like if the tax rate were 40 per cent and at the same time the sales growth rate fell to 11 per cent. Print out your results.

3. Determine what the spreadsheet would look like if interest cost grew at only 4 per cent but the cost of sales percent rose to 71 per cent. Print out your results.

4. Determine what the spreadsheet would look like if the overhead fell to 18 per cent, but the sales growth fell to 10 per cent. Print out your results.

CHAPTER 4

Using SuperCalc³

This chapter will take you through the steps necessary to use SuperCalc³ in solving the case problems in this text and in solving many types of financial problems. Before beginning, a couple of things need to be said. First of all the Supercalc³ program, hereafter referred to as SC3, is a very sophisticated spreadsheet program, capable of doing many more things than those discussed in this chapter. Also, experienced users will find that they can do things faster and easier than the methods discussed here permit. This chapter is not meant to produce an expert SC3 user, or even an efficient one. Its goal is to produce a user with the basic skills that will enable him or her to further develop prowess in the program. When you can master the techniques of this chapter, you should have no difficulty in going on to the advanced skills by reviewing the user's manual, using the Help function, or just plain experimenting.

A second point is that this discussion of SC3 is tailored to the IBM PC and its compatibles. In most cases, each point is applicable to a user no matter what machine is employed; but if the program does not act as it should, and you are using a non-IBM machine, it may be that machine differences are causing the difficulties. You should have no hesitancy in examining the manual if you are having trouble at a particular point.

Finally, the assumption is made that the user has a program which has been properly installed for the computer, monitor and printer that is being used. As discussed in Chapter 1, an installation process is necessary in order to configure a program to your specific system, and in order to use certain programs that belong to the makers of the computer or operating system. This installation process is done just once, so if the program has been used before it should be ready to go. If it has not, the operating manual will take you step by step through the installation process.

GETTING STARTED

In order to begin using SC3, you need the SC3 program disk and a blank, formatted disk which will be used to store the spreadsheet. If you have not formatted the blank disk, do so before you start, as you cannot do it after you have begun. You should insert the program disk in Drive A and the blank disk in Drive B and turn on the machine. In some cases the system will be self-booting, that is, the computer will go through the self-checking routing, possibly ask you to enter the date and time, and then go directly into SC3. If it does not, it will display a DOS prompt, which in the IBM and related systems will look as follows.

A⟩

with a blinking cursor after it. This means the computer is waiting for you to tell it what to do. In this case, type

SC3 ⟨enter⟩

where ⟨enter⟩ means to press the return or enter key, and in this case the SC3 program will be loaded into the RAM of the computer and you are ready to go. At this point the screen will look like Figure 4-1. If you then follow the instructions at the bottom of the screen, you can type ⟨enter⟩ and the screen will show the start of a spreadsheet, as shown in Figure 4-2. You are now ready to begin to create a spreadsheet.

Before beginning there are two things which you should know about the program. SC3 has a built in, on-line help function, which is like a small manual. At any time, a user can get into the Help screens by pressing the F1 key, or by typing a ? before making an entry into a cell. In order to get Help on a specific topic, such as a command, start the command and then type F1 or a ? This will bring up the appropriate Help screen on the topic. To return to the spreadsheet, type F1 again, and the program will pick up where you left off.

The second point is that SC3 has commands that enable you to do such things as save a file, print a spreadsheet, format a spread-

Part VI: Microcomputers and Spreadsheet Programs

Figure 4-1   The Initial Screen in SuperCalc^3

```
                    SuperCalc3(tm)
                    Version 1.00
                      I B M   P C
                 S/N-034210 ,IBM DOS

                    Copyright 1983
                    SORCIM CORP.
                    San Jose, CA.
```

```
Enter "?" for HELP or "return" to start.
F1 = Help; F2 = Erase Line/Return to Spreadsheet; F9 = Plot; F10 =
View
```

Figure 4-2   The Spreadsheet Screen for SuperCalc^3

```
|               A ||    B ||    C ||    D ||    E ||    F ||    G ||    H |
  1
  2
  3
  4
  5
  6
  7
  8
  9
 10
 11
 12
 13
 14
 15
 16
 17
 18
 19
 20
> A1
Width: 9 Memory:382 Last Col/Row:A1    ? for HELP
  1>
F1 = Help; F2 = Erase Line/Return to Spreadsheet; F9 = Plot; F10 = View
```

sheet, and other useful things. These commands are accessed by means of the / key. If this key is pressed prior to making an entry in a cell, the command choices come up in the third line at the bottom of the spreadsheet. To use a command requires typing the / key plus certain letters. In the following discussions the keys to type will be set aside, such as

/FCA12

and are to be typed exactly as seen. Any time you have a question during a / command sequence you can get an explanation by typing the F1 or ? for help.

The key to understanding and working with SC3 involves the three lines at the bottom of the spreadsheet, through which the program communicates to the user. In the first line, which is

⟩ A1

in Figure 4-2, there are two pieces of information. The ⟩ sign tells you which way the cursor will move after making a cell entry and pressing the enter key. When you first start up, the symbol points right, indicating that after you make an entry the cursor will automatically move one cell to the right. The direction of the symbol will be the last movement that the cursor made, so to change it, use the arrow keys to move around the spreadsheet until you have the symbol going in the proper direction. The second piece of information is the location of the cursor. You start in cell A1.

The second line,

Width: 9 Memory:382 Last Col/Row:A1   ? for HELP

gives you four pieces of information. The first is the width of the current column, the second is the memory in terms of K that you have left in the machine (as the spreadsheet increases in size you will use up this memory), the third fact is the bottom right corner of the spreadsheet, and the fourth tells you to press the ? key for help. Obviously this line has useful information which should be checked as you are doing your spreadsheet.

The third line, which is

1⟩

in Figure 4-2, shows the position you are at in the current cell entry. In Figure 4-2, it shows that you are ready to type the first character in the cell entry. As you type characters, the number in this line will increase to show how many characters you have typed. Obviously, this is beneficial in structuring the ultimate width of the column in order to properly display all the information.

MAKING ENTRIES IN THE CELLS

If you have followed the procedures outlined so far, you are now ready to start making entries in the cells. The entries will be either numbers, text, or formulas. For numbers, the procedure is simple: Move the cursor to the cell in which you wish to make the entry, type the number, and press the enter key. The number will appear in the cell, and the cursor will move to the next cell in the direction shown on the status line at the bottom of the spreadsheet. Two points should be made here. The first is that the numbers are entered without any dollar signs, commas, or any other characters except the decimal point. These items are provided for in a formatting process. The second point is that if you are entering a large amount of numbers, you can use the number-lock key to engage the key pad, since the enter key will move you to the next cell.

It is almost as easy to enter text. Text is usually a word or set of words, although occasionally a user might wish to define a number as text. To type text, move the cursor to the correct cell and begin typing the words. Again, pressing the enter key will cause the text to enter the cell and the cursor to move to the next cell in the direction indicated. Capitals and lower-case letters are done in the traditional manner and the capitals lock key can be used.

Sometimes you may confuse the program when you want to type text and it thinks you are typing a number. Consider the example shown in Figure 4-3. In cell D3 we have the year, 1984, which we want the program to recognize as text. In this case we would make the entry

"1984

where the " character is a signal to the program that what follows was text. Notice that the " character is not displayed; the program is smart enough to know what you wanted to do.

Many of the entries you will want to make in SC3 will be formulas that will take an entry in one cell and add or subtract it from the value in another cell. For example, in the spreadsheet shown in Figure 4-3, we want to compute gross profit by taking the value in cell C5 and subtracting the value in cell C7. In cell C9 you would type in

Figure 4-3   Sample Spreadsheet

```
I    A  II    B  II    C  II    D  II    E  II    F  II    G  II    H  I
1                          Partial Income Statement
2                          XYZ Company
3                          1984
4
5  Sales                  100000
6
7  Cost of Goods Sold     60000
8
9  Gross Profit           40000
10
11
12
13
14
15
16
17
18
19
20
< C9 Form=C5—C7
Width:   9  Memory:419 Last Col/Row:D9   ? for HELP
   1>
F1 = Help; F2 = Erase Line/Return to Spreadsheet; F9 = Plot; F10 = View
```

C5−C7. Notice in Figure 4-3 that when the cursor is on the cell with a formula, it shows the nature of that formula in the status lines at the bottom. Thus, on the first status line in Figure 4-3 we have

$$v \ C9 \qquad \text{Form} = C5-C7$$

This indicates the entry in C9 is the formula C5−C7, and the appropriate calculation is made in the spreadsheet. If, for some strange reason you had wanted text to read C5−C7 on the spreadsheet, you could have done so by typing the " character before typing the C5−C7 entry. In that case C5−C7 would have appeared in the cell.

Finally, the SC3 program has a number of preprogrammed formulas that enable you to do many mathematical tasks with a minimum of key strokes. For example, if you wish to compute the average for the values in cells B7 to B11 and put that average in cell B13, you could type the following entry for cell B13

$$(B7+B8+B9+B10+B11)/5$$

making sure you have the parentheses, as otherwise only cell B11 would be divided by 5, or you could use the built in SC3 average formula by typing the formula code, found in the SC3 manual, with the necessary information in parentheses. For example, in the above computation you would enter

average(B7:B11)

In using formulas and ranges in SC3 you must separate the cells indicating the range by a colon. In SC3, formulas exist for most common mathematical and financial applications. Remember, they do not have to be used but they save time and effort.

One final point about cell entries is that the entry may be too long for the cell width. In this case, SC3 will display text by borrowing from the adjacent cell if it is empty. Otherwise it just cuts off the entry at the end of the cell. It still remembers the entire text, though, so that later when the column is widened the entire text will be printed. If the cell is not wide enough for the number, the number will be cut off and as many decimal places as can be displayed will be displayed. If the entire integer cannot be displayed, the 〉〉〉〉〉〉〉〉 will appear, indicating the column must be widened.

THE EDIT FUNCTION

After having made entries into cells, the next logical question is how to correct an entry or change an entry. The simplest way is to write the new entry over the old one—that is, move the cursor to the cell, type the new entry, and press 〈enter〉. This will cause the new entry to replace the old one, and you can continue with the work.

In the event that the entry in the cell is very long and complicated, and the change in it is very small, you may want to use the edit function to change the entry. The edit function allows you to make changes in the entry in a single cell without disturbing the characters in the entry you do not wish to change. In order to access the edit function of SC3,

1. put the cursor on the cell you want to change;
2. type /E〈enter〉

and then you will find the contents on the cell at the third line from the spreadsheet. You are now ready to edit or change the entry.

In the edit mode the arrow keys will move the cursor to the left or right. The up arrow key will insert a space where the cursor is, the down arrow key and the delete key will delete the item above the cursor. The tab key will move the cursor to the beginning of the line, or if it is at the beginning of the line, the tab key will move it to the end of the line. The new characters typed will write over the old ones, unless the keyboard is in insert mode, which occurs when the insert key is pressed. In this mode, when you type a character it will be inserted at the point of the cursor. If you are in insert mode, the word *insert* will appear in the lower right corner of the screen. After you are finished making your changes, press enter key, and the new entry will appear in the cell.

You can do one other thing with the Edit function. You can copy an entry from one cell to another, but make a slight change in it. Put the cursor on the cell you wish to move the entry into and then press /E and the cell address that you wish to modify and copy. If you then hit the enter key, make the changes, and hit it again, the modified entry will appear in the new cell.

THE COMMAND SYSTEM AND COPYING CELL ENTRIES

Making cell entries into a new spreadsheet will probably cause a user to access the SC3 command system in order to copy text, data, or most likely formula logic from one set of cells into another. The SC3 command system is the method by which you can do all of the functions described in Chapter 2—copying, saving, printing, and so on. To first access the command system you must position the cursor at a cell and before any typing is done, depress the / key. This will call up the Command system, as shown in Figure 4-4. You have already used this system in the Edit function.

In SC3, the commands which are selected by choosing a letter, are described extensively in the user's manual. However, since all of the commands prompt and explain the proper response, try each command and see what happens. In most cases, the commands are accessed by a rational letter, for example, the save command is accessed by the pressing /S. If you want to see how a command works, press the / and the letter and then get into the help screens. They will explain how each command works.

In SC3, there are two commands—the replicate and the copy commands—that allow copying from one range to another. Since the

Figure 4-4   The SC3 Command Mode

```
v D8
Enter A,B,C,D,E,F,G,I,L,M,O,P,Q,R,S,T,U,V,W,X,Z,/,?
  2)/
F1 = Help; F2 = Erase Line/Return to Spreadsheet; F9
= Plot; F10 = View
```

Figure 4-5   The First Step of Replicate

```
v D8
From? (Enter Range)
 12>/Replicate,
F1 = Help; F2 = Erase Line/Return to Spreadsheet; F9 = Plot; F10 =
View
```

replicate command encompasses the functions of the copy command, this section will explain the use of the /R, or replicate command. In some cases you will be copying text, but in most cases you
will be copying logic. Since most spreadsheets show more than one
quarter or more than one year, you can use the same logic for as
many time periods as you like simply by copying it into other columns or rows. Remember, though, that the copying process copies
logic in a relative manner; that is, it keeps the relationship between
cells unless you override the relationship by a process discussed later
in this section.

To use the replicate function, go through the following step

1. Depress the /R keys. This will cause the lower part of the
screen to look like Figure 4-5.

The first line shows the location of the cursor, at cell D8. The second
line prompts for the entry in the third line. You should enter the
range to be copied from (the upper left cell:the lower right cell) and
then press the enter key. The lower part of the screen will now look
like Figure 4-6.

At this point a crucial decision must be made with respect to con-
tinuation of the process. Remember, the copying and replicating
functions act on a relational basis. If cell D7 was cell D3−D5, then
copying to cell E7 will result in E3−E5. This copying of the relationship is automatic, and if you want the program to do that, strike
the enter key after entering the range and the copying will be
complete.

However, if you want part or all of the copying to be in absolute
form—that is, for the program not to adjust the relationships—then
put , after the *to* range. In this case, the lower part of the screen will
look like Figure 4-7.

Figure 4-6   The Replicate Command after Entering "From" Range

```
v D8
To? (Enter Range), then <RETURN>; or <,> for Options
 18>/Replicate,d3:d7,
F1 = Help; F2 = Erase Line/Return to Spreadsheet; F9 = Plot; F10 =
View
```

Figure 4-7 Manual Adjustment for Copying

```
v D8
N(o Adjust), A(sk for adjust), V(alues), +, -, *, /
 24>/Replicate,d3:d7,e3:h3,
F1 = Help; F2 = Erase Line/Return to Spreadsheet; F9 = Plot; F10 =
View
```

Figure 4-8 Prompting for Adjustment in the Replicate Command

```
Source cell D7. Adjust D3 (Y or N)?
Replicating...7
 25>D3—D5
F1 = Help; F2 = Erase Line/Return to Spreadsheet; F9 = Plot; F10 =
View
```

After the comma you have to type an *N* if you want no relational adjustment in the copying process—that is, if you want all of the copying to be absolute. If you want a mixture, which will be the case in most situations, then strike the *A* key. The program will then take you through each cell entry and each cell reference and ask if you want to make the copying of that cell absolute or relational. In Figure 4-8, the program is asking if you want to adjust cell D3 in copying it to the *to* range. If you do, type *Y*, otherwise type *N* and the cell reference D3 will stay the same in the copied to range. The program will, in this way, prompt for all of the cells in the *copy from* range until the end is reached, at which time the copying will be complete.

FIXING UP THE SPREADSHEET

After you have constructed your spreadsheet, a number of options are available to "clean up" the spreadsheet and make it more presentable. Three of the more commonly used procedures are changing the column width, having the text justified at the left or right margin, and formatting the display of numbers. Other options are available, and a user is encouraged to explore these through either the manual or experimentation with the various commands and options. Remember, the help screens can always be accessed in the middle of a procedure, and remember to always save important work before you start experimenting with different areas.

Column Width

The column width may be changed either globally, that is, for the entire spreadsheet, or for a single column. In order to change the column width for the entire spreadsheet, you would make the following key strokes:

/FGnumber⟨enter⟩

where the number refers to the width you wish to make all of the columns in the spreadsheet. The program will then widen or narrow every column to the specification. If at any time you wish to return to the default settings, of nine-character-wide columns for example, the key strokes are

/FGD⟨enter⟩

and all columns except those which have been individually set will return to the default value of nine characters wide.

To change the width of an individual column, the keystrokes are

/FCletter,number⟨enter⟩

where letter is the letter of the column and number is the width you wish to make the column. This arrangement will override any global formatting you have done, so the only way to change the width of a column once the above procedure has been done is to redo it to the width you want.

Text or Number Justification

In SC3, you have the option of having your text or numbers flush against either the right or left margin. The default option is flush against the left margin for text and flush against the right margin for numbers. The default may be changed on either a global or individual range basis. To change the text on a global basis, the keystrokes are

/FGTR⟨enter⟩

to have right text justification and

/FGTL⟨enter⟩

to return to left text justification.

To change the numbers, the keystrokes are

/FGL⟨enter⟩

to left justify the numbers and

/FGR⟨enter⟩

to return to right justification.

In order to have left or right justification for a range, the keystrokes are

/FEcell:cell⟨enter⟩letter⟨enter⟩

where the first cell reference is to the upper left corner of the range, the second cell reference to the lower right corner of the range, and the letter *L,R, TL*, or *TR* to justify numbers on the left margin, to justify numbers on the right margin, to justify text on the left or to justify text on the right, respectively.

FORMATTING

The term *formatting* in spreadsheet context refers to putting in dollar signs, commas, parentheses for negative numbers, per cent signs, and so on, in displaying the data. Formatting can be done on a global basis, but in almost all cases you will want to do it on a range basis— that is, format one part of the spreadsheet in one way, another part in another way, and so forth. To do this in SC3, you will use a user-defined format table.

To define the table, first type

/F

This will produce the following at the bottom of the spreadsheet:

Figure 4-9   The F Command Choices

```
>A1
Enter Level: G(lobal), C(olumn), R(ow), E(ntry) or D(efine)
  9>/Format,
F1 = help; F2 = Erase Line/Return to Spreadsheet; F9 = Plot; F10 =
View
```

If you now type the letter D you will get the table shown in Figure 4-10. In effect, you now have eight different formats that you can define and then call up by number. The default options in the user-defined format table are shown in Figure 4-10. When Figure 4-10 is first displayed, the cursor will be on the *Y* in the upper left corner. Basically, the *Y* refers to yes and the *N* to no. If you want the particular item identified on the left to be in the form, type *Y* and that letter will appear on the screen. You can then move the cursor with

Figure 4-10   User Defined Formats—Default

	User-defined formats							
	1	2	3	4	5	6	7	8
Floating $	Y	Y	Y	Y	Y	Y	Y	Y
Embedded Commas	Y	Y	Y	Y	Y	Y	Y	Y
Minus in ( )	N	N	N	N	N	N	N	N
Zero as Blank	N	N	N	N	N	N	N	N
%	N	N	N	N	N	N	N	N
Decimal Places	2	2	2	2	2	2	2	2
Scaling factor	0	0	0	0	0	0	0	0

F2 to return to worksheet.

```
> A1
Y(es) or N(o) ?
  15>/Format,Define
F1 = Help; F2 = Erase Line/Return to Spreadsheet; F9 = Plot; F10 = View
```

the arrow keys around the table and change the *Y*'s and *N*'s to whichever you would like.

In the table, *Y*'s and *N*'s are used except in the last two rows. The decimal places can be determined by a number that indicates how many places will be displayed. The last row scales the numbers and can be ignored for most applications, that is, left as it is displayed.

A typical formatting table for three widely used formats is shown in Figure 4-11. Format 1 has dollar sign, commas, negative numbers in parentheses, and two-decimal places, which is the typical way of displaying the first row of a set of financial data. The second format, under column 2 has the same format but without the dollar signs. This is the typical way of displaying rows other than the first row in financial data. Finally, format 3 would display per cents to two decimal places, that is, .12 would display as 12.00%.

Figure 4-11 $, Commas and % Formats

	User-defined formats							
	1	2	3	4	5	6	7	8
Floating $	Y	N	N	Y	Y	Y	Y	Y
Embedded Commas	Y	Y	Y	Y	Y	Y	Y	Y
Minus in ( )	Y	Y	Y	N	N	N	N	N
Zero as Blank	N	N	N	N	N	N	N	N
%	N	N	Y	N	N	N	N	N
Decimal Places	2	2	2	2	2	2	2	2
Scaling factor	0	0	0	0	0	0	0	0

F2 to return to worksheet.

```
> A1
Enter number from (0 - 7)
  15>/Format,Define
F1 = Help; F2 = Erase Line/Return to Spreadsheet; F9 = Plot; F10 = View
```

Figure 4-12

```
> A1
Enter range
 21>/Format,Entry,a1:d10
F1 = Help; F2 = Erase Line/Return to Spreadsheet; F9 = Plot; F10 =
View
```

Figure 4-13

```
> A1
Define Formats: (I,G,E,$,R,L,TR,TL,*,U(1—8),H,D)
 36>/Format,Entry,a1:d10,User-defined3,
F1 = Help; F2 = Erase Line/Return to Spreadsheet; F9 = Plot; F10 =
View
```

After you have defined up to eight formats, press the F2 key to return to the spreadsheet. Using the print screen command, it is a good idea to print out the table so you can remember what formats are where. You are now ready to format a range in your spreadsheet.

In order to format a particular range of the spreadsheet, the key strokes are begun as follows:

/FEcell:cell

The results are shown in Figure 4-12, where we want to format the range A1:D10 with per cents to two decimal places. If we now continue with ⟨enter⟩, we will get a list of options as shown in the second line in Figure 4-13. To select a user-defined format, type *U* and the number of the format, in this case *3*, and the third line will look like the third line in Figure 4-13. If we now press the enter key the program will format the range and return us to the spreadsheet. In summary, our key strokes were

/FEcell:cell⟨enter⟩Unumber⟨enter⟩

SAVING AND RETRIEVING A FILE

Making a spreadsheet is a lot of work and you probably will not create a final version in a single sitting. Even if you do, the chances are high that you will want to return to the spreadsheet for modifications later on. However, when you turn off the computer, the spreadsheet that resided in the computer's memory will be gone. You must be able to store and retrieve a spreadsheet from a disk in order to work effectively.

In SC3, the storage and retrieval is done with the /S and /L commands. To save a spreadsheet, you do the following:

1. Type /S at which time the program will ask you for a name for your file.

2. Type the name of the file. If it is a spreadsheet you have called up from a disk, strike the ESC key and the name will appear.

3. If the spreadsheet has already been saved under the name, the program will ask if you want to change the name, create a back-up, or overwrite. In most cases you will be updating the file, so type *O*.

4. The program will now determine if you want to save all of the file, the values only, or a part of the file. In most cases you will want to save all of the file, so type *A*, and the file will be saved and you will be returned to the spreadsheet as you left it.

In retrieving a file from a disk, a similar procedure is used. In this case the steps are the following:

1. Type /L and the program will ask for the file name.

2. Type the file name.

3. The program will ask if you want all the file, part of the file, to consolidate the file, or a special function called *. Again, in almost all cases you will want all the file, so typing *A* will load the file, so that you are now ready to edit.

If you do not remember the status of the program, or the file names when you are working with /S and /L, press ⟨enter⟩ after the /S or /L, and you will get a directory of the status and a directory of files. You can recognize SC3 files by the fact that the program has appended .CAL after the name. This .CAL may be ignored in all user actions.

PRINTING THE SPREADSHEET

A large number of options are available in SC3 for printing the spreadsheet. The steps that follow will allow you to print the spreadsheet or a portion of it as it appears on the screen. Your computer has to be properly connected to the printer and the program properly installed for the printing equipment to work. The following steps show only the basics of printing. Consult the manual or the help screens for additional information.

In order to print, the following key stroke sequence is used:

/ODcell:cell⟨enter⟩PP

where the *cell:cell* is the upper left and lower right corners of the range you wish to print. The program will print as shown on the screen, including the row and column headings. In order to eliminate them you should use the following command prior to printing

/GB

which will remove the borders. Repeating the command after printing will restore the borders.

A COMPREHENSIVE EXAMPLE

In order to demonstrate the ability of SC3 to produce a spreadsheet, we will consider how the program might be used to solve the following problem.

Forecasting Net Income for the Smith Company

It is January, 1986, and the Smith Company has just completed a review of its 1985 results. The income statement for 1985 is shown in Table 4-1 below. The company would like to produce a report that compares the actual 1985 income statement with a forecast of the income statement for 1986 through 1988. In doing so it will make the following assumptions.

1. Cost of sales will be 65 per cent of sales each year.
2. Overhead will be 22 per cent of sales in each year.
3. Sales will grow at a rate of 14 per cent each year.
4. Interest will grow at a rate of 8 per cent each year.
5. The tax rate will be 45 per cent.

Based on this information and Table 4-1, use SC3 to produce a

Table 4-1

Income Statement Year Ending Dec. 31, 1985

	Actual
Net Sales	$100,000
Cost of Sales	65,000
Gross Margin	35,000
Overhead	22,000
Income Before Interest and Taxes	13,000
Interest	5,000
Income Before Tax	8,000
Tax	3,600
Net Income	4,400

report showing the current income statement and the forecast for years 1986, 1987, and 1988.

In order to build the spreadsheet we will do the following:

1. Globally set the column width to 11 spaces.
2. Set the width of column A to 20 spaces.
3. Enter the following text

Smith Company
Income Statement
Year Ending Dec. 31,

in cells B1, B2, and B3.

4. We want to enter the critical variables in a separate data section. The reason is to build the spreadsheet by referring to these critical variables by cell address, in case we want to change one. If we do want to change, and the variables are entered in numerical form only once, the one change will reflect throughout the spreadsheet. Thus, we will make the following entries:

Cell	Entry	Cell	Entry
A5	Data:		
A7	Cost of Sales %	C7	.65
A8	Overhead %	C8	.22
A9	Growth in Sales	C9	.14
A10	Growth in Interest Exp.	C10	.08
A11	Tax Rate	C11	.45

5. We are now ready to set up the income statement. We will use the data in Table 4-1 and the four columns, the 1985 actual, 1986, 1987, and 1988. We will first enter the year heading by putting "1985, "1986, "1987, "1988 in cells B14 to E14, consecutively. Putting the " character in front of the year indicates that it is text and not a number. In cell B15 we type the word *actual,* which puts it below the year 1985.

We will now type the income statement accounts as presented in Table 4-1. Net sales goes in cell A17, cost of sales in cell A18, and so on through net income in cell A26. Finally, we type the numbers for 1985 in cells B17 to B26 from the data in Table 4-1. Our spreadsheet now looks like Figure 4-14.

6. The next step is the hardest. Until now, all we have really been doing is entering text and values to introduce the variables into the example and, basically, recreate Table 4-1. We will now create the forecast, and every cell from now on will be a formula. From this point forward, the computer will be doing most of the work.

Creation of the rest of the spreadsheet requires two steps. The first is to create the entries for column C and the second to copy that

Figure 4-14   The Spreadsheet Through Step 5

```
 |           A              ||   B   || C  ||  D  ||  E
1|                          Smith Company
2|                          Income Statement
3|                          Year Ending Dec. 31,
4|
5|Data:
6|
7|Cost of Sales %                           .65
8|Overhead %                                .22
9|Growth in Sales                           .14
10|Growth in Interest Exp.                   .08
11|Tax Rate                                  .45
12|
13|
14|                          1985        1986    1987   1988
15|                          Actual
16|
17|Net Sales                 100000
18|Cost of Sales              65000
19|Gross Margin               35000
20|Overhead                   22000
21|Income Before
22|Interest and Taxes         13000
23|Interest                    5000
24|Income Before Tax           8000
25|Tax                         3600
26|Net Income                  4400
```

logic into columns D and E. The entries in cells C17 to C26 and their explanation are as follows.

Cell	Entry
C17	B17*(1+C9)

This says to take one plus the sales growth in cell C9 and multiply it by the 1985 sales, which is in cell B17.

C18	C7*C17

This says that the cost of goods sold will be the value of sales in cell C17 times the cost-of-goods-sold per cent, which is in cell C7.

C19	C17−C18

This says to create the gross margin, take the sales in cell C17 and subtract the cost of goods sold in cell C18.

C20   C8*C17

This computes overhead by multiplying the overhead per cent times the sales for the year.

C21   empty
C22   C19−C20

This computes the income before interest and taxes by subtracting overhead in C20 from gross margin in C19.

C23   B23*(1+C10)

This computes the interest expense by increasing the interest expense in 1985 by the rate designated in the data section.

C24   C22−C23

This computes income before tax by subtracting interest from income before interest and taxes.

C25   C24*C11

This computes the income-tax expense by multiplying the income before tax by the tax rate in cell C11.

C26   C24−C25

This computes the net income by subtracting the income tax from the income before tax.

At this point we are finished with 1986. Our spreadsheet now has the entries in the cells shown in Figure 4-15, although the 1986 column will not show formulas but the values they have taken on.

We are now ready to fill out the spreadsheet by copying the logic in column C to columns D and E. We will do this with the /R command, as explained in an earlier section. Notice that some of the logic will have to be copied with adjustments, that is, on a relational basis, and some will have to be copied without adjustment. Whenever we want to use a value from the data section, we want the copying to be done without adjustment, that is, the cell reference to stay the same.

The steps for the copying are as follows: First we will press /R for the replicate command. The first entry we have to make is the *copy from,* which will be done by entering C17:C26. The program will now ask for the *copy to* range, which will be answered by giving the

Figure 4-15   The Spreadsheet after the Logic for 1986 is Entered

```
  |         A              ||   B    ||   C    ||      D   ||  E
 1|                        Smith Company
 2|                        Income Statement
 3|                        Year Ending Dec. 31,
 4|
 5|Data:
 6|
 7|Cost of Sales %                      .65
 8|Overhead %                           .22
 9|Growth in Sales                      .14
10|Growth in Interest Exp.              .08
11|Tax Rate                             .45
12|
13|
14|                        1985         1986        1987    1988
15|                        Actual
16|
17|Net Sales               100000    B17*(1+C9)
18|Cost of Sales            65000    C17*C7
19|Gross Margin             35000    C17-C18
20|Overhead                 22000    C8*C17
21|Income Before
22|Interest and Taxes       13000    C19-C20
23|Interest                  5000    B23*(1+C10)
24|Income Before Tax         8000    C22-C23
25|Tax                       3600    C11*C24
26|Net Income                4400    C24-C25
```

Note: The screen will display numbers, not the cell formulas, as shown in this figure

upper left corner and upper right corners, that is D17:E17. After making this entry, type , followed by *A*.

The program will now take you through a prompting of each cell reference in the copy from cells C17 to C26, asking if you want to adjust. You will want to answer *Y* for the cells in the income statement, B17 for example in the first reference, and *N* for the cells that are in the data section. This will keep the cell references in the data section constant in the *copy to* area, and adjust the other cells as required to keep the logic correct. After you have answered the query for all the cells, the copying will be complete and your spreadsheet will be filled out for all four years.

7. The remaining step is to clean up the worksheet by typing /F and then a *D* to set up the format table. In the format table you will create Format 1 with $ signs, commas, and *0* decimal points. Format 2 will be no $ signs, commas, and 0 decimal points. Typing F2 returns you to the spreadsheet.

Figure 4-16   The Final Version

	A	B	C	D	E
1		Smith Company			
2		Income Statement			
3		Year Ending Dec. 31,			
4					
5	Data:				
6					
7	Cost of Sales %		.65		
8	Overhead %		.22		
9	Growth in Sales		.14		
10	Growth in Interest Exp.		.08		
11	Tax Rate		.45		
12					
13					
14		1985	1986	1987	1988
15		Actual			
16					
17	Net Sales	$100,000	$114,000	$129,960	$148,154
18	Cost of Sales	65,000	74,100	84,474	96,300
19	Gross Margin	35,000	39,900	45,486	51,854
20	Overhead	22,000	25,080	28,591	32,594
21	Income Before				
22	Interest and Taxes	13,000	14,820	16,895	19,260
23	Interest	5,000	5,400	5,832	6,299
24	Income Before Tax	8,000	9,420	11,063	12,962
25	Tax	3,600	4,239	4,978	5,833
26	Net Income	4,400	5,181	6,085	7,129

If you now type /F again, and then *E* after the command, you will be prompted for a range. Type B17:E17⟨enter⟩U1 and the first row of the income statement will be formatted with dollar signs, commas, and no decimal places. Typing /FEB18:E26⟨enter⟩U2 will cause the rest of the spreadsheet to be formatted with commas and no decimal places. Your finished spreadsheet will now look like Figure 4-16. Congratulations, you have created your first spreadsheet and are now on your way to doing more with SC3

SUGGESTED QUESTIONS

1. Construct the spreadsheet in the example and print it out.

2. After you have constructed the spreadsheet, print out the results if the tax rate were changed to 40 per cent and at the same time the sales growth rate fell to 11 per cent.

3. Print out the results if interest cost grew at only 4 per cent, but the cost of sales per cent rose to 71 per cent.

4. Print out the results if the overhead fell to 18 per cent, but sales growth fell to 10 per cent.

Note: In questions 2–4 assume you are back at the original values before making the changes.

CHAPTER 5

Using Multiplan

This chapter will take you through the steps necessary to use Multiplan in solving the case problems in this text and in solving many types of financial problems. Before beginning, a couple of things need to be said. First of all, Multiplan is a very sophisticated spreadsheet program, capable of doing many more things than those discussed in this chapter. Also, experienced users will find that they can do things faster and easier than the methods discussed here permit. This chapter is not meant to produce an expert Multiplan user. Its goal is to produce a user who can develop, save, and print spreadsheets, and to provide users with the basic skills that will enable him or her to further develop prowess in the program. When you can master the techniques of this chapter, you should have no difficulty in mastering the advanced skills by reviewing the user's manual, using the help function, or just plain experimenting.

A second point is that this discussion of Multiplan is tailored to the IBM PC and its compatibles. In most cases, each point is applicable to the program no matter what type of machine is employed; but if the program does not work as it should and you are using a non-IBM machine, it may be that machine differences are causing the difficulty. This certainly might be the case when using Multiplan on the Apple Macintosh. You should have no hesitancy in examining the manual if you have trouble at a particular point.

Finally, the assumption is made that the user has a program which has been properly installed for the computer, monitor, and printer that is being used. As discussed in Chapter 1, an installation process

Figure 5-1   The Opening Screen of Multiplan, Version 1.2

```
#1                    1       2       3       4       5       6       7
  1
  2
  3
  4
  5
  6
  7
  8
  9
 10
 11
 12
 13
 14
 15
 16
 17
 18
 19
 20
COMMAND:  Alpha Blank Copy Delete Edit Format Goto Help Insert
          Lock Move Name Options Print Quit Sort Transfer Value
          Window Xternal
Select option or type command letter
R1C1                         100 % Free      Multiplan: TEMP
```

is necessary to configure a program to your specific system and to use certain programs that may belong to the makers of the computer or the operating system. This installation process is done just once, so if the program has been used before it should be ready to go. If it has not, the operating manual will take you step by step through the installation process.

GETTING STARTED

In order to begin using Multiplan you will need Multiplan program disk and a blank, formatted disk, which will be used to store the spreadsheet. If you have not formatted the blank disk, do so before you start, as you cannot do so after you have begun. You should insert the program disk in Drive A and the blank disk in Drive B, and then turn on the machine. In most situations your system will be self-booting and the computer will go through a self-checking routine, possibly asking for the date and time, and then going directly into Multiplan. If it does not, it will display the DOS prompt which in the IBM and related systems will look as follows:

A⟩

with a blinking cursor after it. This means the computer is waiting for you to tell it what to do. In this case type

MP⟨enter⟩

where the ⟨enter⟩ sign means to press the return or enter key and the Multiplan program will be loaded into the system. In the event of any difficulty, put the DOS disk in the machine, turn it on to get the A⟩ prompt, and then type MP⟨enter⟩.

After Multiplan is loaded the screen will show a blank spreadsheet of Multiplan, and you are now ready to go to work. The screen will look like Figure 5-1.

Before beginning, there are several things you should know about Multiplan. The first is that the program has a built in help function, which may be accessed at any time by going to the help selection in the command menu or by typing ?. The help screens tell all about certain aspects of the program and are particularly useful if you get hung up on a certain point in the middle of doing it. By typing ? you will get the appropriate help screen to aid you with the problem. The opening help screen with its directions are shown in Figure 5-2.

Figure 5-2   The Multiplan Initial Help Screen

```
There are three ways to use HELP:

1. You may press the "?" key at any time during your work.
   The help text that appears will apply to the command
   you were using when you pressed "?". When you resume
   (by pressing "R"), your work will be exactly as you
   left it.
2. You may view information on special topics right now by
   selecting one of the topics listed at the bottom of the
   screen. Type the first letter of the desired word.
3. You may familiarize yourself with all the available
   information by paging through the help text right now.
   Select "Next" (press "N") "Previous or "Start" page.

If you need information on a specific command, highlight
the command name on the proper menu (using the space bar)
and press "?".

Applications

The following table provides an index to the commands and
help

HELP: Resume Start Next Previous
      Applications Commands Editing Formulas Keyboard
Select option or type command letter
R1C1                    100% Free    Multiplan: TEMP
```

A second point is that Multiplan allows you to do such things as access the help screens, save and load files, or print a file by means of a command menu. The menu is displayed at the bottom of the screen and one makes a choice by either typing the first letter of the menu item or by moving the cursor with the space bar and then typing ⟨enter⟩ when the space bar is on the appropriate item. The menus will contain several selections. You can move to the different areas of the submenus by means of the tab key. This will be demonstrated in subsequent discussions as we cover topics like formatting a cell, copying, and printing.

Finally, you should be aware of what information the spreadsheet is providing you in its basic screen. In Figure 5-1, the top part of the spreadsheet shows the cells, with both columns and rows designated by numbers. In Multiplan a cell address is written as R1C1, where the numbers after each letter refer to the row and column; thus, R1 signifies row 1 and C1, column 1. The bottom part of the spreadsheet, shown in Figure 5-3, provides the following information:

Figure 5-3   The Lower Part of a Multiplan Spreadsheet Screen

```
COMMAND: Alpha Blank Copy Delete Edit Format Goto Help
         Insert Lock Move Name Options Print Quit Sort
         Transfer Value Window Xternal
Select option or type command letter
R1C1                    100% Free    Multiplan: TEMP
```

The first two lines of Figure 5-3 show the available commands in the Multiplan system. The commands are accessed by either typing the first letter of the command, or by moving the cursor to the command by means of the space bar and then typing ⟨enter⟩. The third line gives you the information on how to access the commands. The fourth line shows the current location of the cursor, in this case in the upper left-hand corner, R1C1 standing for row 1, column 1, how much of the memory is available, and the name of the current file. Since no file has been created, *Multiplan: TEMP* tells you the program does not have a permanent file. When you have called a file from memory, or given the file a name, the name will appear in the lower right corner after *Multiplan*.

MAKING ENTRIES IN THE CELLS

If you have followed the procedures outlined so far you are facing a Multiplan blank spreadsheet that looks like Figure 5-1 and are ready to start making entries into the cells. The entries will be either numbers, text, or formulas, although Multiplan in its designations treats numbers as formulas. For numbers, the procedure is simple: Move the cursor by means of the arrow keys to the cell in which you wish to make the entry; type the number and press either the enter key or an arrow key. The number will appear in the cell, and you can go on to the next thing you want to do. Pressing an arrow key automatically moves the cursor in the direction of the arrow after entering the number. One thing is important, the numbers should be entered without any dollar signs, commas, parentheses, and so on. The program will provide for this in the formatting process.

In order to enter text, usually a word or set of words, although occasionally a set of numbers, you must alert the program that text is coming. This is done by selecting the Alpha command, by typing the letter *A*. The program will indicate at the command level that text is being entered, and you can type in whatever you want to say, even a number. After typing in the text you can move to the next cell and continue typing numbers or text. As long as you use the arrow keys after typing an entry to create a cell, you can type either text or values. If, however, you type a number and strike ⟨enter⟩, you must return to the command menu status of Figure 5-3 and type *A* before typing text again. Once you start typing text, the program will assume you are typing text until you type a number.

Two things should be noted here. If, for example, you want to type a number as text and are in the text/value mode, you have to return to the command menu level, type *A* and then type the number as text. Typing the number as text in the text/value mode will cause the program to think you are typing a number. The second point is that to return to the command menu, you must hit the ESC key. ESC can be thought of as an undo key. It will get you out of the current menu situation and return you to the spreadsheet with the command menus at the bottom.

In Figure 5-4 we are entering the designation *1984-1* as the first quarter of 1984 as text. If we did not designate this as text, the program would think we wanted to subtract 1 from 1,984. By indicating this is text, the 1984 appears in the cell.

Entering formulas introduces us to a unique feature of Multiplan—the ability to make entries by *pointing*. Remember, a formula will in many cases involve cell references. In Multiplan the formula is built by pointing to the cells involved and entering the appropriate

Figure 5-4   1984-1 Entered as Text

```
# 1          1        2        3        4        5        6        7
  1
  2
  3
  4
  5
  6
  7
  8
  9
 10
 11
 12
 13
 14
 15
 16
 17
 18
 19
 20
ALPHA: 1981-1

Enter text (no double quotes)
R7C3                              100% Free      Multiplan: TEMP
```

arithmetic operator symbol. As with many situations, it is easier to show than to explain.

In Figure 5-5 we have started a partial income statement. Column 1 was widened to accommodate the text and the data was entered in the appropriate places. We want the program to compute the gross profit by subtracting the cost of goods sold from the sales and compute the per cent by dividing the gross profit by sales. We start this process by putting the cursor on cell R12C2, as indicated in Figure 5-5.

We want the program to take the value in cell R8C2 and subtract the value in cell R10C2. Thus, we first type *value* to indicate to the program a formula will be entered. Next we use the arrow keys to move the cursor to the first cell of the formula, R8C2. The result is shown in Figure 5-6, in which we see, on the status line, that R[−4]C has been entered in cell R12C2. R[−4]C indicates the entry in the cell is to be the data in the cell four rows up, same column. This, of course is the sales data.

After having moved the cursor up to the cell, we now type the − to indicate we want to subtract something from this value. The program will return the cursor to cell R12C2 to wait for the next step.

Figure 5-5 The Spreadsheet Ready for a Formula

```
#1                 1              2          3    4    5    6
   1
   2 XYZ Company
   3 Partial Income Statement
   4
   5
   6
   7
   8 Sales                     300000
   9
  10 Cost of Goods Sold        200000
  11
  12 Gross Profit
  13
  14 Percent
  15
  16
  17
  18
  19
  20
COMMAND:  Alpha Blank Copy Delete Edit Format Goto Help Insert
          Lock Move Name Options Print Quit Sort Transfer Value
          Window Xternal
Select option or type command letter
R12C2                        99% Free    Multiplan: TEMP
```

Figure 5-6 The First Step in Building the Formula

```
#1               1            2        3   4   5   6
   1
   2 XYZ Company
   3 Partial Income Statement
   4
   5
   6
   7
   8 Sales                   300000
   9
  10 Cost of Goods Sold      200000
  11
  12 Gross Profit
  13
  14 Percent
  15
  16
  17
  18
  19
  20
VALUE: R[−4]C

Enter a formula
R8C2    300000              99% Free   Multiplan: TEMP
```

303

Figure 5-7   The Second Step in Building the Formula

```
#1                    1              2           3   4   5   6
  1
  2 XYZ Company
  3 Partial Income Statement
  4
  5
  6
  7
  8 Sales                      300000
  9
 10 Cost of Goods Sold         200000
 11
 12 Gross Profit
 13
 14 Percent
 15
 16
 17
 18
 19
 20
VALUE: R[−4]C−R[−2]C

Enter a formula
R10C2    200000                99% Free    Multiplan: TEMP
```

If we now move the cursor up to the cell where the cost of goods sold is, the program will look like Figure 5-7. The formula is completed by typing ⟨enter⟩. This makes the cell entry in R12C2, R[−4]C−R[−2]C, which says to take the value in the cell four rows above, same column, and subtract from it the value in the cell two rows above, same column. The screen will show 100000 and you are now ready to continue with the program.

To create the formula for cell R14C2 we will do the same set of steps. We will

1. Place the cursor in cell R14C2.
2. Type *V* to indicate a value is coming.
3. Move the cursor to cell R12C2 and type / .
4. Move the cursor to cell R8C2.

The screen will now look like Figure 5-8. The last step is to put the formula in the cell. This is done by

5. Type ⟨enter⟩.

Now the spreadsheet will look like Figure 5-9. To place dollar and per cent signs, commas, and the like, you will use the formatting function, which will be discussed later in this chapter.

Figure 5-8 The Creation of the Formula for Cell R14C2

```
#1                   1                2             3    4    5    6
  1
  2 XYZ Company
  3 Partial Income Statement
  4
  5
  6
  7
  8 Sales                      300000
  9
 10 Cost of Goods Sold         200000
 11
 12 Gross Profit               100000
 13
 14 Percent
 15
 16
 17
 18
 19
 20
VALUE: R[-2]C/R[-6]C

Enter a formula
R8C2    300000              99% Free     Multiplan: TEMP
```

Figure 5-9 The Completed Spreadsheet with Formulas

```
#1                   1                2             3    4    5    6
  1
  2 XYZ Company
  3 Partial Income Statement
  4
  5
  6
  7
  8 Sales                      300000
  9
 10 Cost of Goods Sold         200000
 11
 12 Gross Profit               100000
 13
 14 Percent                    0.3333333
 15
 16
 17
 18
 19
 20
COMMAND:  Alpha Blank Copy Delete Edit Format Goto Help Insert
          Lock Move Name Options Print Quit Sort Transfer Value
          Window Xternal
Select option or type command letter
R14C2    R[-2]C/R[-6]C                99% Free     Multiplan: TEMP
```

Remember that the entry into the cells has been relational and not absolute. If we were to copy this logic over into other columns, values in row 12 and row 14 would be governed by the values in the cells above them. If we want to make a cell address absolute, we have to type its address. That is, cell R8C2 would be typed R8C2 not as R[−4]C. This distinction is important for the copying activity, and we will discuss it later.

THE EDIT FUNCTION

After having made entries into cells, the next logical question is how to correct or change an entry. The simplest way is to write the new entry over the old one, that is move the cursor to the cell you want to change, make the cell entry you wish, and type ⟨enter⟩ or hit the return. This will cause the new entry to replace the old one in the cell and you can go on with your work. If you make a mistake while you are typing the entry, it can be corrected by using the backspace key which will erase each character as it goes backward.

In the event that the entry in the cell is very long and complicated, and the change in it is relatively small, you may want to use the edit function to change the entry. Depressing the E key when the command menu is showing will put the program in Edit format. The cell entry that the cursor is in will be displayed on the status line at the bottom of the page and you will be ready to Edit. In the Edit mode you can erase by moving backward with the back-space key, or you can move the cursor under the letter you want to change by using cursor movement keys, CTRL K for left, CTRL L for right, CTRL O for word left and CTRL P for word right. The delete key will erase the character above it, and the program will insert any character you type in the line. The enter key allows you to exit from the Edit function and return to the spreadsheet. When you type ⟨enter⟩ the new entry will be made as adjusted.

THE MENU/COMMAND SYSTEM AND COPYING CELL ENTRIES

Making cell entries in a new spreadsheet will almost certainly cause a user to access the Multiplan menu/command system in order to copy cell entries from one range to another. The Multiplan menu/command system is the method by which you can do all of the functions described in Chapter 2—copying, saving, printing, and so on. In accessing the menu/command system you must have the menu/

command displayed as they would be at the bottom of the spreadsheet shown in Figure 5-1. If they are not displayed, typing ESC will cause them to be displayed.

In the Multiplan menu/command system, the choice can be made in one of two ways. The easiest is to type the first letter of the command you want, which will cause the system to go into the command mode and display the next level of menus for selection. A second way is to move the cursor to the item by means of the space bar and then type ⟨enter⟩. Once in the command menus, you skip to new fields by using the tab key to shift to new items. It is a good idea to stroll through the menu commands and look at each one, if you remember that you can always get out by pressing the ESC key.

The copy function speeds up construction of a spreadsheet. In some cases you will be copying text, but in most cases you will be copying the logic of your constructed formulas. Since most spreadsheets show more than one quarter or more than one year, once you have set up the logic for one time period you can make the same logic for as many time periods as you like by simply copying into other columns and rows.

Remember, though, that the copying process will copy either relationships or absolutes, depending upon how you have set up the formulas. Take, for example, the following situation. Suppose you have the following partial spreadsheet:

	1	**2**	**3**
14	200		
15	300		
16			

and you wish the program to add the values of R14C1 and R15C1 to get the value in R16C1. There are two ways you can do this. One is to create the formula $R[-2]C + R[-1]C$ which says to take the value two rows up and add it to the value one row up. If you now copy this logic into columns 2 and 3, the same relationship will hold, that is, the value in Row 16 will always be the value two rows up plus the value one row up in the current column.

Your second choice is first to type *V* to get the value command and then to type the formula R14C1 + R15C1. In column 1 this will result in the same value in cell R16C1 as before. However, when you go to copy the formula to other cells in row 16, the other cells will always be row 14 column 1 plus row 15 column 1. This is what we mean by making the relationship absolute. It is this process which must be correctly decided before you make the copying command do the copying. In the *copy from* range, you must have the cells you want to be relational as relational and the cells you want as absolute be absolute.

Figure 5-10   The Copy Menu Selection

```
COPY:Right Down From

Select option or type command letter
C1                        99% Free    Multiplan: MULTI
```

Assuming that you have correctly set up the spreadsheet so that the formulas you want to be relational are relational and the formulas you want to be absolute are absolute, you are now ready to copy. Selecting the copy function will now present the bottom of the screen as shown in Figure 5-10. The easiest and most general selection to make is the *from* command, which can be done by typing *F* or by moving the cursor to that selection and typing ⟨enter⟩. The copy menu selection now shows as follows.

Figure 5-11   The "From" Selection in Copy

```
6
COPY FROM cells: R37C1                   to cells: R37C1

Enter reference to cell or group of cells
7C1                       99% Free    Multiplan: MULTI
```

Essentially, what you will do here is to define the *from* range and the *to* range. The *from* range is defined by RxCy:RcCd where RxCy is the upper left corner of the range to be copied from and RcCd is the lower left corner. After defining this, use the tab key to move to the *to* selection. You can now define the *to* selection by typing the upper left and upper right corners of the *to* range. In Figure 5-12, for example, we are copying the items in the range row 5 column 3:row 10 column 3 to the range row 5 column 4:row 5 column 8. This will put whatever was in the section of row 5 to row 10 in column 3 into rows 5 through 10 in columns 4, 5, 6, 7, and 8.

Figure 5-12   Completed Copy From Command

```
COPY FROM cells: r5c3:r10c3              to cells:
r5c4:r5c8

Enter reference to cell or group of cells
7C1                       99% Free    Multiplan: MULTI
```

FIXING UP THE SPREADSHEET

After you have constructed your spreadsheet a number of options are available to "clean up" the spreadsheet and make it more presentable. Four of the more commonly used procedures are changing the column width, allowing test entries to run over into unused column space, positioning the text, and formatting the display of the data. Other options are available, and the user is encouraged to explore these through the manual or through experimentation with the commands and the help function. Remember, in the following discussions, that to select a command you can either type the first letter or move through the commands with the space bar and hit ⟨enter⟩. Within the commands, you move through the selection areas with the tab key.

The four things that are to be done in this section will be done with the format command. This command is accessed by typing *F* or moving to it and hitting the return key.

Column Width

The column width is changed by first accessing the format command, after which the screen will show the bottom of the spreadsheet as follows:

Figure 5-13   The Format Command Selections

```
FORMAT: Cells Default Options Width

Select option or type command letter
R50C1               99% Free    Multiplan: MULTI
```

To change the column width, select width by typing a *W*. The screen will now look like Figure 5-14, giving you a choice of setting the column width starting with a certain column and ending with a certain column. The cursor will be in the place after the first colon, which will display the column width of the first column, or *d* for default. The initial default width is ten characters. You should enter the number of the width you wish the column to be, then press the tab

Figure 5-14   The Format Width Selections

```
FORMAT WIDTH in chars or d(efault): d column: 1 through: 1

Enter a number, or d for default
R50C1               99% Free    Multiplan: MULTI
```

key. This will move you to the selection for the first column you want to change. Enter the number of the first column and then press tab again to move the cursor to the last selection, where you will enter the number of the column that completes the list of columns whose width is changed. Pressing the enter key completes the action. If, for example you wish to change the width of columns 8 through 11 to 12 characters wide, the key strokes are *F W 12* TAB *8* TAB *11* ⟨ Enter⟩.

Continuous Text

Occasionally, you will have a situation where you need a wider column in one part of the spreadsheet but not in all parts. You may have text in one part of the column that uses twenty spaces, and data that needs only eleven spaces. In this case, one of the things you can do is to borrow from an adjoining column if there is nothing in that column. To do this you must use the format cont command for the range you wish to be able to borrow from.

To do this, select the format command, and then the cells command within the format command. Your command section of the spreadsheet will now look like Figure 5-15. The cursor will be in the *cells,* space in which you enter the range you wish to do something to. Remember, the range is RxCy:RaCb where the letters before the colon define the upper left corner, and the letters after the colon define the lower right corner. After selecting the range, use the tab key to go to format code by pressing it twice. Then use the space bar to select cont and hit the enter key. Your text will now spill over into the next column. Remember, though, in setting the range you must include the columns the text is in and the columns the text will spill over to.

Positioning the Text

When the text is entered, it will be lined up at the left margin in the cell. You can change this with the format cell command. You start by typing *FC* to get to Figure 5-15. Then set your range as before and then tab to the alignment section. Use the space bar to move through the alignment section. Your choices are:

(Def)   Selects the default alignment.

Ctr   Centers the display in the cell.

Gen   Aligns text left, numbers right.

Left   Left justifies the display.

Right   Right justifies the display.

—   Leaves alignment codes as they are.

Figure 5-15 The Format Cells Selection

```
FORMAT cells: R50C1     alignment:(Def)Ctr Gen Left Right
    — format code:(Def)Cont Exp Fix Gen Int $ * % —
    # of decimals: 0
Enter reference to cell or group of cells
R50C1               99% Free    Multiplan: MULTI
```

After selecting the alignment code, strike ⟨enter⟩ to execute, or use the tab key to move on to the format code.

Formatting

Formatting is the means by which text is displayed in the proper mode: dollar signs, commas, per cent signs, and so on. In Multiplan the formatting is done in the format command in three different parts. Selecting format and then selecting options allow you to do two things. One is to display commas in the appropriate places in the numbers; the second is to display the formulas in the spreadsheet rather than the entries. These selections may be made by typing *FO*, making the appropriate selection with the tab key and space bar, and then hitting ⟨enter⟩. Note that the commas will be displayed only with the format of Fix, Int, $ or %.

To get dollar and per cent signs or other format options, you choose the cells selection in the format command, displaying the command menu as shown in Figure 5-15. Again, you enter the appropriate range, and then tab twice to the format code section. Selecting $ will put dollar signs in front of the numbers, selecting % will put per cent signs after the numbers. The other selections listed are explained in the manual.

Finally, you may want to set the number of decimal points that are displayed. This is done by pressing the tab key a sufficient number of times to get to the *# of decimals:* selection. Then enter the number of decimal points you want displayed. Multiplan will round off to the number shown in its display. Again, typing ⟨enter⟩ completes the command and you are ready to continue. Remember, the formatting will be done for the range specified.

SAVING AND LOADING A FILE

Making a spreadsheet is a lot of work and you probably will not produce a final version in a single sitting. However, when you turn off the computer, the spreadsheet that resided in the computer's mem-

Figure 5-16   The Transfer Command Screen

```
TRANSFER: Load Save Clear Delete Options Rename

Select option or type command letter
R1C1                         100% Free    Multiplan: TEMP
```

ory is gone. Consequently, to work efficiently, you must be able to store the spreadsheet and then load the spreadsheet from a disk.

In Multiplan, saving and loading a spreadsheet is done by means of the transfer command. In order to save a spreadsheet you do the following. Make certain, of course, that you have a formatted disk available to save the spreadsheet. When you select the transfer command you will have what is shown in Figure 15-16 at the bottom of the screen. Before beginning, you should note that the program may assume you are working in Drive A. To get the program to save or load from Drive B, use the options selection. Tab to the "setup" field and type *b:⟨enter⟩*. This will now cause the computer to read and save on the B Drive.

Assuming you have the right default drive and a formatted disk in it, you can save the file by selecting the save option in the transfer command. The program will ask for the name of the file to be saved, which is then typed, making certain there are no spaces in the name. Once you have named your file, or are using a file recalled from a disk, the current name will appear after the file-name request, and all you have to do is hit ⟨enter⟩. The program will ask if you want to override the current version, and typing a *Y* will do so. If you want to make a back-up, use a different name when asked for the file name.

To load a file from a disk, select the load option. The program will then ask for the file name. At this point, hit the left or right arrow key to cause a display of all of the file names on the disk. You can move the cursor with the arrow keys to the file name you desire, and then type ⟨enter⟩ to make the selection. The program will load that worksheet and you can start to work. Remember to save versions of your worksheet frequently throughout a session so that it will not be lost in the event of an interruption to your system.

Figure 5-17   The Load Selection in the Transfer Command

```
TRANSFER LOAD filename:

Enter a filename, or use direction keys to view directory
R1C1                         100% Free    Multiplan: TEMP
```

Figure 5-18   The Print Command Selections

```
PRINT: Printer File Margins Options

Select option or type command letter
R1C1                        100% Free    Multiplan: TEMP
```

PRINTING THE SPREADSHEET

There are a number of options available in Multiplan for printing the spreadsheet. The steps that follow will allow you to print the entire spreadsheet or a portion of it. It is assumed that your computer is properly connected to the printer and that your version of Multiplan will work with the printer you have selected.

To print a spreadsheet you use, naturally enough, the print command. Selecting the print command will give you the screen as shown in Figure 5-18. Selecting the printer option will cause the program to print, but before doing that you will want to go to the options selection to make some choices.

In the options section you can specify the range you want printed, indicate if you want the formulas or values printed, and indicate if you want the row-column numbers printed. In most cases all you will want to change is the area selection, as the default options are *no* on the formulas and *no* on the row-column numbers. In the area selection you should type the range to be printed in the form of RxCy:RaCb, where the items before the colon are the upper left corner of the range and after the colon, the lower right corner.

After you have selected the proper range, the program will remember that range until it is changed. Thus you can now print the range by returning to the print command and selecting the printer option. This will cause the selected range to print.

Figure 5-19   The Options Selection in the Print Command

```
T OPTIONS: area: R1:255    setup:
           formulas: Yes(No) row-col numbers: Yes(No)
r reference to cell or group of cells
                            100% Free    Multiplan: TEMP
```

A COMPREHENSIVE EXAMPLE

In order to demonstrate the ability of Multiplan to produce a spreadsheet, consider how the program might be used to solve the following problem.

Forecasting Net Income
for the Smith Company

It is January, 1986, and the Smith Company has just completed a review of its 1985 results. The income statement for 1985 is shown in Table 5-1. The company would like to produce a report which compares the actual 1985 income statement with a forecast of the income statement for years 1986 through 1988. In doing so, it will make the following assumptions:

1. Cost of sales will be 65 per cent of sales in each year.
2. Overhead will be 22 per cent of sales in each year.
3. Sales will grow at an annual rate of 14 per cent over the forecast period.
4. Interest expense will grow at a rate of 8 per cent over the forecast period.
5. The tax rate will be 45 per cent.

Based on the above information and the information in Table 5-1, use Multiplan to produce a report showing the current income statement and a forecast for years 1986, 1987, and 1988.

To build the spreadsheet we will do the following:

1. Set column width of columns 2–5 to 12 characters.
2. Set column width of column 1 to 28 characters.
3. Enter the heading

Smith Company
Income Statement
Year Ending Dec. 31,

in cells R1C1, R2C1, and R3C1.

Table 5-1

Income Statement Year Ending Dec. 31, 1985

	Actual
Net Sales	$100,000
Cost of Sales	65,000
Gross Margin	35,000
Overhead	22,000
Income Before Interest and Taxes	13,000
Interest	5,000
Income Before Tax	8,000
Tax	3,600
Net Income	4,400

4. We want to enter the critical variables in a separate data section. The reason for this is that we want to build the spreadsheet by making reference to the critical variables in case we have to change one. If we do it this way, and the variables are typed only once, then one change will reflect throughout the spreadsheet. Thus, we will make the following entries.

Cell	Entry	Cell	Entry
R5C1	Data:		
R7C1	Cost of Sales	R7C3	.65
R8C1	Overhead %	R8C3	.22
R9C1	Growth in Sales	R8C3	.14
R10C1	Growth in Interest Exp.	R10C3	.08
R11C1	Tax Rate	R11C3	.45

5. We are now ready to set up the income statement. We will put the accounts in Table 5-1 in column 1 and use the next four columns for the data. We will enter the year headings by putting 1985, 1986, 1987, and 1988 in row 14 columns 2 through 5 and the term *Actual* in row 15 column 2. We will now type the income statement accounts as they are presented in Table 5-1. Net sales goes in cell R17C1, cost of sales in R18C1, and so on through net income in cell R26C1. Finally, we would type the numbers for the 1985 actual in cells R17C2 to R26C2 from the data in Table 5-1. Our spreadsheet now looks like Figure 5-20.

6. The next step is the hardest. Until now all we have really been doing is entering text and values to introduce the variables into the example and re-create Table 5-1. We will now create the forecast, and from this point forward every cell will be a formula. From this point forward the computer will do most of the work.

Our creation of the rest of the spreadsheet will be in two steps. In the first step we will create the entries for column 3 and in the second step we will copy that logic into columns 4 and 5.

Cell	Entry
R17C3	RC[−1]*(1+R9C3)

This takes the previous year's sales and multiplies it by one plus the sales-growth rate. Notice that the previous year's sales logic is relational and the growth rate, absolute.

| R18C3 | R[−1]C*R7C3 |

This takes the sales and multiplies it by the cost of sales per cent, which is in cell R7C3.

| R19C3 | R[−2]C−R[−1]C |

Figure 5-20 Partial Spreadsheet

	1	2	3	4	5
1	Smith Company				
2	Income Statement				
3	Year Ending Dec. 31,				
4					
5	Data:				
6					
7	Cost of Sales %		0.65		
8	Overhead %		0.22		
9	Growth in Sales		0.14		
10	Growth in Int. Exp.		0.08		
11	Tax Rate		0.45		
12					
13		1985	1986	1987	1988
14		Actual			
15					
16					
17	Net Sales	100000			
18	Cost of Sales	65000			
19	Gross Margin	35000			
20	Overhead	22000			
21	Income Before				
22	Interest and Taxes	13000			
23	Interest	5000			
24	Income Before Tax	8000			
25	Tax	3600			
26	Net Income	4400			

This takes the value two rows up and subtracts the value one row up, i.e., sales minus cost of sales.

$$R20C3 \qquad R[-3]C*R8C3$$

This takes the value three rows up (sales) and multiplies it by the overhead per cent in cell R8C3.

$$R21C3 \qquad empty$$
$$R22C3 \qquad R[-3]C-R[-2]C$$

This takes the value three rows up (gross margin) and subtracts the value two rows up to get income before interest and taxes.

$$R23C3 \qquad RC[-1]*(1+R10C3)$$

This takes the previous year's interest expense and multiplies it by one plus the interest expense growth rate to get this year's interest expense. Again, notice which reference is relative and which is absolute.

R24C3   R[−2]C−R[−1]C

This computes income before tax as the difference between the values two rows up and the value one row up.

R25C3   R[−1]C*R11C3

This computes the tax by multiplying income before tax by the tax rate, which is housed in R11C3.

R26C3   R[−2]C−R[−1]C

This computes net income by taking the value two rows up and subtracting the value one row up.

The spreadsheet now looks like Figure 5-21. Notice that Figure 5-21 shows the formulas in each cell, although on the screen you have the value of each cell as computed by the formula. We are now ready to do the second step of filling out the spreadsheet. This consists of copying the logic into columns 4 and 5. This is done by the *copy*

Figure 5-21   The Spreadsheet with Formulas

	1	2	3	4	5
1	Smith Company				
2	Income Statement				
3	Year Ending Dec. 31,				
4					
5	Data:				
6					
7	Cost of Sales %		0.65		
8	Overhead %		0.22		
9	Growth in Sales		0.14		
10	Growth in Int. Exp.		0.08		
11	Tax Rate		0.45		
12					
13					
14		1985	1986	1987	1988
15		Actual			
16					
17	Net Sales	100000	RC[−1]*(1+R9C3)		
18	Cost of Sales	65000	R[−1]C*R7C3		
19	Gross Margin	35000	R[−2]C−R[−1]C		
20	Overhead	22000	R[−3]C*R8C3		
21	Income Before				
22	Interest and Taxes	13000	R[−3]C−R[−2]C		
23	Interest	5000	RC[−1]*(1+R10C3)		
24	Income Before Tax	8000	R[−2]C−R[−1]C		
25	Tax	3600	R[−1]C*R11C3		
26	Net Income	4400	R[−2]C−R[−1]C		

from command. In the *from* selection we put the range R17C3:R26:C3 and then we tab over to the *to* section and put R17C4:R17C5 and press the enter key. At this point all of the spreadsheet will be filled in with the proper numbers.

7. The remaining step is to clean up the spreadsheet with the format command. We will first of all format the range R17C2:R17C5 for dollar signs, *0* decimal places, then format the range R17C2:R26C5 for commas, zero decimal points.

Your spreadsheet is finished and now looks like Figure 5-22. Congratulations, you have created your first spreadsheet with Multiplan, and you are on your way.

Figure 5-22 The Final Version

	1	2	3	4	5
1	Smith Company				
2	Income Statement				
3	Year Ending Dec. 31,				
4					
5	Data:				
6					
7	Cost of Sales %		0.65		
8	Overhead %		0.22		
9	Growth in Sales		0.14		
10	Growth in Int. Exp.		0.08		
11	Tax Rate		0.45		
12					
13					
14		1985	1986	1987	1988
15		Actual			
16					
17	Net Sales	$100,000	$114,000	$129,960	$148,154
18	Cost of Sales	65,000	74,100	84,474	96,300
19	Gross Margin	35,000	39,900	45,486	51,854
20	Overhead	22,000	25,080	28,591	32,594
21	Income Before				
22	Interest and Taxes	13,000	14,820	16,895	19,260
23	Interest	5,000	5,400	5,832	6,299
24	Income Before Tax	8,000	9,420	11,063	12,962
25	Tax	3,600	4,239	4,978	5,833
26	Net Income	4,400	5,181	6,085	7,129

SUGGESTED QUESTIONS

1. Construct the spreadsheet in the example and print it out.

2. After you have constructed the spreadsheet, determine what it would look like if the tax rate were 40 per cent and at the same time the sales growth rate fell to 11 per cent. Print out your results.

3. Determine what the spreadsheet would look like if interest cost grew at only 4 per cent, but the cost of sales rose to 71 per cent. Print out your results.

4. Determine what the spreadsheet would look like if the overhead fell to 18 per cent but the sales growth fell to 10 per cent. Print out your results.

PART VII

Appendixes

APPENDIX A

Tables of Present-Value and Future-Value Factors

Table 1
Future Value Factors $(1+i)^n$

Interest Rate

Period	0.01	0.02	0.04	0.05	0.06	0.08	0.10	0.12	0.14	0.15	0.16	0.18	0.20	0.25	0.30
1	1.010	1.020	1.040	1.050	1.060	1.080	1.100	1.120	1.140	1.150	1.160	1.180	1.200	1.250	1.300
2	1.020	1.040	1.082	1.103	1.124	1.166	1.210	1.254	1.300	1.323	1.346	1.392	1.440	1.563	1.690
3	1.030	1.061	1.125	1.158	1.191	1.260	1.331	1.405	1.482	1.521	1.561	1.643	1.728	1.953	2.197
4	1.041	1.082	1.170	1.216	1.262	1.360	1.464	1.574	1.689	1.749	1.811	1.939	2.074	2.441	2.856
5	1.051	1.104	1.217	1.276	1.338	1.469	1.611	1.762	1.925	2.011	2.100	2.288	2.488	3.052	3.713
6	1.062	1.126	1.265	1.340	1.419	1.587	1.772	1.974	2.195	2.313	2.436	2.700	2.986	3.815	4.827
7	1.072	1.149	1.316	1.407	1.504	1.714	1.949	2.211	2.502	2.660	2.826	3.185	3.583	4.768	6.275
8	1.083	1.172	1.369	1.477	1.594	1.851	2.144	2.476	2.853	3.059	3.278	3.759	4.300	5.960	8.157
9	1.094	1.195	1.423	1.551	1.689	1.999	2.358	2.773	3.252	3.518	3.803	4.435	5.160	7.451	10.604
10	1.105	1.219	1.480	1.629	1.791	2.159	2.594	3.106	3.707	4.046	4.411	5.234	6.192	9.313	13.786
11	1.116	1.243	1.539	1.710	1.898	2.332	2.853	3.479	4.226	4.652	5.117	6.176	7.430	11.642	17.922
12	1.127	1.268	1.601	1.796	2.012	2.518	3.138	3.896	4.818	5.350	5.936	7.288	8.916	14.552	23.298
13	1.138	1.294	1.665	1.886	2.133	2.720	3.452	4.363	5.492	6.153	6.886	8.599	10.699	18.190	30.288
14	1.149	1.319	1.732	1.980	2.261	2.937	3.797	4.887	6.261	7.076	7.988	10.147	12.839	22.737	39.374
15	1.161	1.346	1.801	2.079	2.397	3.172	4.177	5.474	7.138	8.137	9.266	11.974	15.407	28.422	51.186
16	1.173	1.373	1.873	2.183	2.540	3.426	4.595	6.130	8.137	9.358	10.748	14.129	18.488	35.527	66.542
17	1.184	1.400	1.948	2.292	2.693	3.700	5.054	6.866	9.276	10.761	12.468	16.672	22.186	44.409	86.504
18	1.196	1.428	2.026	2.407	2.854	3.996	5.560	7.690	10.575	12.375	14.463	19.673	26.623	55.511	112.455
19	1.208	1.457	2.107	2.527	3.026	4.316	6.116	8.613	12.056	14.232	16.777	23.214	31.948	69.389	146.192
20	1.220	1.486	2.191	2.653	3.207	4.661	6.727	9.646	13.743	16.367	19.461	27.393	38.338	86.736	190.050
21	1.232	1.516	2.279	2.786	3.400	5.034	7.400	10.804	15.668	18.822	22.574	32.324	46.005	108.420	247.065
22	1.245	1.546	2.370	2.925	3.604	5.437	8.140	12.100	17.861	21.645	26.186	38.142	55.206	135.525	321.184
23	1.257	1.577	2.465	3.072	3.820	5.871	8.954	13.552	20.362	24.891	30.376	45.008	66.247	169.407	417.539
24	1.270	1.608	2.563	3.225	4.049	6.341	9.850	15.179	23.212	28.625	35.236	53.109	79.497	211.758	542.801
25	1.282	1.641	2.666	3.386	4.292	6.848	10.835	17.000	26.462	32.919	40.874	62.669	95.396	264.698	705.641
30	1.348	1.811	3.243	4.322	5.743	10.063	17.449	29.960	50.950	66.212	85.850	143.371	237.376	807.794	2619.996
35	1.417	2.000	3.946	5.516	7.686	14.785	28.102	52.800	98.100	133.176	180.314	327.997	590.668	2465.190	9727.860
40	1.489	2.208	4.801	7.040	10.286	21.725	45.259	93.051	188.884	267.864	378.721	750.378	1469.772	7523.164	*********
45	1.565	2.438	5.841	8.985	13.765	31.920	72.890	163.988	363.679	538.769	795.444	1716.684	3657.262	****************	****************
50	1.645	2.692	7.107	11.467	18.420	46.902	117.391	289.002	700.233	1083.657	1670.704	3927.357	9100.438	****************	****************

Table 2
Present Value Factors $1/(1+i)^n$

Interest Rate

Period	0.01	0.02	0.04	0.05	0.06	0.08	0.10	0.12	0.14	0.15	0.16	0.18	0.20	0.25	0.30
1	0.990	0.980	0.962	0.952	0.943	0.926	0.909	0.893	0.877	0.870	0.862	0.847	0.833	0.800	0.769
2	0.980	0.961	0.925	0.907	0.890	0.857	0.826	0.797	0.769	0.756	0.743	0.718	0.694	0.640	0.592
3	0.971	0.942	0.889	0.864	0.840	0.794	0.751	0.712	0.675	0.658	0.641	0.609	0.579	0.512	0.455
4	0.961	0.924	0.855	0.823	0.792	0.735	0.683	0.636	0.592	0.572	0.552	0.516	0.482	0.410	0.350
5	0.951	0.906	0.822	0.784	0.747	0.681	0.621	0.567	0.519	0.497	0.476	0.437	0.402	0.328	0.269
6	0.942	0.888	0.790	0.746	0.705	0.630	0.564	0.507	0.456	0.432	0.410	0.370	0.335	0.262	0.207
7	0.933	0.871	0.760	0.711	0.665	0.583	0.513	0.452	0.400	0.376	0.354	0.314	0.279	0.210	0.159
8	0.923	0.853	0.731	0.677	0.627	0.540	0.467	0.404	0.351	0.327	0.305	0.266	0.233	0.168	0.123
9	0.914	0.837	0.703	0.645	0.592	0.500	0.424	0.361	0.308	0.284	0.263	0.225	0.194	0.134	0.094
10	0.905	0.820	0.676	0.614	0.558	0.463	0.386	0.322	0.270	0.247	0.227	0.191	0.162	0.107	0.073
11	0.896	0.804	0.650	0.585	0.527	0.429	0.350	0.287	0.237	0.215	0.195	0.162	0.135	0.086	0.056
12	0.887	0.788	0.625	0.557	0.497	0.397	0.319	0.257	0.208	0.187	0.168	0.137	0.112	0.069	0.043
13	0.879	0.773	0.601	0.530	0.469	0.368	0.290	0.229	0.182	0.163	0.145	0.116	0.093	0.055	0.033
14	0.870	0.758	0.577	0.505	0.442	0.340	0.263	0.205	0.160	0.141	0.125	0.099	0.078	0.044	0.025
15	0.861	0.743	0.555	0.481	0.417	0.315	0.239	0.183	0.140	0.123	0.108	0.084	0.065	0.035	0.020
16	0.853	0.728	0.534	0.458	0.394	0.292	0.218	0.163	0.123	0.107	0.093	0.071	0.054	0.028	0.015
17	0.844	0.714	0.513	0.436	0.371	0.270	0.198	0.146	0.108	0.093	0.080	0.060	0.045	0.023	0.012
18	0.836	0.700	0.494	0.416	0.350	0.250	0.180	0.130	0.095	0.081	0.069	0.051	0.038	0.018	0.009
19	0.828	0.686	0.475	0.396	0.331	0.232	0.164	0.116	0.083	0.070	0.060	0.043	0.031	0.014	0.007
20	0.820	0.673	0.456	0.377	0.312	0.215	0.149	0.104	0.073	0.061	0.051	0.037	0.026	0.012	0.005
21	0.811	0.660	0.439	0.359	0.294	0.199	0.135	0.093	0.064	0.053	0.044	0.031	0.022	0.009	0.004
22	0.803	0.647	0.422	0.342	0.278	0.184	0.123	0.083	0.056	0.046	0.038	0.026	0.018	0.007	0.003
23	0.795	0.634	0.406	0.326	0.262	0.170	0.112	0.074	0.049	0.040	0.033	0.022	0.015	0.006	0.002
24	0.788	0.622	0.390	0.310	0.247	0.158	0.102	0.066	0.043	0.035	0.028	0.019	0.013	0.005	0.002
25	0.780	0.610	0.375	0.295	0.233	0.146	0.092	0.059	0.038	0.030	0.024	0.016	0.010	0.004	0.001
30	0.742	0.552	0.308	0.231	0.174	0.099	0.057	0.033	0.020	0.015	0.012	0.007	0.004	0.001	.000
35	0.706	0.500	0.253	0.181	0.130	0.068	0.036	0.019	0.010	0.008	0.006	0.003	0.002	.000	.000
40	0.672	0.453	0.208	0.142	0.097	0.046	0.022	0.011	0.005	0.004	0.003	0.001	0.001	.000	.000
45	0.639	0.410	0.171	0.111	0.073	0.031	0.014	0.006	0.003	0.002	0.001	0.001	.000	.000	.000
50	0.608	0.372	0.141	0.087	0.054	0.021	0.009	0.003	0.001	0.001	0.001	.000	.000	.000	.000

Table 3
Future Value of An Annuity Factor (1st Payment End of Year)
$((1+i)^n-1)/i$

Period	Interest Rate														
	0.01	0.02	0.04	0.05	0.06	0.08	0.10	0.12	0.14	0.15	0.16	0.18	0.20	0.25	0.30
1	1.000	1.000	1.000	1.000	1.000	1.000	1.000	1.000	1.000	1.000	1.000	1.000	1.000	1.000	1.000
2	2.010	2.020	2.040	2.050	2.060	2.080	2.100	2.120	2.140	2.150	2.160	2.180	2.200	2.250	2.300
3	3.030	3.060	3.122	3.153	3.184	3.246	3.310	3.374	3.440	3.473	3.506	3.572	3.640	3.813	3.990
4	4.060	4.122	4.246	4.310	4.375	4.506	4.641	4.779	4.921	4.993	5.066	5.215	5.368	5.766	6.187
5	5.101	5.204	5.416	5.526	5.637	5.867	6.105	6.353	6.610	6.742	6.877	7.154	7.442	8.207	9.043
6	6.152	6.308	6.633	6.802	6.975	7.336	7.716	8.115	8.536	8.754	8.977	9.442	9.930	11.259	12.756
7	7.214	7.434	7.898	8.142	8.394	8.923	9.487	10.089	10.730	11.067	11.414	12.142	12.916	15.073	17.583
8	8.286	8.583	9.214	9.549	9.897	10.637	11.436	12.300	13.233	13.727	14.240	15.327	16.499	19.842	23.858
9	9.369	9.755	10.583	11.027	11.491	12.488	13.579	14.776	16.085	16.786	17.519	19.086	20.799	25.802	32.015
10	10.462	10.950	12.006	12.578	13.181	14.487	15.937	17.549	19.337	20.304	21.321	23.521	25.959	33.253	42.619
11	11.567	12.169	13.486	14.207	14.972	16.645	18.531	20.655	23.045	24.349	25.733	28.755	32.150	42.566	56.405
12	12.683	13.412	15.026	15.917	16.870	18.977	21.384	24.133	27.271	29.002	30.850	34.931	39.581	54.208	74.327
13	13.809	14.680	16.627	17.713	18.882	21.495	24.523	28.029	32.089	34.352	36.786	42.219	48.497	68.760	97.625
14	14.947	15.974	18.292	19.599	21.015	24.215	27.975	32.393	37.581	40.505	43.672	50.818	59.196	86.949	127.913
15	16.097	17.293	20.024	21.579	23.276	27.152	31.772	37.280	43.842	47.580	51.660	60.965	72.035	109.687	167.286
16	17.258	18.639	21.825	23.657	25.673	30.324	35.950	42.753	50.980	55.717	60.925	72.939	87.442	138.109	218.472
17	18.430	20.012	23.698	25.840	28.213	33.750	40.545	48.884	59.118	65.075	71.673	87.068	105.931	173.636	285.014
18	19.615	21.412	25.645	28.132	30.906	37.450	45.599	55.750	68.394	75.836	84.141	103.740	128.117	218.045	371.518
19	20.811	22.841	27.671	30.539	33.760	41.446	51.159	63.440	78.969	88.212	98.603	123.414	154.740	273.556	483.973
20	22.019	24.297	29.778	33.066	36.786	45.762	57.275	72.052	91.025	102.444	115.380	146.628	186.688	342.945	630.165
21	23.239	25.783	31.969	35.719	39.993	50.423	64.002	81.699	104.768	118.810	134.841	174.021	225.026	429.681	820.215
22	24.472	27.299	34.248	38.505	43.392	55.457	71.403	92.503	120.436	137.632	157.415	206.345	271.031	538.101	1067.280
23	25.716	28.845	36.618	41.430	46.996	60.893	79.543	104.603	138.297	159.276	183.601	244.487	326.237	673.626	1388.464
24	26.973	30.422	39.083	44.502	50.816	66.765	88.497	118.155	158.659	184.168	213.978	289.494	392.484	843.033	1806.003
25	28.243	32.030	41.646	47.727	54.865	73.106	98.347	133.334	181.871	212.793	249.214	342.603	471.981	1054.791	2348.803
30	34.785	40.568	56.085	66.439	79.058	113.283	164.494	241.333	356.787	434.745	530.312	790.948	1181.882	3227.174	8729.985
35	41.660	49.994	73.652	90.320	111.435	172.317	271.024	431.663	693.573	881.170	1120.713	1816.652	2948.341	9856.761	*********
40	48.886	60.402	95.026	120.800	154.762	259.057	442.593	767.091	1342.025	1779.090	2360.757	4163.213	7343.858	*********	*********
45	56.481	71.893	121.029	159.700	212.744	386.506	718.905	1358.230	2590.565	3585.128	4965.274	9531.577	*********	*********	*********
50	64.463	84.579	152.667	209.348	290.336	573.770	1163.909	2400.018	4994.521	7217.716	*********	*********	*********	*********	*********

Table 4
Present Value of An Annuity Factor
$(1-1/(1+i)^n)/i$

Interest Rate

Period	0.01	0.02	0.04	0.05	0.06	0.08	0.10	0.12	0.14	0.15	0.16	0.18	0.20	0.25	0.30
1	0.990	0.980	0.962	0.952	0.943	0.926	0.909	0.893	0.877	0.870	0.862	0.847	0.833	0.800	0.769
2	1.970	1.942	1.886	1.859	1.833	1.783	1.736	1.690	1.647	1.626	1.605	1.566	1.528	1.440	1.361
3	2.941	2.884	2.775	2.723	2.673	2.577	2.487	2.402	2.322	2.283	2.246	2.174	2.106	1.952	1.816
4	3.902	3.808	3.630	3.546	3.465	3.312	3.170	3.037	2.914	2.855	2.798	2.690	2.589	2.362	2.166
5	4.853	4.713	4.452	4.329	4.212	3.993	3.791	3.605	3.433	3.352	3.274	3.127	2.991	2.689	2.436
6	5.795	5.601	5.242	5.076	4.917	4.623	4.355	4.111	3.889	3.784	3.685	3.498	3.326	2.951	2.643
7	6.728	6.472	6.002	5.786	5.582	5.206	4.868	4.564	4.288	4.160	4.039	3.812	3.605	3.161	2.802
8	7.652	7.325	6.733	6.463	6.210	5.747	5.335	4.968	4.639	4.487	4.344	4.078	3.837	3.329	2.925
9	8.566	8.162	7.435	7.108	6.802	6.247	5.759	5.328	4.946	4.772	4.607	4.303	4.031	3.463	3.019
10	9.471	8.983	8.111	7.722	7.360	6.710	6.145	5.650	5.216	5.019	4.833	4.494	4.192	3.571	3.092
11	10.368	9.787	8.760	8.306	7.887	7.139	6.495	5.938	5.453	5.234	5.029	4.656	4.327	3.656	3.147
12	11.255	10.575	9.385	8.863	8.384	7.536	6.814	6.194	5.660	5.421	5.197	4.793	4.439	3.725	3.190
13	12.134	11.348	9.986	9.394	8.853	7.904	7.103	6.424	5.842	5.583	5.342	4.910	4.533	3.780	3.223
14	13.004	12.106	10.563	9.899	9.295	8.244	7.367	6.628	6.002	5.724	5.468	5.008	4.611	3.824	3.249
15	13.865	12.849	11.118	10.380	9.712	8.559	7.606	6.811	6.142	5.847	5.575	5.092	4.675	3.859	3.268
16	14.718	13.578	11.652	10.838	10.106	8.851	7.824	6.974	6.265	5.954	5.668	5.162	4.730	3.887	3.283
17	15.562	14.292	12.166	11.274	10.477	9.122	8.022	7.120	6.373	6.047	5.749	5.222	4.775	3.910	3.295
18	16.398	14.992	12.659	11.690	10.828	9.372	8.201	7.250	6.467	6.128	5.818	5.273	4.812	3.928	3.304
19	17.226	15.678	13.134	12.085	11.158	9.604	8.365	7.366	6.550	6.198	5.877	5.316	4.843	3.942	3.311
20	18.046	16.351	13.590	12.462	11.470	9.818	8.514	7.469	6.623	6.259	5.929	5.353	4.870	3.954	3.316
21	18.857	17.011	14.029	12.821	11.764	10.017	8.649	7.562	6.687	6.312	5.973	5.384	4.891	3.963	3.320
22	19.660	17.658	14.451	13.163	12.042	10.201	8.772	7.645	6.743	6.359	6.011	5.410	4.909	3.970	3.323
23	20.456	18.292	14.857	13.489	12.303	10.371	8.883	7.718	6.792	6.399	6.044	5.432	4.925	3.976	3.325
24	21.243	18.914	15.247	13.799	12.550	10.529	8.985	7.784	6.835	6.434	6.073	5.451	4.937	3.981	3.327
25	22.023	19.523	15.622	14.094	12.783	10.675	9.077	7.843	6.873	6.464	6.097	5.467	4.948	3.985	3.329
30	25.808	22.396	17.292	15.372	13.765	11.258	9.427	8.055	7.003	6.566	6.177	5.517	4.979	3.995	3.332
35	29.409	24.999	18.665	16.374	14.498	11.655	9.644	8.176	7.070	6.617	6.215	5.539	4.992	3.998	3.332
40	32.835	27.355	19.793	17.159	15.046	11.925	9.779	8.244	7.105	6.642	6.233	5.548	4.997	3.999	3.333
45	36.095	29.490	20.720	17.774	15.456	12.108	9.863	8.283	7.123	6.654	6.242	5.552	4.999	4.000	3.333
50	39.196	31.424	21.482	18.256	15.762	12.233	9.915	8.304	7.133	6.661	6.246	5.554	4.999	4.000	3.333

ACRS Rates

The cases in this study are based on ACRS rules and regulations in effect in 1985. Basically, ACRS replaced accelerated depreciation for tax purposes in 1982, and current practices are to use ACRS methods unless an optional straight-line method is used. Since the straight-line method is not economical except where companies have significant operating losses and no tax carry-back, it is ignored for the case studies.

Under ACRS an asset is classified into a life class, and the rates in the class are applied against the basis. The basis is determined by whether or not the investment tax credit was taken. For the three-year life, if ITC was taken the basis is 97 per cent of the installed cost of the asset. For other lives, if ITC was taken, the basis is 95 per cent of the installed cost. ACRS rates are as follows:

Year	3 Year Life	5 Year Life	10 Year Life
1	.25	.15	.08
2	.38	.22	.14
3	.37	.21	.12
4		.21	.10
5		.21	.10
6			.10
7–10			.09 each year